On Your Mark

On Your Mark

Reading Scripture without a Teacher

William J. O'Malley, SJ

LITURGICAL PRESS
Collegeville, Minnesota

www.litpress.org

1   2   3   4   5   6   7   8   9

Library of Congress Cataloging-in-Publication Data

O'Malley, William J.
   On your Mark : reading Scripture without a teacher / William J. O'Malley.
      p. cm.
   ISBN 978-0-8146-3350-2 — ISBN 978-0-8146-3944-3 (e-book)
   1. Bible. N.T. Mark—Commentaries.   I. Title.

   BS2585.53.O42   2011
   226.3'077—dc22   2010030983

For Dr. Thomas Doyle

Contents

Introduction

Scripture from Scratch

When I began to teach, I came armed with a master's thesis on Dostoevsky's vision of human nature. I'd gotten an A+ for it (and A+s, for me, were rare!). Since I'd been given glop as a high-school English student, I was going to give my eleventh-grade students the real stuff! So I dumped *Crime and Punishment* on them. Disastrous. It took me awhile to realize I wasn't there to teach what excited me but what my students needed to learn. Humbling.

Similarly, when I began teaching theology, I found students looking up at me with glazed eyes, as if they'd had their previous period in Opium 103. As my first teaching experience indicates, I must be a slow learner—or stubborn about yielding my own interests to the needs of those I teach. When I talked about the gospel, about justice and love, about being apostles and healers, I might as well have been speaking Mandarin. I was as thickheaded as a salesman offering sand to Bedouins. The audience wasn't interested, in the first place, because the topics were (as far as they could see) completely pointless to their experience, and, in the second place, because they didn't know what the heck I was talking about in the first place!

After awhile, I found at least part of the cause: I was doing the same thing in religion class that I'd done in my first English classes. I was "dumping." I was giving them Mark when I never would have dreamed of giving them *Macbeth*—not without a rabbit warren of notes on the facing pages, the way the wise Folger people present Shakespeare. So that's what makes this book different from all other versions of Mark's gospel: It is devised for beginners at reading the scriptures without a teacher, whether the beginner is fifteen or fifty.

For the untrained reader, young or old, there are as many mystifying historical references, cultural presuppositions, and symbolic devices in Mark as there are in *Macbeth*. So, this text treats Mark as if it were *Macbeth*.

As Raymond Brown, SS, puts it tersely in *The Jerome Biblical Commentary* (71:15):

Because Scripture is inspired and presumably this inspiration is for the good of all, there has arisen the fallacy that everyone should be able to pick up the Bible and read it profitably. If this implies that everyone should be able to find out what the sacred author is saying, without preparation or study, it really demands of God in each instance a miraculous dispensation from the limitations imposed by differences of time and circumstances.

Think about a time in the future, after an atomic war, when people have been so enraged against the science and scientists who perpetrated this horror (see Miller, *A Canticle for Leibowitz*, or Bradbury, *Fahrenheit 451*), that they outlaw books, kill teachers, and confine language to mere utilitarian business exchanges. Now think of a person who has unearthed a New Testament. He or she is fascinated by this alien thing. It needs to be deciphered. That's what we are setting out to do in this book: Get rid of all you've heard before; get rid of all the old assumptions, all the classes and homilies you've been present for but never really listened to. Discover the Jesus story for the first time, as the first non-Palestinian converts did: through Mark.

From the best of motives, the church has tried to give you "the whole thing, all at once," as I tried to give my classes *Crime and Punishment* and a gospel-all-at-once. No one begins an introduction to science with the quantum theory. No one begins English as a Second Language with *King Lear*. For too long, we have given you—old or young—all the answers you'll *never* need, most of which were meaningless, at least at the time. This book is an attempt to change that, to let you discover for yourself.

Mao Zedong once said that if you give a fish to someone starving, you give them a day's life. If you give them a fishing pole instead, you teach them how to fish for themselves. You give them not merely a day but a life.

This book is a fishing pole.

Part I

The Gospels

1

Reading Scripture on Your Own

Let's start honestly: Most ordinary people find scripture boring. Anybody who says otherwise at least seems to have a self-deceiving motive, like being pretentious, cozying up to the teacher, sounding intellectual—or worse, "holy." But since over the last twenty-five centuries uncountable human beings, from the most brilliant to the least learned, have professed a profound debt to these scriptures, there simply must be "something" in there that engages their hearts and minds.

Few would say that Einstein is "boring" or that Shakespeare is "stupid." So many bright people praise them that it would make me feel stupid myself (or it ought to) if I disagreed about something they seem to know a great deal about but which I just can't seem to "get into."

There's the core problem: not that what's in those authors' books is worthless, but that I myself just can't find a way in. It's at least something like trying to eavesdrop on a bus where everyone else speaks a foreign language.

But if you've read those last three paragraphs you *do* speak the same language as Einstein and Shakespeare, Darwin and Dickens, Lamentations and Luke (at least in English translations). Well, yes and no. Truth to tell, most people read on a pretty elementary level. Just because you can follow the directions for a recipe doesn't mean you could follow the plans to build a rocket. There's a broadening perspective of vocabulary, complex sentence constructions, and subject matter that demands a gradual easing into. That's what this book tries to do.

For the moment, trust that people whose opinions on other important aspects of life sincerely believe the gospels have something life-giving to offer. Then, ask yourself if it might be worth some effort to widen your present reading skills, simply because you could be missing out on something those people you respect believe is important and enriching.

Eisegesis / Exegesis

Every English teacher has heard, "Do you want what we *really* think the poem means or *your* interpretation?" Many beginning readers will take a verse of a poem or scripture the teacher has pored over again and again—but which the student is usually seeing for the first time—and spin out an "interpretation" that tells more about what's going on in the student's mind than it does about what was going on in the mind of the writer. For instance:

Wind and Silver

Greatly shining,
The Autumn moon floats in the thin sky;
And the fish-ponds shake their backs
   and flash their dragon scales
As she passes over them.
              —Amy Lowell (1874–1925)

Consider this actual case in regard to that little poem:

Teacher: No profound meaning there; just a pretty picture of a pond in the moonlight. The wind flicks up little wavelets that catch the moonlight and remind her of dragon scales.

Student: I have another interpretation.

Teacher: Okay, as long as the poem has the evidence to support it. A poem's not a Rorschach test, you know, where you look at the inkblots and say, "This makes me think of . . ."

Student: I think it's about a U-2 flight over Red China.

Teacher: (jaw sagging) What? Where's the evidence in the *poem*?

Student: It's right there. "Dragon scales."

Teacher: But you've just taken two words and spun out your *own* poem.

Student: That's *your* opinion.

Teacher: (teeth clenched) Why couldn't it be about a U-2 flight over medieval England? Apparently *they* had dragons too!

Student: That's *your* opinion.

Teacher: (simmering) Look at the *bottom*! The poet *died* in 1925! There *was* no Red China! There were no U-2's!!!

Student: That's *your* opinion.

(Stout football players attempt to pry
the teacher's thumbs from that kid's windpipe.)

What the student was engaging in was *eisegesis*: reading *into* the poem his own feelings at the moment, provoked only by two words, "dragon scales," and ignoring all the other evidence in the poem. Each of us is free to write our own poems, or our own spiritual thoughts about Jesus and his message, but we're not legitimately free to rewrite someone *else's* poem—or scripture—and give it *our* meaning rather than the writer's intended meaning. That would be like scrawling our own imaginative graffiti all over Michelangelo's Sistine Ceiling.

What this book attempts to do is allow the inexperienced reader of scripture to read the gospel of Mark as *Mark* intended it to be read: *exegesis*, reading *out from* the book only what's *there*. If Mark's gospel provokes you to further insights, all well and good; the church has been doing that for two thousand years: finding truths that go beyond what even Mark could have understood about Jesus, enriching his insights with our growing understanding not only of Jesus but also of human and divine nature. But before you make a claim about Mark's thought—or Jesus'—you have to make sure there's evidence *in* Mark's writing to support your claim.

On the other hand, the gospel of Jesus is not the sole monopoly of the clergy. It was written for all people, even for not-yet-Christians. What's more, people with the ability to cope with Shakespeare, chemistry, and calculus ought to be able to read the greatest book ever written without a teacher or homilist at their elbows to interpret for them. It's good to check your opinions about what Mark says with a commentary, but there's no reason you can't read it on your own with a few hints about the mind-set a first-century Greek writer would have that would be quite different from our mind-set, after two thousand years of theologizing.

It's important to remember also that Mark didn't write in English; he wrote in Greek, often translating from Aramaic, the dialect of Hebrew Jesus used. Words that have fixed meanings for us meant something quite different for Mark. For instance, translations often render the Greek word *hubris* as "pride," as in "Pride goes before the fall." Thus, people are afraid to seem conceited if they have genuine and legitimate pride in a job well done. But a Greek-speaking Roman like Mark did not mean justifiable self-esteem—which is a virtue. He meant *arrogance*, self-absorption, rejection of all others, including any need for help from God. *Hubris* is the original sin of Adam and Eve, which is the pattern of all others.

Similarly, when the gospel writers speak of "perfect," they by no means intend "flawless," as the word might mean to us; they meant "whole," having it all together. You needn't know Greek to read the New Testament, but not knowing Greek is another reason for having a good commentary.

Figurative Language

Consider the following dialogue between Bob and his older sister Erin:

Bob: It's the end of the world! My chick just gave me my walking papers.
   She's got a brick for a heart.
Erin: None so blind as those who will not see, baby brother. I *told* you she was
   a vampire.
Bob: I'm gonna kill myself.
Erin: Brilliant idea!
Bob: Why not? She's already killed me a thousand times.
Erin: Bobby, she's just not worth all this agony.
Bob: Who are you all of a sudden, Dear Abby?

If you read that with literalist (fundamentalist) eyes, the exchange is insane. Here's a young man saying one of the signs of the end of the world is that the chicken he's dating has hopped onto a typewriter and tapped out formal papers severing their relationship. Not only that, but this chicken has a heart made out of brick and not flesh. His sister counters that he's blind (which he's not) and that blind people see better than people with vision. What's more, this girl now appears to be not only a baby hen but a blood-sucking bat. When Erin's own flesh and blood threatens suicide, she counters with her opinion that suicide sounds just peachy to her. Then Bob reveals he's already been dead and (apparently) resurrected one thousand times already and that his sister writes a nationally syndicated advice column.

We're so used to speaking and listening to figurative language we're no longer aware we're "translating" in our heads all the time. Jesus did the same thing, and if we take him literally we end up believing rich people don't have a snowball's chance in hell to be Christian ("for a camel to go through the eye of a needle"; Mark 10:25) and that anyone who has had sexual thoughts ought to be groping around blind ("And if your eye causes you to stumble, tear it out"; Mark 9:47).

Figurative language makes communication more fun. It also holds attention longer than:

Bob: I feel unhappy. My girlfriend separated from me. She is very unkind.
Erin: You're not seeing her for what she has always been. Did I not warn you?
Bob: I feel awful, etc.

That sounds like a conversation between Mister Spock and a computer. Perhaps you're already aware of the ways in which we brighten up our exchanges and hint at meanings and attitudes that literal words can't quite capture—such as Bob's deep-seated hurt, far more than merely "unhappy," and

Erin's loving attempt to jolly his feelings back into perspective. But it might be worthwhile to recap figurative language briefly and show how Jesus used the same indirect ways of communicating too.

At risk of oversimplification, figurative language falls into two categories: *comparison* and *distortion*.

Comparison tries to explain realities we're not familiar with in terms of realities we are familiar with. For instance, Erin calls Bob's girlfriend "a vampire." She's not, but you get a better idea at least of what Erin thinks of her. Similarly, "You can't understand the kingdom of God? Well, think of a wedding reception!"

Distortion tries to explain realities we *think* we understand by twisting them around or exaggerating them so that we get a new perspective. For instance, "Brilliant idea!" when her tone of voice is inviting him to see how stupidly he's acting. Similarly, "If you want the first place, take the last place."

The trouble with figurative language is that it does take effort on the part of the reader or listener to de-compact the comparison or to untwist the distortion in order to find the literal insight that lies beneath it. For instance, how is Bob's girlfriend "like" a vampire; what insights into her personality can you find by looking—not directly at her, as he does, blinded by romance —but at a lady out of a Dracula movie.

GIRL   like   VAMPIRE
cold-hearted
self-centered
using others

And what can you learn about the kingdom from thinking about wedding parties:

KINGDOM   like   WEDDING
joy
freedom from care
music, food, drink

Most people might be puzzled by the oddity of winning a race by losing it, but they'd immediately move on to other things. But how can you be *both* first *and* last, unless of course you're the only person in the race? Simple: there are *two* races, each heading in exactly the opposite direction from one another. The world's race is heading toward monopoly, conspicuous consumption, "Me, first!" The kingdom's race is heading toward healing, concern for outcasts, forgiveness of debts. Those who are in the lead in the one race are close to dead last in the other.

A knowledge of figurative language can help a reader get a lot more out of the scriptures because that sensitivity uncovers more than merely the surface meanings. Be patient for a very quick refresher course:

COMPARISON	DISTORTION
—Metaphor	—Hyperbole
—Symbol	—Irony
—Allusion	—Paradox

Metaphor is more than merely "a comparison without using 'like' or 'as.'" It's a comparison of two basically *unlike* things: Sylvia's a warthog; war is hell; finding the kingdom is like finding a treasure in a field.

A *symbol* is more than "something to stand for something else." It tries to capture—physicalize—something *real* but not itself physical: flowers embody real love; flags embody a country's spirit; men wrapped in shining white garments physicalize real contacts with God.

Allusion is more than merely an irritating learned reference to a person or event in the past. Allusion is a specific form of symbol, trying to enrich the meaning of a current person or event by suggesting common characteristics or purposes with a person or event from the past: Samson symbolizes strength; Solomon = wisdom; Elijah = all the prophets; Moses = the Law. The trouble with allusions is that, if you don't know history or literature, they're less than helpful.

Hyperbole is more than merely exaggeration; it's *obviously* stretching the truth in order to reveal more than the obvious: It's raining cats and dogs; I'm starving; it's as easy for a rich man to get into the kingdom as for a camel to get through the eye of a needle.

Irony is not the same as sarcasm; it is purposely saying the *opposite* of what one really means, tongue-in-cheek: Brilliant idea; nice dress—Salvation Army?; it is not fitting for the food of the children to be given to dogs.

Paradox is an *apparent* contradiction in which, if you ponder a bit, you realize that words were used in a different sense from what one might first have heard: There's none so blind as those who will not see; if you want the first place, take the last place; anyone who will keep his life must lose it.

As with any poet, we can't legitimately hold Jesus to literal statements when he was making figurative statements.

Story Truth

Literalists have very little engagement with their intuitive right brains, demanding that everything that claims to deliver truth has to have at best mathematical proof or at least a line of clear linear logic grounded in reality. No problem with rigid left-brain logic at all, except that it goes only part way. There are realities with which left-brain logic just can't cope adequately enough. For instance, the left-brain dictionary takes forty-three lines to define "love," and when you come to the end of it, you're really not that close to what loving really means. On the other hand, a little kid standing in the doorway holding out a bunch of droopy dandelions to his mother also "says" love, and says it far more satisfyingly.

Literalists also believe that stories are either provably historical or they are merely "entertainments." Some stories, to be sure, like detective novels and Westerns, are most often just that: ways to pass the time. But other stories have a far more serious purpose: to give an insight into reality that you just can't get as satisfyingly from a cold left-brain analysis, like philosophy or theology. *Catcher in the Rye* never historically happened, and yet it gives more insight into adolescent male psychology than most psychology textbooks; *The Color Purple* never historically happened either, and yet it allows us to *experience* better than reams of cold statistics the life of an impoverished, abused, courageous black woman.

Jesus didn't teach in cut-and-dry treatises; he taught in stories. So did the gospel writers who followed in his footsteps. So it should trouble no one's faith to hear, "The story of the Magi is 'only' a myth," or "I can't believe Jesus actually walked on the water." To say such things is to miss the whole point of the stories.

Most people—including the editors of *Time* magazine—equate the word "myth" to some naive belief that has been proven to be false, like "Vietnam destroyed the myth that America could never lose a war." There's a far more positive—in fact essential—meaning to the word "myth." A genuine myth is a story that acts like a metaphor or a symbol. Start with an unarguable truth: Life is difficult. Change that to a metaphor: Life is a war, and you just hope you win more battles than you lose. The two statements say exactly the same thing, one literally, the other figuratively, and both are legitimate. But the second one gives just a bit more insight into the actual struggles involved. Now go one step further and spin the metaphor out into a story:

> Once upon a time there was a boy named Youth, eager to go out and do battle with dragons and trolls. He had a rather dithery old tutor, Scholasticus, who droned on all day about this and that, but Youth hardly listened except just before a test. He spent most of his time daydreaming of a damsel he had heard the minstrel sing of: Perfecta the Impeccable, locked away in the Castle Perilous by the jealous witch, Time, and guarded by the giant, Fear, who squashed dragons into dog food to pass the time.

One day, Youth slipped away with his squire, Hope, and set off through the mountains of Doubt and the swamp of Puberty, where lilies and poisonous snakes abound. Finally, they arrived at Castle Perilous, called forth the giant, and waded into the fray. Fall after fall, they were defeated and crawled away into the woods, where they were found by the Good Witch Pride who bound up their wounds and sent them back into battle with a secret potion called Faith.

While Hope distracted the giant, Fear, by telling him naughty—and totally untrue—stories, Youth crept up behind him and stabbed him right in his fat gizzard, and Fear fell face-forward into the fen. Of course, Youth and Perfecta fell instantly in love, were married and crowned king and queen on the very same day, and lived happily ever after. Or so we are told.

That story never happened, but it tells something about the trials and tribulations of being a young boy. It is no more than an extrapolation of the original metaphor, Life is a war, but it gives a lot more about the specific battles, and it says the same thing as the literal statement, Life is difficult. If you took the basic statement even further, gave the characters less obvious names, filled in the adventures with more detailed, realistic events, you would have a novel like *The Red Badge of Courage*—which never happened but nonetheless tells truths about human life more richly and more appealingly than a literal textbook could.

Aesop did the same thing in his fables. He never thought his listeners believed rabbits actually, literally, made bets—any more than the author of Genesis expected his readers to believe snakes once talked to naked ladies in the park. Stories capture the attention more readily than sermons; what's more, they distract listeners from their preconceptions by sugarcoating the moral pill with adventure. No child wants to hear, one more time, "You may not be as talented as the others, but if you stick to it, you can beat them." But the child will sit still for the story of the tortoise and the hare, which tells the same truth. For the sake of those too dense to figure out the moral for themselves, Aesop prints it out for them at the end.

Folktales like "Beauty and the Beast" and "The Three Little Pigs" never happened either, but they still tell very profound truths about growing from a child into an adult human being. "Beauty and the Beast" physicalizes the real truth that anything ugly, once it is loved, becomes beautiful. "The Three Little Pigs" says not only that you have to learn that hard work pays off more than playing games does but also that you have to conquer and harness the wolf—the Beast —within yourself.

The parables of Jesus serve the same purpose. They're stories that never, historically, occurred; Jesus made them up *in order* to tell a truth he couldn't convey to them in any other acceptable way. And yet they do convey a truth about what being a human being and a Christian truly mean. The story of the Good Samaritan (which appears only in Luke) never happened, and yet it sugarcoats a quite unpalatable pill: when Jesus says we must love the neighbor as ourselves, he means we cannot limit "neighbor" merely to our attractive neighbors. The story of the prodigal father (which, again, appears only in Luke) tells us that, to be true Christians, we must forgive those who "come home" even though they haven't "paid up their debts in full." Jesus told the truth in the form of stories simply because his audiences wouldn't have "bought" the truth had he said it straight out.

The word "parable" comes from the Greek *para-* (around) + *ballein* (to throw), which pretty much translates into "curveball." It's a story that seems at first to the listener to say something he or she finds unthreatening till, all of a sudden: Thud! The ball's in the catcher's glove, and the batter's fallen for a sucker pitch.

The same is true of later additions that might have been made by the authors of the gospels—or their sources. Is it necessary to be a full-fledged Christian that you believe that, on a given night, the sky was *literally* filled with angels singing at the tops of their lungs? Not really. When Luke wrote that episode, he was trying to show how important the birth of the Messiah was. How does Steven Spielberg show that something in one of his films is important? He lays on the music and the special effects; so do those who design rock concerts; so does Luke. The point is not whether you can find an independent source to corroborate the presence of these fire-folk in the sky that particular night. The point is whether the birth of Jesus was really important.

Scholars quibble over whether the wise men actually showed up at Jesus' birth, as Matthew says they did. Many people get their ideas of the wise men more from shopping mall windows than from the gospel. They don't realize that the wise men appear in only one gospel, that there is no designation of them as "kings"; it merely says "some stargazers" or some "wise men" showed up. Nor does it ever say there were three or that they were different races. We get the idea there were three from the three gifts: gold, frankincense, and myrrh. There could have been twelve who chipped in to buy three gifts; there could have been two. But the point of the story is not how many or even that they actually showed up. The point is the same as the story of the boy named Youth, a truth that can be conveyed better with a story than with a televised documentary: Jesus came not only to the poor, uneducated, Jewish shepherds, but also to the rich, learned, and Gentile peoples. Is that the truth? Yes. And even the legendary additions, like the different colors of the visitors and their names—Gaspar, Melchior, and Balthazar—"fit" the truth of the story, even though they are not historical, and not even in the gospel itself! Jesus also came for people who are not white.

So too with the story about walking on water—which is not so much about Jesus walking on water but on *Peter* walking on the water. The point of the story, whether it is historically true or not, is nonetheless an embodiment of the truth: If you keep your eyes on Jesus and forget your shortcomings, you can do what you thought was impossible. As soon as you focus on what *you* think you're capable of, you sink. Perhaps Peter never did literally, historically walk on the water, but the coward of Good Friday went on to be crucified for refusing to deny that Jesus had risen from the dead. That's a miracle greater than walking on water! To say that there must have been a sandbar and it only *appeared* that Jesus and Peter were walking on the water is as left-brain blind as trying to argue that no Fairy Godmother could turn a pumpkin into a carriage, or no boy could be as articulate and cutesy-flip as Holden Caulfield, or no snake could have talked to a naked lady in a park, or no young man thirty-years-old could have been as indecisive as Hamlet.

Literalists (fundamentalists) have to dance around and try to twist the facts, like making up a story that there was a certain gate in the Jerusalem Wall so narrow it was called The Needle's Eye, and rich people *could* get into the kingdom with a little rearranging of their loads—so *that* big benefactors would stay and support the parish! Crazy! It was hyperbole. Just like, "I'll wipe that smirk off your face with my fist!" It's not literal, but it's a lot more forceful than "I'm angry." Rich people are welcome in Christ's kingdom—Martha, Mary, and Lazarus were rich; so was Joseph of Arimathea who gave Jesus his tomb. The Good Samaritan would have been no good to the man in the ditch without money. Money won't bar the gate into heaven, but it's bound to be a very, very big distraction.

Ease up on Jesus. Let him talk in figurative language and not in the terms of an abstract theologian. But also let him talk in terms which he—and Mark— understood. *Yield* to them, rather than writing your own "acceptable" version of the gospel, like that kid with "Wind and Silver." That's why Jesus got so angry—and so often—at his own apostles, because they wanted to hear what Jesus said in terms *they* found acceptable, rather than in the terms he actually chose. When Jesus said "kingdom," they kept insisting on taking him literally, filling their heads with hopes of golden crowns and influence. As you'll see in reading Mark's gospel, again and again the problem is not with what God says but with what we're willing to hear.

2

How the Gospel Became the Gospels

Jesus didn't write the gospels. The first Christian communities did. In fact, the first explanation of the Good News was not written by Matthew, Mark, Luke, or John, but by St. Paul in his letters to the churches around the eastern Mediterranean.

> For I handed on to you as of first importance what I in turn had received: that Christ died for our sins in accordance with the scriptures, and that he was buried, and that he was raised on the third day in accordance with the scriptures, and that he appeared to Cephas, then to the twelve. . . . Last of all, as to one untimely born, he appeared also to me. (1 Cor 15:3-8)

Many good Christians are surprised the church came *before* the gospels. Of course they realize Jesus didn't write things like, "And then Jesus said," but they're shocked when someone suggests that every word quoted by a gospel writer as coming from Jesus' mouth is not necessarily a perfectly accurate quotation. In AD 30, there were no camcorders or tape machines—although because of memorizing lessons from the rabbis, the people had remarkably better memories than our own.

Perhaps this will be clearer if we look at an actual passage that "covers" the same event but in quite different ways. (RSV; Burton Throckmorton, *Gospel Parallels* [New York: Nelson, 1957]. Because John is so much different from the other three, we will restrict ourselves to the three Synoptics—Matthew, Mark, and Luke, who are called "Synoptics" [*synoptikos*, seeing the whole thing together] because you can put them side-by-side and read them in parallel.)

MATTHEW	MARK	LUKE
[51]And behold, the curtain of the temple was torn in two, from top to bottom; and the earth shook, and the rocks were split; [52]and the tombs were opened, and many bodies of the saints who had fallen asleep were raised, [53]and coming out of the tombs after his resurrection they went into the holy city and appeared to many.	[38]And the curtain of the temple was torn in two, from top to bottom.	[See v. 45—curtain]
[54]When the centurion and those who were with him, keeping watch over Jesus, saw the earthquake and what took place, they were filled with awe, and said, "Truly this was the Son of God!"	[39]And when the centurion who stood facing him, saw that he thus breathed his last, he said, "Truly this was the Son of God!"	[47]Now when the centurion saw what had taken place, he praised God, and said, "Certainly this man was innocent!"

As an exercise:

(1) Draw a solid line under words and phrases where all three agree verbatim.

(2) Draw a wavy line under words and phrases where all three agree but with just a difference in vocabulary or style.

(3) Draw a broken line under words where at least two agree (usually Matthew and Luke and not Mark).

(4) Finally, circle the places where only *one* of the three has an entry.

All three have similarities. They're all speaking of the death of Jesus and with many of the same details, though not in the same places in their narration.

Luke has already put the detail of the torn curtain in his verse 45, at the moment *before* Jesus died. The event itself is probably not historical but rather symbolic. The curtain hung in the doorway to the holy of holies, the most sacred place in the Jewish cult. But why does Luke put it *before* Jesus' death while the other two put it after? Probably to say in symbolic terms that Judaism was "defeated" before Jesus. Note that Luke, who is writing for well-educated Greek-speaking Romans, changes the centurion's declaration to "this man was innocent," rather than "this man was the Son of God." Luke is emphasizing that Jesus is not guilty of any crime against the Roman state. And the "multitudes," the Jews, return to their homes acknowledging their guilt.

Matthew adds far more symbolic and hyperbolic details: earthquake, tombs opening and yielding up their dead, and even the Hebrew saints coming alive again after Jesus' resurrection. Matthew is the Steven Spielberg of the gospel writers; throughout his gospel he has a fondness for the grand scale. The earthquake—which Old Testament poetry said figuratively was the tread of Yahweh's feet as he passed by—is a sign that says God is leaving Israel behind. Also, it is one of the signs of the beginning of the Day of Yahweh, when the remnant of Israel would be freed. Moreover, through the symbolism of the risen dead, Matthew can connect the resurrection of the believer—even the pre-Christian believer—with the resurrection of Jesus. That is *why* the Messiah had to die. And Matthew is writing for a primarily Jewish audience who would grasp these Old Testament allusions more readily than Gentiles or ourselves.

Mark is the briefest and, as we shall see in more detail later, was most likely the first gospel and the one Matthew and Luke used as a "base text" to which they added material that they had discovered from later sources unavailable to Mark.

Each tells the same event, but each from a different point of view, for a different audience, and for a different purpose. Historically, who knows what the people who actually stood at the cross thought or said? The point is that Jesus did actually die, and that the event and its aftermath, the resurrection, calls for a response. When reading the Synoptic Gospels, it's important to remember three very important facts:

(1) The gospel writers were not just reporters; they were also *commentators*. They were not merely setting down facts but, by their treatment, trying to bring out their *significance*.

(2) The gospel writers had quite different personalities and were writing for quite different audiences with different receptivities and concerns: Matthew wrote for Jews with a deep knowledge of the Old Testament; Luke wrote for well-educated Romans with no knowledge of Hebrew or its scriptures; Mark

wrote "on the run" during the persecution of Christians by Nero (AD 60) and his style is quite breathless and unpolished.

(3) Each gospel writer had his own sources of information. Mark's source was quite possibly Peter himself, since tradition says that he was Peter's interpreter to Greek-speaking audiences, plus an already-written account of Jesus' passion, plus various accounts he picked up from eyewitnesses or oral reports; Matthew and Luke reproduce nearly every verse of Mark and thus probably used his book as a base text. But they also have identical material Mark did not have and they both use, indicating they shared at least one common source (called Q). Further, Matthew and Luke have sections unique to each (M and L) and therefore had sources exclusively their own. Finally, since Matthew doesn't use items unique to Luke—and vice versa—they probably did not know of one another's work, or they would have used that "good stuff."

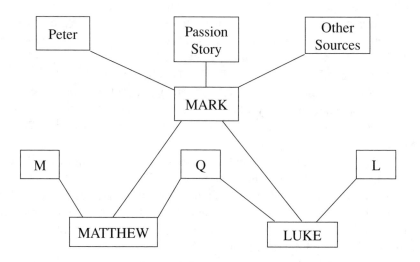

Q = *Quelle*, 250 verses of sayings of Jesus common to Matthew and Luke but not found in Mark.

M = Matthew's exclusive sources, unknown to Mark or Luke (e.g., the wise men at Jesus' birth).

L = Luke's exclusive sources, unknown to Mark or Matthew (e.g., the shepherds at Jesus' birth).

3

Mark: Collector and Editor

The Emperor Nero began a persecution of Christians in the Roman Empire in AD 64 and it did not end until Nero's death in 68. It was the persecution in which the Apostle Paul was most likely beheaded in about 67. At nearly the same time, the Jews in Palestine revolted against Rome in AD 66, beginning a war they hoped Yahweh would help them win. When the war ended tragically in the complete destruction of Jerusalem in the year 70, Palestinian Christians were caught in the middle. The Romans considered them one more sect of Jews, and the Jews considered them deserters—plus a mixed bag of half-assimilated Gentiles. Many Jewish Christians fled to other Christian communities around the Mediterranean, taking with them their collections of Jesus' sayings and deeds. The audience outside Palestine was used to more philosophical and theological handling of new ideas. Therefore, the message from missionaries like Paul was intriguing. And this interaction of theological understanding with historical-mythic material was certainly responsible in large part for the writing of the later gospels of Luke and Matthew.

But first came Mark. In about AD 65, just after the beginning of Nero's persecution, Mark wrote his small volume. Looking at events around him, Mark must have seen the dreadful prophecies that make up his own chapter 13 literally being fulfilled: there were, in fact, wars and rumors of war coming from Palestine and elsewhere; there were (and always are) earthquakes and droughts; Christians were being persecuted by emigrated Jews and martyred by Romans; before his death in AD 41, the Emperor Caligula had vowed to erect a heroic statue of himself within the holy of holies of the Jewish temple ("the desolating sacrilege," 13:14). Mark could not have helped but think that the prophecies of the end were literally coming true, though at the time the Apostle Paul in his letters was drawing back from his own previous belief in an almost immediate end of the world.

But other concerns were reflected in Mark's gospel version as well as preparing for the end. With a previously written brief account of Jesus' passion, Peter's recollections, scattered anecdotes, sayings, and brief collections of writings, he set out to construct a book that would explain "The Way" of Christian belief. Nearly 20 percent of Mark's gospel (about 117 verses) is taken up with so-called controversy stories (ostensibly between Jesus and the temple officials) that give us a very good idea of the issues that troubled the people of the later Christian community, at least in Rome, for whom Mark was writing.

The treatment Mark gives the passion account that he inherited attempts to answer the question: *Why* did Jesus die? And why the ugly death Romans reserved only for runaway slaves and revolutionaries? Why would his own people desire his death, and why would a good God allow it? To these questions Mark attempts an answer. First of all, Jesus died because the Jewish leaders refused to believe his claims and, out of envy (15:10), handed him over to the Roman governor. (The reasons for this envy will become clear when we consider the controversy stories with which Mark prefaces his treatment of the passion/death narrative.)

Jesus died because he *willed* to die: "For the Son of Man came not to be served but to serve, and to give his life a ransom for many" (10:45). If Jesus did *not* die and rise, we would never have known that we too will die but rise. Most important, Jesus died because God willed it and had expressed his will throughout the Hebrew Scriptures: Jesus said, "The Son of Man goes as it is written of him" (14:21). In the garden, Jesus said, "Yet, not what I want, but what you want" (14:36b). And at his crucifixion, the details Mark point out are taken from the psalms of the Suffering Servant in Isaiah (chap. 53).

In the controversy stories that occupy almost a fifth of his gospel, Mark attempts to answer other questions by using the literary device of placing the question in the mouths of Jesus' antagonists, the temple officials, and giving either the answer Jesus gave himself historically or one that was consistent with his message. This is a method Christian theologians have used for the last two thousand years to deal with problems Jesus simply could not have anticipated: nuclear war, planetary pollution, etc.

These can be grouped into three types of disputes Mark's audience later had: (1) with Jews, (2) with the Greco Roman environment, or (3) with both. Remember, too, that these answers of Mark were not merely defensive against attack from Jews or Hellenists (Greek-speaking converts) but also offensive, seeking out converts and instructing the already converted.

(1) *For Jews*: the Sabbath observance, divorce, the "greatest commandment: Love God, love neighbor," the Davidic descent of the Messiah, food regulations, and the relationship of Jesus' doctrine to John the Baptist's teachings.

(2) *For non-Jews*: the problem of paying tribute to Caesar when that money could be used for immoral purposes (exactly the same moral problem many had over paying taxes during the Vietnam War).

(3) *For both*: the source of Jesus' power and authority, the need for signs to prove beyond doubt Jesus was Lord, defense of eating with pagans and "sinners." Who were the true leaders of the church? Mark's answer is simple: "the Twelve" (3:13-19). It's clear John the Baptist wasn't a rival to Jesus but his herald. Was martyrdom for the sake of others, as Jesus' was, the only true test of discipleship? Throughout his gospel version, Mark's Jesus gives a demand far less terrifying than martyrdom: faith in Jesus as Lord (Yahweh), humbling oneself, giving a cup of water, living in peace, being wary of the enticement of riches, childlike vulnerability. In other words, the true test of Christian discipleship is renunciation of selfishness. Still, for Mark's audiences in and around the Rome of the ferocious Nero, the complete renunciation embodied in martyrdom was not out of the question.

But one can imagine the effect of this gospel on the meetings of frightened, persecuted Christians in Rome and throughout the empire, in danger at any moment of being hanged up as living torches in Nero's gardens or thrown to the beasts in the arena. Here is a Jesus, compassionate and willing to help, a friend of sinners; here is a Jesus also hated and despised, betrayed by his own friends, deserted by his disciples, and sent to shameful death at the hands of the Jews and Romans. Surely it was a precious document to them.

Besides the end of the world passage that became Mark's chapter 13, the passion account, and the collections of controversies handed on to him, Mark quite likely had a fourth source of material: Peter himself. Papias, writing in the early second century:

> When Mark became Peter's interpreter, he wrote down accurately although not in order, all that he [Peter] remembered of what the Lord had said or done. For he [Mark] had not heard or followed the Lord, but later, as I said [heard and followed] Peter, who used to adapt his teaching to the needs [of the moment and audience], without making any sort of arrangement of the Lord's oracles. Consequently, Mark made no mistake in thus writing down certain things as he remembered them. For he was careful not to omit or falsify anything of what he had heard. (*The Jerome Biblical Commentary*, 42:1)

Mark's gospel was written (between AD 65 and 70) only a few years after Peter's death in Rome (about AD 64). When it was written, the character of Peter had been transfigured by martyrdom, and it was easy to see how readily those threatened by persecution would understand this model disciple, who believed so fiercely and yet doubted so often, who loved Jesus dearly and yet failed so frequently to grasp anything, who stood breathless at the transfiguration and snored through the agony in the garden, who three times denied the Jesus he loved and yet wept bitterly at his weakness and became a missioner of the message of resurrection.

The Jesus of Mark is the Son of God, equipped with divine power right from the first verse. But he is also a Jewish teacher and prophet, with human feelings of anger and disappointment and limited knowledge. Divinity and humanity interpenetrate each other in Jesus in an inseparable unity. He is more than the Messiah; he is also the Son of God. Mark never reflects *how* one could be both God and human at the same time, nor how God's son arrived or departed. But in his rugged Greek prose—so different from the elegance of Luke—he affirmed his belief in a forthright tone that seems to say, "Don't ask me to explain it, but that's the way things *are*." It is the same tone as Peter's answer to Jesus' question of who they thought Jesus was (8:29): " 'But who do you say that I am?' Peter answered him, 'You are the Messiah.' " Period. It is the same tone as the tough Gentile centurion's at the cross in the statement that climaxes Mark's gospel: "This man was God's Son!" Period.

The Messianic Secret

The focus of Mark's unique approach to the gospel is in his question to Peter quoted above: "Who do you say I am?" Right from his opening statement, Mark doesn't keep the answer to that question a secret from the reader: "The beginning of the good news of Jesus Christ, the *Son of God*" (1:1). No dodging there. But the development of Mark's book is shaped by showing Jesus slowly establishing a basis for that opening claim.

Such care is, to say the least, prudent. You can imagine Jesus starting out his mission by revealing his true identity from the start: "Who am I? I'm the Messiah you've all been waiting for for the last thousand years. Oh, yes, and by the way, I'm also God. Don't look so surprised!" There quite likely would have been no gospels and no Christianity.

Right! Everyone reading this page has already heard, again and again (and again) that Jesus claimed to be equal to God. It has little power to shock anymore. But imagine hearing it for the very first time! Especially a crowd of rigidly monotheistic Jews who for their entire history prided themselves on having only *one* God, as opposed to their polytheistic neighbors. He would have been stoned to death on the spot, and there never would have been a Christian gospel, no cathedrals or hospitals or libraries, and all that we mean by "Western civilization" would have been unimaginably otherwise.

What's more, it took the Christian Church over two hundred years of speculating and arguing and excommunicating back and forth to settle on an even
remotely satisfying (and terribly complex!) explanation of just *how* there could
be only one God and yet a Father, Son, and Holy Spirit. Mark, with Roman
soldiers roaming the streets looking for Christians, did not have that luxury.
The historical Jesus who trudged the rocky roads of Palestine long before
anything was written about him would have been a colossal fool to walk boldly
into the Nazareth synagogue and declare his divinity! In fact, a case can be
made—and we will explore it later—that the historical Jesus himself discovered
who he really was only gradually, just as we must discover our real selves.

The secret that emerges through Mark's gospel is that Jesus is an extraordinary person, capable of miraculous cures and speaking as no man had ever
spoken before. The first revelation comes at the mini-climax when Peter re-
sponds: "You are the Messiah." But then it reaches its fullest climax when Jesus
is questioned by the high priest at the Jewish trial (14:61-62): "Are you the
Messiah, the Son of the Blessed One?" And Jesus answers unhesitatingly, "I
AM." He is not only the Messiah; he is also the unique Son of God, and he
does not hesitate to use the words no Jew would dare to use—the unpronounceable name of Yahweh—at which, the high priest rips his garment at the blatant
blasphemy and says, "You have heard his blasphemy." Finally, when it is all
over, the quiet climax that ends the story, the *pagan* centurion's declaration
(15:39) answering that same question: "Truly this man was God's Son!"

It is precisely the *impossibility* of Jesus' claim that forms the whole structure
of Mark's gospel. The temple authorities simply cannot accept what they realize
more and more Jesus is starting to claim. His own disciples resent all that Jesus
claims he and they must undergo. It is the conflict of two points of view: this
world's (the Antagonist) and God's (the Kingdom).

Jesus gives the resolution after the rich man has walked away from the
invitation to become an apostle, after he has made his hyperbolic claim about
the rich man and the camel through the needle: "For mortals it is impossible,
but not for God" (10:27).

There is the radical conflict: trying to limit God to what we are capable of
understanding.

An Outline of Mark

    (1) **Overture** 1:1-13: The Desert

        (a) John and Jesus

        (b) The Prototype Temptation

    (2) **Galilean Ministry** 1:14–8:21

        (a) Inauguration Platform 1:14-15: "The kingdom is here."

(b) Disciples 1:16-45

(c) Conflicts with the Antagonist 2:1–3:6

(d) Ministry 3:7–4:34

(e) Beyond Galilee to the Gentiles 4:35–8:26

(3) **From Galilee to Jerusalem** 8:27–10:52

(a) Focusing the conflict with the Antagonist

(b) Begins and ends with cures of blindness

(4) **Passion and Resurrection** 11:1–16:8

(a) Rejection of Judaism 11:1–13:37

(b) Passion 14:1–15:47

(c) Victory over Death 16:1-8

4

Jesus' Consciousness of His Divinity

A theme throughout Mark's gospel is the antagonism between our perspective on reality and God's, the limitation of our point of view because of our human, space-time limitations, in contrast to God's limitlessness. That very antagonism, however, raises a significant problem in understanding Jesus himself. How could Jesus' knowledge of the truth—especially of the future—be *both* limitless (his divinity) *and* limited (his humanity)? That seems a radical contradiction.

In a trivial way, for instance, when Jesus was a boy and Joseph took him into the carpenter shop, did Jesus just *pretend* he didn't know a thousand better ways to make a chest than Joseph did? Homilists frequently say, "Ah, Jesus had the cross looming before his eyes from the very days of his childhood." If so, he had far longer to prepare for his agonies than most humans do; one of the bitterest prices for being human is *not* knowing when tragedy will befall us. In the agony in the garden, Jesus begs his Father not to make him go through with the passion he knows is beginning. But if he had full use of the divine knowledge, he'd *know* the future; he'd know that he would get through it; he'd not be limited by the boxed-in, space-time perspective. This conflict is most disturbing when Jesus was dying: He cried out, "My God, my God, why have you abandoned me?" If he enjoyed the divine knowledge, he'd have known with total certainty that he had *not* been abandoned. Was he merely quoting a psalm for the edification of the crowd? Put at its rawest: was Jesus merely *faking* despair?

Similarly, when people tell us our lives should imitate Jesus' life, there is at least a temptation to say, "It was *easy* for Jesus. He was God. He *knew* what was going to happen. I don't!" For every human being ever born, the most painful difficulty of *being* human is coping with imperfection, uncertainty, doubt. How could Jesus have been authentically human if he never knew doubt?

23

How could the temptations in the desert have been real if Jesus could "see right through them" in a way we can't when we are faced with temptation?

What's more, of all the natures we know, human nature is the only one that is an invitation and not a command. Growth *as* human beings involves freely responding to the invitation to mature every day as *more* human, more able to know and love. If Jesus were in possession of the fullness of knowledge and love, growth would be impossible. God is perfect. By that very fact, God has no growing to do. But the gospel says explicitly that Jesus "increased in wisdom and in years, and in divine and human favor" (Luke 2:52). God "increased"? How is that possible?

Finally, one of the greatest continuing crises in human life, especially in adolescence, is the search for a unique identity, not the smallest part of which is coping with the bewilderment of sexuality. As Richard McBrien says, "To accept a Jesus who is at once human—yet immune to sexual desires—is to stretch not only one's imagination but also one's theological convictions about the incarnation and the fundamental goodness of creation, the human body, and human sexuality."

Jesus must have faced all of this if he was, as dogma says he was, not only fully divine but also *fully human*. Further, he had to have a *growing* (human) realization not only of who he was as a human being, as we all do, but also a growing realization of who he was as the Son of God!

The answer—or at least an answer—lies in an insight of Paul to the Philippians (2:6-7):

> Though he was in the form of God, [he] did not regard equality with
> God as something to be exploited, but emptied himself, taking the form
> of a slave, being born in human likeness.

Jesus most definitely did not stop *being* God. It was as if a king had tried in vain for years to make his people understand what would make them happy and came down and *became* a peasant himself. Everything he did, he did as a peasant. But he couldn't stop *being* king.

But the metaphor of the king, like all metaphors, limps: the king-peasant in the metaphor would still *remember* he was king. But Jesus—if you will allow another clumsy metaphor—freely became *amnesiac* about being God and about the divine knowledge: "he *emptied* himself," gave up all the prerogatives of divinity (without giving up divinity itself) and became fully immersed in humanity, with all its limitations.

Nor did Jesus-the-Man *become* more and more divine as he aged; what changed was not Jesus' divinity but Jesus' growing *understanding* of his divinity.

Thus Jesus grew like any other boy of his place and time. He was genuinely ignorant about how to tie his sandals until Mary taught him how. He learned how to wash, how to control his bladder and bowels, how to read, just as any normal Jewish boy did. Leaving aside the Angel Gabriel appearing to Mary as an attempt to embody her realization of the source of her pregnancy, and leaving aside the extravagance of Matthew's description of the angelic hosts at Jesus' birth, Jesus lived a normal childhood. There must have been something "special" about him, as indicated in Luke's description of Jesus astonishing the rabbis in the temple with his insight into scripture, but otherwise his boyhood was so normal no record remains of it.

But then at Jesus' baptism by John, it all came together in a thunderous realization (symbolized by the opening of the heavens, the dove, the voice): "You are my Son, the Beloved; with you I am well pleased" (Mark 1:11). The effect within him must have been stunning. It simply couldn't be true. As a result, his spirit "drove" him into the wilderness to test that realization, and it was precisely that question on which he was tested: "If you *are* the Son of God, command this stone to become a loaf of bread" (Luke 4:3; emphasis added). They would all come running after it. But Jesus resisted the easy way of trickery. But the temptation couldn't have been a temptation if Jesus had foolproof divine knowledge. To be genuinely "tempting," it had to seem truly desirable.

When he had conquered the temptations, he came resolutely into the synagogue and, according to Luke (4:18-19), read to the worshipers from the scroll of Isaiah:

> The Spirit of the Lord is upon me, because he has anointed me to bring good news to the poor. He has sent me to proclaim release to the captives and recovery of sight to the blind, to let the oppressed go free, to proclaim the year of the Lord's favor.

From that moment, Jesus went on, *trusting* that his mission was empowered and authenticated by his Father, and he spoke with his Father's authority. Yet he always insisted that it was his *Father* who worked *through* him. He says, too, in regard to his knowledge of the future, "No one knows, neither the angels in heaven, *nor the Son*, but only the Father" (Mark 13:32; emphasis added).

Thus, Jesus worked as we all must work, trusting in God and in our mission from God. After the agony in the garden (14:51-52), *after* "*All* of them deserted him and fled," Mark—and only Mark—pictures a "young man . . . wearing nothing but a linen cloth." The temple soldiers "caught hold of him, but he left the linen cloth and ran off naked." This puzzling person was clearly not one of the regular disciples, since they had "all" already deserted him. As we saw before, young men in bright white garments were *symbols* for the presence of

God: angels. If everything so far has been correct about Jesus' consciousness of his divinity, at that moment Jesus' inflexible conviction of his Father's protection faced a shattering test, and Jesus went through his passion alone, on nothing but guts and faith. Just as we must.

At the next-to-last moment of his life, when he cried, "My God, my God, why have you forsaken me?" he truly felt despair. Was he wrong? Had he deluded himself? But Luke shows Jesus' very last statement, "Father, into your hands I commend my spirit!" (23:46).

Not only does this explanation begin to resolve the conflict between Jesus' divine and human intelligence, but it even more importantly makes the person of Jesus so much more approachable, cuts down the intimidating distance between what Jesus was capable of and what God asks us to be capable of.

It is a most profound difference between Christianity and any other religion: only our God has been tempted to despair, just as we sometimes are. Our God felt his heart pound with terror and despair, knew what it was like to be abandoned by his friends, wondered at times if he was a self-deluded fool, put his faith in his Father's hands when he was genuinely tempted to despair.

This Jesus has a Secret worth looking into.

"The Son of Man *Must* Suffer" (9:12)

Like a musical theme in a minor key, the "necessity" of Jesus' suffering threads its way through Mark's gospel. From hearing it so often, most of us take that for granted—that Jesus' mission was to suffer in our place. But why? God could have repaired whatever is wrong in human life with a flick of his (nonexistent) fingers. Why did Jesus "have to" suffer? In fact, why does *anybody* have to suffer? Just because the first pair of fools didn't realize they had the best of all possible worlds—and screwed up everything? For *one* piece of fruit?

God is faithful, no matter what. But what of the obverse, rarely broached? How long are we to cleave to a God who ambushes us with tragedy, often just as we've improvised some shaky equanimity from the last surprise? How do we assess a God who invented both breathtaking sunsets and emphysema? Who "demanded" the suffering even of the One he loved best? In order to satisfy his own bruised ego? As Robert Frost quipped: "Forgive, O Lord, my little jokes on Thee, and I'll forgive Thy great big joke on me."

In the broadest sense, "suffering" means losing anything we love or even just presume. In that sense, getting out of bed is suffering, leaving the serenity of sleep to face the day's surprises. Suffering is given. But can any insight make the forfeitures *worth* it? Every thinker since Buddha began with that primal unfairness, the *lachrymae rerum*. That search feeds our dreams with paradisial islands where no one has to work or be watchful. Most stories, however, suggest suffering is the path to growth as a human being, that *purpose* comes from surpassing challenges.

At least in the cold light of reason, if you grant that the Creator intends humans freely to foster the growth of their souls, some suffering "makes sense." On one hand, *natural retribution* is etched into the natures of things. Violate those ingrained natures, and you discover that. Like hearing the tilt buzzer in pinball, intelligent people sense a "wrongness" defying limits too often. If you act the S.O.B, you *become* an S.O.B., and few will dare tell you. On the other hand, if Whoever Made the Rules invites free evolution *beyond* animal nature by scaling predictable obstacles, each crisis in physical growth is a *natural invitation* to broader and deeper participation in being human, independent of parents. In that perspective, such inequities as adolescence are certainly unpleasant but "legitimate," more readily acceptable, an invitation to a larger life.

Contrarily, *unmerited* suffering is unpredictable, an affliction for which no victim was responsible: My parents split, my house burned, my friend betrayed my confidence, my mother's alcoholic, I got hit by necrotizing fasciitis. None of them my fault, but either live with them or go mad trying to make the truth untrue.

Another way to study our common burden subdivides that unmerited suffering into *physical* suffering—hurricanes, cancer, death—results of living in this world rather than another. No human is responsible for those, only Whoever set up this environment with those pitfalls. The other unmerited suffering is *moral* evil: "Man's inhumanity"—war, murder, rape—results of human will, freely degrading others and oneself. Although this places the rebel human as the *immediate* cause, it still doesn't absolve the kindly Creator. If God is The Ultimate Cause of *Everything*, He/She freely gave wits and freedom to inadequately evolved apes. Some thinking people find that so contradictory they deny such a careless Cause can exist.

Each of us, merely by being born (for which none of us was responsible), is by that fact *condemned* to death. Samuel Beckett makes that absurdity clear: "Astride of a grave and a difficult birth. Down in the hole, lingeringly, the grave-digger puts on the forceps." In a godless universe, the greatest curses are intelligence and hope: hungers—by our very nature—for answers and survival. But in the godless universe, there are no answers and we won't survive! Better a pig that never asks why or yearns to outwit death.

Who can justify a God who allows cancer to devour a saint? (Or permits his only Son to be insulted, scourged, and executed?)

That question underlies the book of Job: the mystery of suffering for which the victim is not culpable. God allows subjection of "the perfect and upright man" to one physical and moral evil after another. Natural disasters and marauders destroy his children, animals, and crops. His skin erupts in boils. His wife deserts him. Yet despite his friends' insistence God makes *only* the guilty suffer, Job knows unarguably he did nothing wicked enough to justify suffering such as his.

Unmerited Suffering

Whether one suffers innocently from the whims of the environment (physical evil) or from others' callous use of freedom (moral evil), God's "answer" is the same. It comes at the end of the book of Job, and at (almost) the end of each gospel. But God's answer is *not* "fair" or "just." Nor is it, in any strict sense, an "answer." In the first place, when God finally arrives to respond to Job's accusations of mistreatment, God turns up in a *hurricane*, which is not quite fair. But that's God's whole *point.* Job's situation is not a question of *justice* but a matter of *trust*, as was Abraham's. In the second place, the answer is not rational at all, but rather a person-to-Person experiential *encounter* between a creature and his Creator—which is what "religion" means.

"Gird up your loins," says God's imperious voice to Job from the windstorm. "Where were you when I laid the foundation of the earth? Tell me, if you have understanding" (Job 38:3-4). In effect, God is saying, "Have you forgotten who I AM and who you are? Is there some ground on which you presume I should check my plans with you? Is it just possible I have reasons your space-time mind is incapable of fathoming?"

If the "patience of Job" means fidelity despite boundless doubt, then Job was truly a patient, trusting man. But if "patience" means silent acquiescence, he was anything but. For thirty-seven chapters he relentlessly challenges his friends who insist he is guilty. Since scripture is the word of God, and Job is rewarded in the end for his perseverance, God seems to have no problem with our using the wits he gave us to challenge him. (A wonderful Jewish belief says, when we use our God-given wits to dispute with him, God dances for joy!)

God finds no objection to our yelling at him, wrestling with him as Jacob did, even bawling him out for a fare-thee-well like Jeremiah, using every curse in our arsenal as we would with any lifelong friend—*provided*, when we calm down, we *forgive* God, for the good times. Because good times have far outnumbered and outweighed the bad times.

For instance, in classes of all boys, if you argue the manifest differences between human and animal sex, you can guess who the sexually active are, because they defend a vested interest with no pretense at fair exchange. At those times, I say, "Look, don't be mad at me because I know more than you do, because I've read more, because I've given these questions more thought."

That's at least remotely like our crying, "Unfair!" to the very Person who gave us the means to see inequity and the skills to voice our objections. Therefore, if forgiveness is the hardest loving, perhaps the way in which we love God most profoundly is forgiving God, for *being* God, for having reasons and a perspective we are simply, humblingly unable to grasp.

Wisdom makes peace with the unchangeable. We're free to face the unavoidable with dignity, to understand the transformational value *attitude* works on suffering. We're not responsible for our predicament as its cause—cancer, job loss, the death of a spouse. But we are responsible for what we *do* with the effects, with what we build from the rubble.

Psychiatrist Viktor Frankl, who survived the Nazi camps, echoes Nietzsche: "Whoever has a *why* to live for can bear with almost any *how*." Whoever could sustain his or her own inalienable soul—clinging to the memory of a loved one, a life-goal, a purposive God—could survive. The ultimate freedom is the *attitude* with which we face unpleasant challenges. But it's a free response. We *can* settle for bitter endurance.

What suffering—accepted as challenge—redeems us from is our misplaced feeling of uselessness, of meaninglessness, of being dismissible as human beings. With that understanding, experience of suffering is essential! Would we exult in good health if we had never been sick? Would we appreciate living without a felt realization of death? Would we feel grateful unless all happiness were precarious? "Shall we receive the good at the hand of God, and not receive the bad?" (Job 2:10).

Jesus' Passion

Personally, I find an iron wall between the Father revealed by Jesus in the parable of the prodigal son and the image of God theologians have offered for centuries, a God who required Jesus' sufferings as an "atonement" for sins. I resist accepting Jesus as a "ransom" for us to an offended and unbending God. Isn't ransom paid only to a *hostile* power?

The God revealed in Jesus' unvarying treatment of sinners—the woman who wept on his feet, the adulterous woman, the woman at the well, cowardly Peter, the kindly thief crucified with him—offers simple, uncritical *acceptance*. Never a need to crawl, to list species and number, no compensatory penance. How to square that kindly Father with a vindictive God who demands blood in recompense for two simpletons (whom he himself gave the freedom) eating one piece of fruit? Could the God who asks us to forgive seventy times seven times hold a grudge so long?

Note well: I'm not denying that centuries-old teaching on atonement. I just no longer pretend I understand it. Not even a fool could deny the *effects* of "original sin": arrogance, covetousness, lust, anger, gluttony, envy, and sloth. But I balk at the Economic Metaphor—an almost irreparable debt to God for one primeval sin—to explain what caused human inconstancy.

I simply have enormous difficulty harmonizing the open-handed God embodied in Jesus and the fault-finding God I accepted until my thirties. I accept that those two seemingly incompatible views must have a way of coexisting, but I have yet to grasp it.

But if the enormous degradation God endured for us on the cross hasn't been deadened by repetition, I wonder if we can find a depth *beyond* atonement. In his forthright confrontation with evil and suffering, Christ did indeed free us—from *fear*: fear that our sins might defy forgiveness, fear that our sufferings have no meaning, fear that only a few loved ones truly *care*. To my mind, our liberation comes in the very nature of a God who *is* Love, who dotes on us neither despite our faults nor because of our good deeds but because we're *his*. Such love eludes any science, even theology.

The "scandal" of the cross—the contradiction of an omnipotent God, by nature inaccessible to anything remotely negative, much less helpless agony (*the omnipotent God of Job!*), willingly yielding to such degradation—defies rational explanation! To those not dulled by familiarity, the cross staggers the mind. What could motivate such abasement? The only response is no rational answer: love—freely given, prompted by nothing more than a Father's death-less infatuation.

The passion declares: "Here! *Look!* Is *this* enough to prove how important you are to me? If wonderment at the carouse of the universe doesn't prove it, if the centuries of my faithful waiting for you outside your bordello isn't enough, is *this* enough? Does this demonstrate you're too *precious* to degrade yourselves with paganism, the momentary bread-and-circuses, the illusory pleasures that tempt you so easily?"

Bewildering as that love is, it is truly comprehensible—and more congruous with the God embodied in Jesus—than a God placated by blood sacrifice, as was accepted in a barbarian world. What's more, it checkmates the two basest motives for choices: fear and hope of reward—tooth and fang, survival of the fittest, the animal in us. It also allows of a God who goes beyond even "Conventional Morality," group loyalty and law and order—quid pro quo, the just balance, the human in us. It provides a model beyond ordinary *human* motivation: unbridled altruism, which is neither rational nor irrational but beyond logic. Difficult as it might be for those whose scope is at those lower levels, this is the God "in whose image" we're fashioned—invited *beyond* the self-centered animal, even *beyond* the self-governed human, into the freewheeling love life of the Trinity Family. Into holiness.

Look at a crucifix. Reflect on whom that corpse embodies. The Architect of the Universe, compacted into that bleeding mass. Can I honestly say—and accept in the depths of myself—"Yes. It's inescapable. God believes *I* am worth that. Who am I even to have second thoughts about that evaluation?" For that, I think I can forgive God's unfathomable intentions.

Part II

The Gospel
of
Jesus Christ
According to
Mark

Text and Commentary

1 ¹The beginning of the good news of Jesus Christ, the Son of God. ²As it is written in the prophet Isaiah,

"See, I am sending my
    messenger ahead of you,
who will prepare your way;
³the voice of one crying out in the
    wilderness:
'Prepare the way of the Lord,
    make his paths straight,'"

Introduction: VV1-8

V1. *The beginning*: In Mark's gospel, there are no genealogies, no stories of Jesus' birth, childhood, or early adulthood. They would most likely have distorted his focus; ***good news***: Mark is the only evangelist to call his book *euangelion*, "gospel, good news," a proclamation of the person and message of Jesus. He IS the good news; ***Jesus***: the Greek form of the Hebrew, *Joshua*— who in the Hebrew scripture succeeded Moses; ***Christ***: (Greek: *christos* = anointed), *the Messiah,* symbolically consecrated with oil, as priests were; ***Son of God***: Right from the top, Mark forthrightly declares Jesus is not merely one more prophet. As Mark later shows at Jesus' trial, he was not executed for being "a godly man" or for forming a new sect of Judaism—since there were already many—but for blasphemy, claiming to be equal to Yahweh. In this first sentence Mark reveals the "Messianic Secret," the answer to the climax questions of his book ("Who *are* you?"): Peter's answer (8:29) is Mark's turning point. Jesus' answer to the high priest's question at his trial—"Are you the Messiah [Anointed One, Christ], the Son of the Blessed One [Yahweh]?" (14:61)—is Mark's climax. And the Gentile centurion's statement—"Truly this man was God's Son" (15:39)—is Mark's culmination. Along the way, only demons acknowledge Jesus' true status (3:11; 5:7). This is testimony from heaven and hell, from Jerusalem and Rome. Jesus' true identity is hidden only from characters in the story, not from the reader.

V2. *As it is written*: Allusions to the Hebrew scripture are used throughout the New Testament (NT) to validate claims of divine authenticity; ***Isaiah***: This first part of the sentence source is actually from Malachi, 3:1; ***messenger***: Note the tiny but crucial comma after the quotation; the entire reference is not to Jesus but to John, the wilderness messenger. The prophet Elijah was to return to purify Israel for the Day of Yahweh (the Lord). Thus, again, the person awaited is now revealed to be not merely another prophet or great hero, but Yahweh himself. The paths are to be made straight for God. God is on his way!

V3. *the voice, etc.*: This is from Isaiah, 40:3. Here, in a kind of prologue, Mark gives preliminary testimonies to Jesus' role: the Old Testament (OT)

⁴John the baptizer appeared in the wilderness, proclaiming a baptism of repentance for the forgiveness of sins. ⁵And people from the whole Judean countryside and all the people of Jerusalem were going out to him, and were baptized by him in the river Jordan, confessing their sins. ⁶Now John was clothed with camel's hair, with a leather belt around his waist, and he ate locusts and wild honey. ⁷He proclaimed, "The one who is more powerful than I is coming after me; I am not worthy to stoop

---

prophets, the Baptist, the Father at Jesus' baptism, and the test given by Satan himself; *wilderness*: this need not be some specific location, but any barren place where God is less easily avoided, where Moses first heard the voice of God and Yahweh betrothed Israel, where Elijah heard God's still, small voice (1 Kgs 19:3-12); *Prepare*: The One coming will make himself known only to those willing to accept him; *Lord*: Greek *Kurios*, Hebrew *Adonai*, as in Psalm 18:1, "Yahweh is Lord." The Hebrew Scriptures are often referred to as "the Law and the Prophets." In the transfiguration (9:2-13), both Moses (the Law) and Elijah (the Prophets) appear as witnesses for Jesus' authenticity.

V4. *John*: Elijah/John heralds Yahweh/Jesus. According to Luke, John and Jesus were second cousins. John might have been a former Essene, a sect of Judaism whose monks retired to wilderness communes to acknowledge their sins and purify themselves, using water as a symbol. Qumran, the most famous Essene commune, was only a few miles from Jericho, the spot on the Jordan where John most likely baptized. Later in Mark (9:12), Jesus himself identifies John's role as the same as Elijah's. As with Jesus, the factual existence of John is attested to from outside the gospels by the Jewish historian Josephus (AD 37–100); *the baptizer*: An evocative translation for "baptizing" is "drenching"—thoroughly cleansing.

V5. *all*: surely hyperbole. The initial response to Jesus was enthusiastic too, but it splintered when he revealed who he truly was; *were going*: Mark often uses this repetitive form to show a continuous activity over some time; *Jordan*: the river running the eastern length of Palestine, emptying into the Dead Sea, the lowest place on earth, 2,750 feet below sea level. The Israelites crossed the Jordan into the Land of Promise.

V6. *camel's hair*: In 2 Kgs 1:8, Elijah wears a hairy coat and a leather loincloth. The official Greek translation (Septuagint—or LXX) uses the same Greek words both there and here in Mark.

V7. *more powerful than I*: Some of John's disciples did not transfer their loyalties to Jesus, which resulted in friction between the two different sects. Mark takes pains to show that John's sole function in the kingdom of God is to point away from himself, to Jesus. This is also the reason for the hyperbole about the sandal strap—since John does baptize Jesus; *untie . . . sandals*:

down and untie the thong of his sandals. ⁸I have baptized you with water; but he will baptize you with the Holy Spirit."

⁹In those days Jesus came from Nazareth of Galilee and was baptized by John in the Jordan. ¹⁰And just as he was coming

---

Work given only to the lowest slaves, removing sandals and washing the feet of visitors.

V8. *Holy Spirit*: Essene writings say that when Yahweh comes he will "cleanse of all impurity with a holy spirit. Like waters of purification, he shall pour over him [humankind] the spirit of truth." The differences between John's baptism and the new baptism is, first, that the new baptism is less about cleansing from sin and more about a new aliveness and, second, that this aliveness came about *through* the death and resurrection of Jesus: "Therefore we have been buried with him by baptism into death, so that, just as Christ was raised from the dead by the glory of the Father, so we too might walk in newness of life" (Rom 6:4). Mark clearly does not presume people immediately grasped Jesus' divinity before the resurrection.

Preparation: VV9-15

V9. *Nazareth*: A small village of perhaps five hundred people, twenty miles east of the Mediterranean Sea and twenty miles west of the Jordan; *of Galilee*: The north section of Palestine, about 1,500 square miles (about the size of Monroe County, NY) in the time of Antipas. Here Jesus begins his mission and makes his final appearance to the disciples after the resurrection; *was baptized*: Jesus was sinless and didn't "have to," nor did he "have to" assume the shortcomings of being human. He shared our baptism, just as he shared our death. That identity of Jesus with ordinary people is underlined by the perfect parallel of V9 with V5; just like "the people," Jesus "came . . . baptized . . . Jordan." Only "confessing sins" is omitted. Matthew makes the point more sharply (3:14) by having John say Jesus should rather baptize John. St. Paul writes (2 Cor 5:21): "For our sake he made him to be sin who knew no sin, so that in him we might become the righteousness of God." The fact that the early church was forced to explain why Jesus was baptized (when they could simply have ignored and omitted it) argues that it historically did happen.

V10. *out of the water*: An allusion to the Israelites set free by crossing the Red Sea led by Moses and then the Jordan led by Joshua (another form of the name "Jesus"); *he saw*: Visions are a common literary device in the Bible. They try to capture a genuine spiritual experience—thus in no way physical—in physical terms, for people who have never had such an experience. Just as

up out of the water, he saw the heavens torn apart and the Spirit descending like a dove on him. ¹¹And a voice came from heaven, "You are my Son, the Beloved; with you I am well pleased."

¹²And the Spirit immediately drove him out into the wilderness. ¹³He was in the wilderness forty days, tempted by Satan; and he was with the wild beasts; and the angels waited on him.

---

awareness of the real but not physical presence of God is concretized elsewhere in the Bible as an angel or "men in white garments," here God's presence is concretized as a dove; *heavens torn apart*: Foreshadows the "tearing open" of the temple curtain (15:38) at Jesus' death, erasing the barrier between God and humanity. Note: unlike Matthew and Luke, Mark restricts the knowledge of Jesus' true identity and mission, revealed in this event, only to Jesus, not to the bystanders. The rest of Mark's version is the gradual unfolding to Jesus' disciples of the Messianic Secret of what "Messiah" and "Son of God" really mean, climaxing in the question of the high priest and the testimony of the centurion; *on him*: Mark actually uses the Greek *eis*, which means "into" rather than something external like "upon." This is an "invasion" or "possession" by God's Spirit.

V11. *a voice came from heaven*: This, too, need not be taken literally; it was a profound awareness within the spirit of Jesus of Yahweh missioning him and validating that mission. No one could deny that conviction of such a unique calling would be astounding; *You are my Son*: Not merely the expected Suffering Servant or David Hero Messiah, but a fusion of Messiah and Yahweh; *the Beloved*: Probably translates the Hebrew *yahid*, "unique"; *with you . . . pleased*: Foreshadows a second epiphany (divine meeting) at the transfiguration (9:7).

V12. *the Spirit . . . drove him*: Suggests a fierce compulsion within Jesus for his first clash with his Antagonist; *the wilderness*: Not necessarily a place of sand, but a "deserted" place. This is an allusion to the purification of Israel in the wilderness. Just as the first Israel was tested, so will Jesus, the seed of the New Israel.

V13. *forty:* Used for an indeterminate period, as "day" is used at the beginning of Genesis. Israel spent forty years; Jesus spent forty days, the time a Jewish man was tested before becoming a rabbi; *tempted*: Just as the original humans had been tempted. A better translation might be "tested," which avoids the connotations of inducement to moral sin rather than a trial of Jesus' conviction and resolve about his divine calling. Remember that Mark's readers, a generation after Jesus, were themselves facing gruesome tests too; *Satan*: "the Adversary, the Antagonist." The versions of the temptation in Matthew (4:1-11) and Luke (4:1-13) are longer and more detailed. In Mark, the event is used as a prologue-summary to a cosmic battle between good and evil: to show from the start pre-

¹⁴Now after John was arrested, Jesus came to Galilee, proclaiming the good news of God, ¹⁵and saying, "The time is fulfilled, and the kingdom of God has come near; repent, and believe in the good news."

---

cisely who the protagonist and antagonist are. During his life, Jesus will meet Satan not only in exorcisms but in the hearts of his enemies; *wild beasts*: After his trial, Jesus is as "at home" with fearsome beasts as Adam and Eve were before the Fall, the beginning of a New Creation; *angels*: Awareness of the protective presence and power of God goes with Jesus from this moment until the moment when that awareness deserts him in the agony in the garden. In 1 Kings 19, angels serve the prophet Elijah, preparing him to return to his mission.

V14. *was arrested*: In 6:17-29, Mark describes this in detail. It foreshadows Jesus' arrest.

V15. *The time*: Greek *kairos*, "the perfectly opportune moment," the critical instant when an opening appears; "the time is ripe," as the motto, *Carpe diem*, "Seize the day!" *the kingdom of God*: A revolutionary new era in the relationship between Yahweh and humankind has begun; a heavenly reality has descended into human history; *has come near*: The kingdom of God is present, in Jesus, but will not reach earthly fulfillment until his death and glorification; *repent*: This new era must also work a revolutionary change in humankind's consistent refusal to submit to the will of God, not so much cataloguing and regretting specific sins so much as a complete change of heart, a turnabout in one's whole life-view; *good news*: An allusion back to Isaiah: "he has sent me to bring good news to the oppressed" (61:2); and "How beautiful upon the mountains are the feet of the messenger who announces peace" (52:7). Later, at what we now call Palm Sunday (Mark 11:10), when the crowds shout, "Blessed is the coming kingdom of our ancestor David," they mean an entirely different kind of realm from what Jesus embodies—which is proven when they finally grasp what he is claiming and crucify him for it. As early as St. Paul, "Good News" has been a summary of Jesus *and* his message.

First Disciples: VV16-20

V16. *As Jesus passed along*: This sounds as if it were merely a chance meeting, but it is possible Simon and Andrew had also been disciples of John. Understanding that Mark "telescopes" here settles the possible doubt that tough workmen would merely drop everything and follow a total stranger "immediately," after a single sentence; *Sea of Galilee:* actually a lake, about thirteen by eight miles. It also divided pagan Gentiles on the eastern shore (The Ten

16As Jesus passed along the Sea of Galilee, he saw Simon and his brother Andrew casting a net into the sea—for they were fishermen. 17And Jesus said to them, "Follow me and I will make you fish for people." 18And immediately they left their nets and followed him. 19As he went a little farther, he saw James son of Zebedee and his brother John, who were in their boat mending the nets. 20Immediately he called them; and they left their father Zebedee in the boat with the hired men, and followed him.

Cities) from the mainly Jewish towns on the western shores. Jesus travels often between the two, showing his mission to both groups; **Simon . . . Andrew**: John (1:40) suggests Andrew brought his brother to Jesus; *fishermen*: There is a point to the fact that those Jesus chose were clearly not well educated (though he well could have chosen such). In 14:70, when Peter denies Jesus, the bystanders pick him out as a Galilean, probably from his rustic accent.

V17. *Follow me*: Like the British, "Onward!" it denotes a previous training that makes the order less likely to be challenged.

V18. *immediately*: Without prior connection, this is stunning—a real disruption in a family's business when, in both cases, they lose the work of two brothers. Peter was also married (since he has a mother-in-law [1:30] living in his house). This abrupt uprooting recalls again the summons the prophet Elijah gave to his disciple Elisha (1 Kgs 19). Whatever presuppositions about the disciples' readiness, this surely testifies to Jesus' charismatic presence.

V19. *James . . . and . . . John*: Many paintings wrongly picture the apostle John as delicate, but he was a fisherman, and Jesus later (3:17) calls James and John "Boanerges," Sons of Thunder. Their departure is even more shocking because they leave their father right there in their boat! The two pairs of brothers, called first, will be the most prominent in this gospel; *mending the nets*: Usually, fishing was at night, working on their gear in the day.

V20. *Zebedee*: This segment shows that the kingdom must be more important not only than an apostle's business but also than his or her family. It is a total conversion—reversal—of our own values. Compare to the Abraham-Isaac story when God goaded Abraham to decide whether God's will was more important to him than any other reality, even his son; *with the hired men*: Suggests that these recruits were not paupers or rude peasants but rather prosperous. Perhaps this is also why in Mark the two brothers corner Jesus (10:37) and jockey for privileged positions.

This pair of calls is the model for the other vocations in Mark's gospel (Levi/Matthew, 2:13-15; all twelve, 3:13-19). In each, (1) Jesus takes the initiative, (2) calling from ordinary work, (3) to "follow" and share in Jesus' mission, (4) without hesitation or excuses, (5) not to solitary service but to communal work with others.

²¹They went to Capernaum; and when the sabbath came, he entered the synagogue and taught. ²²They were astounded at his teaching, for he taught them as one having authority, and not as the scribes. ²³Just then there was in their synagogue a man with an

---

The First Day: VV21-32

V21. *Capernaum*: On the NW shore of the Sea of Galilee, a toll station on the road between the east and Damascus to the north, which might explain why the tax collector, Levi, lived there. For a while, it will be Jesus' base; *taught*: In the first half of his book, Mark says that Jesus taught, and whom he taught, but does not say explicitly *what* he taught. Mark's gospel contains relatively little "teaching" compared to the other gospels. It is more a story of actions. The content of his parables and deeds is now to establish that the kingdom of God has begun. Only later does he speak of his unique relationship with his Father and his mission to die and rise. This day in Capernaum is a thumbnail sketch of a typical day for Jesus: healing—with his words and hands; *synagogue*: Jewish worship may take place anywhere that ten Jews (a *minyan*) assemble. After his rejection from his home synagogue in Nazareth (6:2), in Mark's story Jesus will never preach in a synagogue again but only out in the open or in private homes. The official synagogue will have become a part of the Antagonist.

V22. *authority*: There are two kinds of "authority": (1) political: because of election or inheritance and power to compel; (2) moral: the power to persuade because of the speaker's reasoning, character, and conviction. Obviously, because of the remarks made about the scribes and Pharisees—who had power to compel—Jesus has authority in the second sense, such that even demons obey him. The unclean spirit cannot resist the Holy Spirit who is in Jesus, and Jesus' power comes not from dominance but from service; *scribes*: Teachers of Hebrew scripture and oral tradition, of lower rank than rabbis. This is a hint of the antagonism to come; obviously, the official, trained teachers would not react graciously to challenges from an untrained layman.

V23. *an unclean spirit*: The affliction is not morally evil, but rather the polar opposite of "holy, godly, peaceful," therefore, "ungodly, incomplete, out of order." In Mark, Jesus' first miracle is an exorcism, to underscore the fact that evil is helpless before him. In a less sophisticated age, it was common even for educated people to attribute sickness to evil spirits. Obviously, two thousand years later it is impossible to tell which are which in the gospels, but exorcisms still take place today, attested to even by psychiatric witnesses. [See M. Scott Peck, *People of the Lie*.] Modern sophistication is (rightly) skeptical about a literal extraterrestrial, personal source of evil. However, it is not too great a

unclean spirit, [24]and he cried out, "What have you to do with us, Jesus of Nazareth? Have you come to destroy us? I know who you are, the Holy One of God." [25]But Jesus rebuked him, saying, "Be silent, and come out of him!" [26]And the unclean spirit, convulsing him and crying with a loud voice, came out of him. [27]They were all amazed, and they kept on asking one another, "What is this? A new teaching—with authority! He commands even the unclean spirits, and they obey him." [28]At once his fame began to spread throughout the surrounding region of Galilee.

[29]As soon as they left the synagogue, they entered the house of Simon and Andrew, with James and John. [30]Now Simon's mother-in-law was in bed with a fever, and they told him about her at once. [31]He came and took her by the hand and

---

strain when we speak of genuinely troubled souls as "wrestling with their demons," and psychiatrists will never lack patients.

V24. *What have you to do*: "We have absolutely nothing in common"; *us*: Either an assumption of kingly power or a declaration that the demons infesting the victim are multiple; *who you are*: Again, a reference to the gradually emerging Messianic Secret and a declaration that even the Antagonist admits who Jesus truly is. Also, in Judaism, to name someone is equivalent to understanding thoroughly that person's power and function and to have some kind of magical power over him or her.

V25. *rebuked*: Mark uses the same word when Jesus silences the storm at sea (4:39), a term used for a judge chastising a defendant; *Be silent*: Literally "muzzle yourself!" Jesus shows no fear, merely tells the demon to shut up. Note that, unlike ritual exorcisms one sees in films, Jesus does not invoke God's assistance. His command comes from himself; *come out*: No complex ritual of prayers or magical motions to beg or "compel" God to intervene, but a command given with the conviction that the speaker himself has an authority that expects the listener to obey. And the results show Jesus had it and that the eyewitnesses recognized it. Note the constant insistence on Jesus' authority, a figure of mystery and power. In Mark, this is Jesus' very first public act: a direct confrontation with a concrete manifestation of the Antagonist.

V28. *his fame began to spread*: This, despite Jesus' insistence on secrecy. Successful exorcisms are difficult to keep hidden! But the Secret could also reflect Jesus' prudent attempts to delay open conflict with the temple officials.

V30. *Simon's mother-in-law*: Obviously, the first pope was—or had been— a married man. Paul (1 Cor 9:5) suggests that Peter (Cephas) is "accompanied by a believing wife."

V31. *lifted her up*: The Greek verb (*egeiro*) is much stronger than most English translations; it is better as "raised her up," which is the Greek verb often used of the resurrection; *serve them*: The detail shows not only how

lifted her up. Then the fever left her, and she began to serve them.

³²That evening, at sundown, they brought to him all who were sick or possessed with demons. ³³And the whole city was gathered around the door. ³⁴And he cured many who were sick with various diseases, and cast out many demons; and he would not permit the demons to speak, because they knew him.

³⁵In the morning, while it was still very dark, he got up and went out to a deserted place, and there he prayed. ³⁶And Simon and his companions hunted for him. ³⁷When they found him, they said to him, "Everyone is searching for you." ³⁸He answered,

---

complete was the woman's cure but also what being a Christian means. Later (10:45), Jesus uses the same verb to describe his mission: "The Son of Man came not to be served but to serve." Serving is not demeaning but an honor.

V32. *at sundown*: Therefore, the end of the Sabbath when people could move about freely and carry the helpless to Simon's yard. Note that Jesus has, nonetheless, had a long day, and yet there are still people in need.

V33. *the whole city*: Again, hyperbole for effect.

V34. *would not permit*: Still holding back the Messianic Secret, which—if revealed at this point—would have sent those who trusted Jesus away. Too much, too soon.

Jesus' Work in Galilee: VV35-45

V35. *prayed*: [See chap. 4: "Jesus' Consciousness of His Divinity."] Just as Jesus, though sinless, accepted baptism and death, he also accepted the need to depend on his Father. Try to imagine what would go on in the mind of a man who had always thought he was somewhat gifted but basically ordinary. He has just had a day in which he has done quite extraordinary things. Surely he would feel confused and need help—if not to understand, at least not to become arrogant. Or lose his mind.

V36. *Simon and his companions*: From the beginning, in all the gospels, Simon Peter is given the place of eminence; *hunted for him*: The words suggest a mild irritation in the one "tracked down," as anyone who has sought the healing of solitude can testify.

V37. *Everyone is searching for you*: In a remote way, Jesus' reputation calls to mind the intrusive demands the "public" lays on present-day celebrities, an insight wildly overworked in *Jesus Christ Superstar*.

V38. *Let us go*: Clearly, Jesus did not stay in an "office" and wait for people to come to him. Following his example may take more aggressiveness than many feel comfortable with; *I came out to do*: His mission is to share the new kingdom.

"Let us go on to the neighboring towns, so that I may proclaim the message there also; for that is what I came out to do." ³⁹And he went throughout Galilee, proclaiming the message in their synagogues and casting out demons.

⁴⁰A leper came to him begging him, and kneeling he said to him, "If you choose, you can make me clean." ⁴¹Moved with pity, Jesus stretched out his hand and touched him, and said to him, "I do choose. Be made clean!" ⁴²Immediately the leprosy left him, and he was made clean. ⁴³After

---

V39. *their synagogues*: This is a place that reflects a term introduced later than the time of Jesus himself. It could be translated more clumsily as "their usual meeting places."

V40. *a leper*: Leprosy is an infection resulting in sores, loss of fingers, toes, sensation. Lepers were excluded not only from dealing with other people but also from Jewish ritual. No Jew would even acknowledge the leper's presence, yet Jesus does. He even touches the leper. Just as more primitive societies often confused mental illness with possession, they also confused many skin diseases with leprosy. To argue that case misses the point. In modern terms, the present victims could suffer from AIDS. Leprosy was a "living death." Whether the victim was a genuine leper or not, the people thought he was and thus rejected him. Jesus didn't.

V41. *Moved with pity*: The particular Greek verb is really packed with the adverb "deeply," like "profoundly stirred," a gut feeling. Throughout the gospels, Jesus is one who is in no way ashamed of his emotions. It is remarkable how he, who was gifted and sinless, felt such empathy for the sick and sinful; *Be made clean*: In contrast, Moses (Num 5:1-2) commanded: "Put out of the camp everyone who is leprous, or has a discharge [bleeding], and everyone who is unclean through contact with a corpse." Jesus ignores that here (a leper) and soon after (a woman with a discharge [5:25]), and immediately after that (a dead girl [5:41]). He clearly did not believe contact could transfer "evil." Experts express doubts that the common people were as finicky as the Jewish clergy about such details. If Jesus had no respect for that tradition (since he defies ritual impurity even by talking to the leper, much less touching him), he was at least prudent.

V42. *Immediately*: Instantly. There is no ritual incantation. It is Jesus' "will." This is no ordinary healer.

V43. *sternly warning*: The Greek word is more like "growling," which is puzzling, more suitable for the disease than for the leper. Some critics suggest it might signal Jesus' anger that the victim could not be accepted back into society without the "certification" of the clergy.

sternly warning him he sent him away at once, [44]saying to him, "See that you say nothing to anyone; but go, show yourself to the priest, and offer for your cleansing what Moses commanded, as a testimony to them." [45]But he went out and began to proclaim it freely, and to spread the word, so that Jesus could no longer go into a town openly, but stayed out in the country; and people came to him from every quarter.

V44. *say nothing to anyone*: Again, the Messianic Secret; *show yourself to the priest*: In order to prove the victim was no longer to be shunned, socially or liturgically, and to show that Jesus was not totally rejecting the laws of Moses.

V45. *spread the word*: One of many places where an author's purpose conflicts with realism. As an author, Mark wants to open the Messianic Secret only slowly, but how could one be cured of leprosy and reasonably be asked to be silent about it? At least in terms of "plot," however, this episode triggers the next segment: the confrontations with the Pharisees.

Review Questions for Chapter 1

1. There are three testimonies to Jesus' mission in this chapter: from John the Baptist (Elijah), from God, and from Satan. What different forms of verification of Jesus' mission does each give witness to?
2. Mark is writing about the Messianic Secret. On the one hand, his gospel is a kind of mystery story, gradually revealing clues that will climax at Jesus' trial. What purpose could he have, just as a writer, for doing that?
3. Go through the text carefully and pick out every bit of evidence indicating that Jesus is making a dramatic breakaway from Israel—just as Israel itself had made a dramatic break away from slavery in Egypt.
4. As in every mystery story, there is a protagonist whose fortunes form the plotline of the story and an antagonist whose purpose is to frustrate the attempts of the hero to succeed. Who are the obvious protagonist and antagonist of this story? For most of the story, the protagonist does in fact succeed—though not without visible opposition. What are those encounters in this chapter?
5. In modern life, where do we find the differences between political authority and moral authority? Show in what ways Jesus and the scribes differ in their approaches to authority. Give evidence from the chapter to show that Jesus did not have—or even want—political authority. Would that indicate that Jesus did not believe Christians should engage in elected public service?
6. Here and throughout the gospel, Jesus' principal task is healing—in many varying ways. What does that persistent preoccupation of Jesus with healing say about Jesus as a model for our own Christian lives?

For Reflection

(1) *Verses 2-3*. John the Baptist was not the One Who Is to Come, "just" a messenger boy. He dressed for the part, as people expected a prophet to look: sort of a Clint Eastwood character in camel hide, emerging from the heat haze. But prophets needn't be stripped to their bare bones. Many prophets—the Empress Helena, Thomas More, Oscar Romero—were learned, complex, embroiled in politics. The liberating message of Christ is more important than one's clothes. Prophets gear their costumes and props to the audience to whom they are sent.

At your baptism, you were ordained a prophet and a healer; at your confirmation, you supposedly personally "confirmed" that vocation—not to be a priest or nun but to be, nonetheless, someone to "make straight the way of the Lord." To use a perhaps clumsy analogy: to be a paramedic until a professional could take over.

Describe the people with whom you live and work. What are their susceptibilities—and resistances—to the announcement that Jesus Christ has set us free from fear of death, right here and now? Do those people take themselves too seriously? How could you—concretely, not abstractly—lure them to be less afraid to become truly alive? What are the resistances within *yourself* to your mission to be a prophet and healer?

(2) *Verse 9*. Jesus was baptized. But why? He was without sin. What was he trying to *share* with us in being baptized? Considering what was said about Jesus' consciousness of his divinity, try to expand on Mark's hit-and-run style, and describe what might have been going through Jesus' mind at the moment of the stunning enlightenment about his person and his mission at his baptism—pictured symbolically as a dove and a thunderous voice from heaven. Have you personally ever suspected, perhaps skeptically, that *you* might be called to a bigger life, a larger contribution than what you might have safely contented yourself with before?

(3) *Verse 18*. "Immediately": Quite possibly, this is an example of hyperbole. It is difficult to imagine a group of hardhanded and tough-minded fishermen being instantly "zapped" and dropping everything to follow Jesus. What's more, their later stubbornness to believe backs that up. There must have been more preparation; perhaps these four had been disciples of the Baptist. Quickly or gradually, they did come, but this description of the apostles' almost instant conversion might have an effect on our own expectations of what a call from God might be like.

Now, as you read this passage, you have for perhaps the first time a chance to hear that call and respond to it. What inside you might tend to resist it, to turn your mind quickly to other things so that it can't "get to you"? If you did respond to it, what person nearest to you would you have the likeliest chance of "healing" if you heeded that call?

(4) *Verses 23-24*. It is interesting to note that the first people to understand Jesus and his mission were his enemies. At the trial before the Jewish elders in chapter 14, we will see that his enemies were much more clearly aware of precisely what Jesus was claiming to be than his own disciples. Unlike the Jesus of holy pictures, the real Jesus didn't have a gold halo around his head; he looked, walked, and smelled like any other man of his time. What do you suspect there might have been about him that made him stand out as someone "special"? Can you think of anyone you know who radiates that kind of magnetism? If Jesus clothed himself in the ordinary when he first came among us, he quite likely hasn't changed his mode of operation. Just pick one person you know, at random, and muse on how Jesus might be lurking within him or her, sending you messages like "Help me" or "Stop me."

(5) *Verse 35*. Jesus went to a lonely place and prayed. When many of us pray, we spend the time "saying prayers," which isn't at all bad. But we also spend much of the time asking God for favors, many of them quite important to us, but basically attempts to change God's mind, influence God's choices, perhaps even bribe God with promises. Nothing wrong with that, either; Jesus himself pleaded with his Father in the agony in the garden to change his mind.

Many say, though, that God never gives them answers when they pray. A likely reason is that the petitioner doesn't keep quiet and give God a chance; the petitioner's prayers monopolize the conversation, trying to dominate God. During a time of prayer, do you ever just "let go," center yourself, empty yourself, and invite God in? Do you ever sit, as nonintrusive and receptive as a tape recorder, and let God manipulate your thoughts in any direction God wishes? If so, what happens? If not, why not?

2 ¹When he returned to Capernaum after some days, it was reported that he was at home. ²So many gathered around that there was no longer room for them, not even in front of the door; and he was speaking the word to them. ³Then some people came, bringing to him a paralyzed man, carried by four of them. ⁴And when they could not bring him to Jesus because of the crowd, they removed the roof above him; and after having dug through it, they let down the mat on which the paralytic lay. ⁵When Jesus saw their faith, he said to the paralytic, "Son, your sins are forgiven." ⁶Now some of the scribes were sitting there, questioning in their hearts,

---

A Paralyzed Man: VV1-12

V1. *at home*: For some time, Jesus and his friends made Capernaum a home base, most likely the duplex house of Simon and Andrew from the previous chapter.

V2. *speaking the word*: Again, like a stand-up comic, Mark connects one segment to another with "hook words." Here the word "word" hooks back to 1:45 where the leper, against Jesus' request, "spread the word."

V3. *paralyzed man*: A victim of injury or disease of the nerves or spine, which kills the ability to feel and move limbs. This man cannot walk and must be carried.

V4. *roof*: Roofs were flat, made of clay and straw tramped down on wooden rafters. Homely details like this may seem unimportant, but they give a sense of concrete realism lacking in most legendary stories. They seem to have no particular symbolism, as in such stories, but suggest a genuinely recollected event. Here the relentlessness of the paralytic and his four bearers is an indication not only of their determination but also of their faith in what they've heard of Jesus' mysterious power.

V5. *their faith*: Jesus never performs a miracle to compel belief, only in response to belief. Later, in Nazareth (6:5) where they scoff at him, he is powerless. Here, obviously, it was not the bearers' faith in Jesus as divine but in Jesus as a "man of God" and healer; *sins*: The Bible has a constant and pervasive awareness of sin. Both the Hebrew and Greek terms mean "missing the mark" or "out of kilter." Sin is not merely an inward, personal, subjective sense of guilt, but an objective reality—as real as the diseases a simpler culture believed embodied sin; *are forgiven*: Nowhere in the gospels, when Jesus forgives sins, does he demand a list, nor does he assign a penance. Only two requirements: that we seek out Jesus and that we want to be healed.

V6. *were sitting there*: Given the wall-to-wall crowd, they presumably got there early! Jesus has begun to draw not only curious or needy audiences.

⁷"Why does this fellow speak in this way? It is blasphemy! Who can forgive sins but God alone?" ⁸At once Jesus perceived in his spirit that they were discussing these questions among themselves; and he said to them, "Why do you raise such questions in your hearts? ⁹Which is easier, to say to the paralytic, 'Your sins are forgiven,' or to say, 'Stand up and take your mat and walk'? ¹⁰But so that you may know that the Son of Man has authority on earth to forgive sins"—he said to the paralytic— ¹¹"I say to you, stand up, take your mat and go to your home." ¹²And he stood up, and immediately took the mat and went out before all of them; so that they were all amazed and glorified God, saying, "We have never seen anything like this!"

V7. *this fellow*: The tone is like the present day, "Who does this guy think he is?"; ***blasphemy***: Assuming to oneself equality with God. This, of course, foreshadows the charge that the high priest will repeat at Jesus' trial. This antagonism could well reflect one in the early churches because they made bold to forgive sins in Christ's name and stead.

V8. *perceived . . . discussing*: One need not read this literally as some form of ESP. Just as Jesus was shrewd enough to know that, if he continued to preach, the vested interests of the temple were going to stop him, so he knew without any divine insight the effect such a statement would have on such men. One detects something of a "sneer" in their disapproval. Note that the scribes have yet to develop the courage to challenge Jesus openly, but he brings the antagonism right out into the awareness of the bystanders.

V9. *Which is easier*: A clever debater, Jesus does not hesitate to answer a question with another question. Note that the scribes are more interested in purity of doctrine than in offering hope to a hopeless man. A physical cure is immediately verifiable; accepting the banishment of guilt requires faith.

V10. *so that you may know*: This cannot be addressed to the scribes, since they would not have accepted it; rather, it is addressed to the Christian reader; ***Son of Man***: Daniel (7:13-14) pictures an Ancient One sitting on a fiery throne (Yahweh) giving "dominion and glory and kingship, that all peoples . . . should serve him" to "a human being" (Aramaic: "one like a Son of Man"). What is puzzling—in light of Mark's stylistic insistence on only revealing the Messianic Secret gradually—is that Jesus would openly use the term "Son of Man" of himself this early, or that he would do so in the presence of scribes.

V11. *stand up*: The same verb used at Jesus' resurrection. Outward cure of the body is symbolic of inward cure of the soul; Jesus has power over both.

V12. *all amazed*: Like people anywhere, the villagers are more interested in the cure of the body than the cure of the soul. This is in sharp contrast to the stiff skepticism of the scribes. It is important to note that Jewish opposition to Jesus was on the part of the few, not the many. Further, as scholars stress, the opposition to Jesus that culminated in his death was willed by God (8:31; 9:31; 10:33). As

¹³Jesus went out again beside the sea; the whole crowd gathered around him, and he taught them. ¹⁴As he was walking along, he saw Levi son of Alphaeus sitting at the tax booth, and he said to him, "Follow me." And he got up and followed him. ¹⁵And as he sat at dinner in Levi's house, many tax collectors and sinners were also sitting with Jesus and his disciples—for there were many who followed him. ¹⁶When the scribes of the Pharisees saw that he was eating with sinners and tax collectors, they

---

Raymond E. Brown suggests (*Death of the Messiah*, 393), if Jesus returned today with the same claim, he would probably be executed as an imposter.

A Preference for Sinners: VV13-17

V13. *beside the sea*: The Sea of Galilee; *taught them*: Again, Mark does not specify what Jesus taught in this half of his book. He is more interested in establishing the *person* of Jesus.

V14. *the tax booth*: A kiosk to collect tolls along the trade route. Such men offered a bid and paid the colonial Romans a fee to collect taxes for the invaders, skimming their share off the top. Unlike Judea in the south, Galilee was not under direct Roman rule, so the taxes would go to Herod Antipas (21 BC–AD 30), the detested Roman confederate who beheaded John the Baptist and mocked Jesus when Pilate shunted him, as Galilean, off to Herod for judgment. Tax collectors were not only gougers but also traitors to their own people and detested by every Jew without exception, like French collaborators with the Nazis. They were classed with beggars, robbers, and sexual sinners; *Levi*: A lapse for Mark here, which Luke (5:27) copies. In the full list of apostles Mark himself omits the name "Levi" but inserts "Matthew" instead and calls a different apostle "son of Alphaeus." Matthew calls him "Matthew," as do all the gospel writers' lists of apostles; *Follow me*: This could be misread as merely, "Follow me to your house for dinner." Rather, it is the same call as that given Simon and the others: to become an apostle. What is important is that Jesus can make an apostle out of the least likely, even someone as detestable as a tax collector. Again, an immediate, unreflective response.

V15. *sat at dinner*: Actually, "reclined," on one's left elbow; *tax collectors . . . sinners*: Many of Jesus' followers were outcasts from official Judaism, people whom the more proper folk considered degraded and sinful—the equivalent in our time of ex-convicts, call girls, and victims of AIDS. Think of a cardinal archbishop dining at a mafioso's compound. God's ideas of worthiness are quite different from our own.

V16. *scribes*: The scribes were surely not among the guests, since no law-abiding Jew would incur ritual uncleanness by associating with such blatant sin-

said to his disciples, "Why does he eat with tax collectors and sinners?" [17]When Jesus heard this, he said to them, "Those who are well have no need of a physician, but those who are sick; I have come to call not the righteous but sinners."

[18]Now John's disciples and the Pharisees were fasting; and people came and

---

ners. Most likely the group at Levi's house was eating outside. This episode also shows what a sharp eye the local clergy were keeping on Jesus from the start; *his disciples*: So far there are only five explicitly called. In Mark, Jesus does not designate them officially until 3:13; *Pharisees*: The word "pharisee" means "set apart," because—like the present-day Hasidim—they avoided any ritual contamination from sinners, Gentiles, and less observant Jews and were rigorous in their meticulous observance. Like the Essenes, Sadducees, etc., they were a sect under the overall umbrella of "Judaism." Unlike the conservative, literalist Sadducees who were tightly identified with the Jerusalem temple but also, ironically, more open and accommodating to Roman influences, Pharisees would argue for leeway "around" OT strictures. Because the gospels were written at a time when Pharisees were persecuting converted Jewish Christians, the evangelists are perhaps a bit one-sided in their bitter criticism. Actually, because of their creative interpretations of the law, which allowed for welcome "exceptions," they were probably the most popular spiritual leaders of the day. Note, however, that there were in fact several different "brands" of Judaism—like the different denominations of Christianity today, but with a marked difference: they were all in the same organizational religion. Thus, if Jesus were merely initiating a new sect of Judaism, with its own unique slant, he might have expected the same toleration. On the contrary, he was killed, and the reason for his death is the Messianic Secret.

V17. *need of a physician*: This is the point of the story: Jesus has a mission to heal souls, but only those can be healed who—unlike the scribes—admit they need forgiveness and realize they cannot "merit" forgiveness by good works or observing the law. The scribes are also given the invitation, but they refuse to believe they need it. In contrast, Pharisaic writings claim that when he comes the Messiah will "expel sinners from the inheritance." Neither with the paralytic nor with these sinners does Jesus—in contrast to John the Baptist—demand anything more than admission of need. Nor is forgiveness some kind of external "legal" action but an inner transformation and a new connection ("religion") to God. After the resurrection, Peter, the leader, refused to eat with Gentiles (Gal 2:11-14), but Paul "opposed him to his face, because he stood self-condemned."

Old Insights and New: VV18-28

V18. *fasting*: The only annual national fast was the Day of Atonement, Yom Kippur. Luke 18:12 suggests that at least some Pharisees fasted twice a week,

said to him, "Why do John's disciples and the disciples of the Pharisees fast, but your disciples do not fast?" ¹⁹Jesus said to them, "The wedding guests cannot fast while the bridegroom is with them, can they? As long as they have the bridegroom with them, they cannot fast. ²⁰The days will come when the bridegroom is taken away from them, and then they will fast on that day.

²¹"No one sews a piece of unshrunk cloth on an old cloak; otherwise, the patch pulls away from it, the new from the old, and a worse tear is made. ²²And no one

---

and also that Jesus was accused of being "a glutton and drunkard" (7:34). However, this inquiry, coming from "people," not scribes, need not be an underhanded one, as in the last episode, but genuine puzzlement.

V19. *wedding guests*: Jesus frequently explains the kingdom of God by comparing it to a wedding reception, which is rooted in the frequent comparisons in the OT of Yahweh's relationship to Israel as a marriage covenant. Anyone who has been to a wedding party knows what they are like; thus, Jesus is saying that being Christian is most definitely not a gloomy affair, and that if "Christians" are in fact gloomy types, they quite likely have not really found the kingdom of God yet; *while the bridegroom is with them*: Much is compacted here: (1) the kingdom of God (wedding banquet) *is* here from the moment Jesus declared his mission; (2) just as Yahweh was the bridegroom of Israel, Jesus is the bridegroom of the New Israel; (3) Jesus has greater authority than any Jewish tradition; (4) followers of Jesus are a breakaway from the Jewish Law; *can they?*: again, Jesus counters a question with a question. An early treatise (*Didache*, ca. AD 200) suggests Christians fasted on Wednesdays and Fridays.

V20. *is taken away*: Ordinarily, a groom would leave the reception, but this implies a forcible removal and is therefore probably a foreshadowing of Jesus' death; *they will fast*: Some biblical scholars suspect this verse may have been added later, since the later, more institutionalized church had returned to the custom of ritual fasting. Yet in Matthew 6:16 Jesus does say that, when his followers fast, they should not make a show of it, putting ashes on their foreheads—which nonetheless was later ritualized in Ash Wednesday.

V21. *cloak*: a rectangular outer garment draped around a two-piece tunic with openings for head and arms; *unshrunk cloth*: When the patched garment is washed, the patch—which covered the hole smoothly before—will now shrink and pull the garment out of shape. Jesus did not come to patch up; he came to begin anew. Jesus speaks to ordinary folks, since rich people would not need to patch their clothing.

V22. *old wineskins*: Overused skins would have swollen to their limit. Says the same as the cloak metaphor—a new beginning, which underlines the point of the episode: the kingdom of God is a breakaway from the exclusivity, legal-

puts new wine into old wineskins; otherwise, the wine will burst the skins, and the wine is lost, and so are the skins; but one puts new wine into fresh wineskins."

²³One sabbath he was going through the grainfields; and as they made their way his disciples began to pluck heads of grain. ²⁴The Pharisees said to him, "Look, why are they doing what is not lawful on the sabbath?" ²⁵And he said to them, "Have you never read what David did when he and his companions were hungry and in need of food? ²⁶He entered the house of God, when Abiathar was high priest, and ate the bread of the Presence, which it is not lawful for any but the priests to eat, and he gave some to his companions." ²⁷Then he said to them, "The sabbath was made for humankind, and not humankind for the sabbath; ²⁸so the Son of Man is lord even of the sabbath."

---

ism, and justification by rule keeping of Judaism. There is a basic incompatibility between the law and the message of Jesus. Mark's audience is experiencing just such a rending antagonism with their Jewish neighbors.

V23. *pluck heads of grain*: Continuing from the previous episode, Jesus' disciples are freed of the strictures of the law, which forbade even such necessary work as lighting a fire on the Sabbath. Idly picking off and nibbling grains of wheat seems hardly a serious offense. The Sabbath rest was essential to Jewish identity all over the known world, however, and violations were a very sensitive matter.

V24. *The Pharisees*: Here and elsewhere we see the author's hand intruding on realism. It is hardly likely that the Pharisees dogged Jesus' heels into a cornfield and just "popped up."

V25. *Have you never read:* A question for a question; *what David did*: Jesus justifies himself from the OT, since David, the greatest of Jewish heroes after Moses, exempted himself from the law when observing the law caused harm. There is a general principle here: God gave us common sense before he found it necessary to give us commandments and laws.

V26. *He entered, etc.*: Mark is again inaccurate here in explaining Jewish customs to his readers. In the David episode (1 Sam 21:2-6), David was alone and did not enter the house of God. The priest (not the high priest) was Ahimelech, not Abiathar; *the bread*: twelve loaves set before the tabernacle every Sabbath.

V27. *made for humankind*: Jesus does not negate the need to honor God one day a week, but there are times when that requirement must yield to a stronger, more immediate need. Extreme legalism suffers from the belief that only lawmakers know what is good for people, and that even good people are incapable of thinking for themselves.

V28. *Son of Man is lord even of the sabbath*: The real problem is not the holiness of the Sabbath but how scrupulously "work" should be analyzed. As before, there is also a question of the source of authority. Unlike Jesus' previous reliance on the OT to justify what he does, he now further justifies what his followers are doing on his own authority. Equivalently, he is claiming authority at least as powerful as the OT. As with Mark 2:11, it is puzzling that Jesus would again make such a strong claim—and to Pharisees—this early in the revelation of the Messianic Secret.

Review Questions for Chapter 2

1. Throughout the gospels, physical illness is used as a concrete embodiment of spiritual illness. How is that shown in this chapter? Why do we feel real compassion for someone who is physically ill and yet feel revulsion for someone who is spiritually, morally ill?
2. In the last chapter, we saw that the Antagonist in this story is Satan—that father of lies and deception. In what forms does the Antagonist emerge in this chapter?
3. The apostles recruited so far were, as far as we can tell, orthodox Jews. Try to describe their inner feelings when Jesus invites Levi to join their group and when Jesus takes them to dine with people no pious Jew would associate with. It might be enlightening to rewrite the scene in a modern setting, with guests who are Mafia bosses and their girlfriends, AIDS victims, street people, homosexuals. What would be your own personal response to sitting down for dinner with such people—and Jesus?
4. How were the various legitimate sects of Judaism different from the various sects of modern-day Christianity?
5. Explain: "Those who are well have no need of a physician, but those who are sick." What admission does anyone have to make in order to be healed?
6. Consistently in the Old and New Testaments, the union of God with human beings is compared to a wedding. De-compact that metaphor: what things can you say about a wedding party that you can also say about being a member of the Body of Christ?
7. Again, comb this chapter for concrete evidence that Christianity is in fact not merely another different sect of Judaism but a complete breakaway.

For Reflection

(1) *Verse 4*. The friends of the paralyzed man were good friends indeed. Most of us would avoid thinking about taking just a friend to seek such help. One's child, perhaps, or one's parent, but not just a pal from the local tavern or from work. These four men not only do that but also aren't daunted by the crowd at

the door. They lug their friend up the outside stairs and pull away the daubed slats of the ceiling (apparently so zealous about their task that they are willing to take on the anger of the owner!).

Are you that kind of friend? If not, it needn't be that you don't care that much about your friends, but perhaps that you are too shy, too lacking in self-confidence to see that you *can* make a difference in the lives of those around you. Pick out one person either in school or at work or in the neighborhood who is in need of some kind of "healing"—and it needn't be the most repulsive! Choose someone you at least have a hunch you might be able to make less shy, or less anonymous, or less pushy. Picture the person's face in your mind. Now what?

(2) *Verse 9*. Sometimes it seems almost easier to think of ourselves performing a physical miracle than to think of ourselves actually forgiving, letting go of a long-term (or short-term) grudge. And yet, if we genuinely call ourselves followers of Jesus Christ who forgave sins so readily, it seems inescapable that we have to forgive sins readily too. Even leaving Christianity aside for a moment, forgiving is in our own *self*-interest. When you're nursing a grudge (and the word "nursing" is worth meditating on all by itself), does it make you happy? Or does it dog your day like a low-grade headache? Why not get rid of it? What would it cost? Your bruised ego? In forgiving the offender—at no matter what cost—you are healing yourself.

(3) *Verse 14*. Jesus certainly wasn't very picky about his friends. Even the fisherman apostles must have felt a bit pesky about taking this low-life collaborator and victimizer, Levi, into their midst. And, like forgiveness, it occurs in Jesus' public life too often not to be an integral component of his personality—and of his hopes for us. He consorts with all kinds of riffraff: tax gougers, prostitutes, lepers, Samaritans, people unwelcome even at the lowest levels of decent society. This troubled not only his own converts but also the self-righteous elders of Judaism. Like inviting the smelly peasants from steerage to come up into first class with "us."

Who are the people in your office or school or neighborhood whom most of the "decent" people shun? The woman with the tarnished reputation, the man who doesn't bathe or dress properly, the student with a chip on his shoulder? As someone who patterns life along the lines of Jesus' life, what do you do for that person? Not "sometime." Today.

(4) *Verse 19*. Jesus, the Bridegroom, is with us still. The kingdom of God is a *party*! It would be difficult to attend a Sunday liturgy in most parishes and come away with that impression. The reason is that the participants are so reserved, so shy, so uptight—in direct contradiction to what Jesus expected of us. When

Claire Booth Luce considered conversion, she watched Catholics—especially seminarians—and she said to herself, "You say you have the truth. Well, the truth should set you free, give you joy. Can I *see* your freedom? Can I *feel* your joy?" Well?

(5) *Verse 27.* Another touchstone of the Good News of Jesus is freedom from fear of breaking rules. And yet well-intentioned Christian leaders and teachers have tried to codify authentic Christian behavior into a great many rules—for people they honestly believe are too undisciplined or too simpleminded to behave in a Christian way. Even though at times it seems that Pharisees have co-opted Christianity, such people's motives are sincere; they don't want people to be hurt or to fail to fulfill the obligations they took on themselves in baptism and confirmation.

Which end of the spectrum are you closer to: The overly strict or the overly lax? Are you too judgmental about others—and yourself—too picky, too unfree? Or are you too easy on others—and yourself—refusing to admonish friends who are hurting themselves, which is also a violation of freedom?

3 ¹Again he entered the synagogue, and a man was there who had a withered hand. ²They watched him to see whether he would cure him on the sabbath, so that they might accuse him. ³And he said to the man who had the withered hand, "Come forward." ⁴Then he said to them, "Is it lawful to do good or to do harm on the sabbath, to save life or to kill?" But they were silent. ⁵He looked around at them with anger; he was grieved at their hardness of heart and said to the man, "Stretch out your hand." He stretched it out, and his hand was restored. ⁶The Pharisees went

---

Healings: VV1-12

V1. *withered hand*: Perhaps a birth defect because of which one hand never developed.

V2. *They watched him*: He is becoming an object of concern; *to see whether . . .*: Note the ruthless cynicism of Jesus' enemies, the degree to which their religious righteousness overcame their compassion. There was a wide variance among the sects about what constituted Sabbath violation. Some rigorists felt even *talking* about work one was *going* to do violated it.

V3. *Come forward*: It is clear Jesus is not one to hide from challenge.

V4. *them:* Presumably the Pharisees mentioned in verse 6; *Is it lawful*: In Matthew (12:1-8), Jesus says the Talmud (traditions of the rabbis) allows a Jew to save a helpless animal, even on the Sabbath; then why not a man? Here, he uses a broader principle: good vs. evil, life vs. death. But the cripple is not in danger of physical death. The irony of Jesus' tone alone is enough to show the Pharisees' hypocrisy; *they were silent*: How could they answer without indicting themselves?

V5. *with anger*: Mark is the only evangelist to mention Jesus' anger explicitly. Note: It is not their plotting against him that grieves him but the hardness of heart that keeps them from the liberating truth. The only people Jesus is helpless to help are those who refuse to admit they need it. This is a frequent theme for Mark: our resistance to our own salvation; *Stretch out your hand*: like the paralytic who had to rise by himself, cripples and sinners must reach out to be healed. We must meet him halfway; *and his hand was restored*: Jesus performs no "action" on the Sabbath—not even touching the hand; speaking does not violate it.

V6. *conspired*: Obviously Mark is editorializing, since no follower of Jesus witnessed this. The hitherto vague antagonism of Jesus' enemies is now focused; the battle is joined; the plot is begun; the conflict between the two forces will climax at Jesus' trial before the Sanhedrin; *Herodians*: Jewish followers of King Herod Antipas, the current puppet king of Galilee, who collaborated with the

out and immediately conspired with the Herodians against him, how to destroy him.

⁷Jesus departed with his disciples to the sea, and a great multitude from Galilee followed him;⁸hearing all that he was doing, they came to him in great numbers from Judea, Jerusalem, Idumea, beyond the Jordan, and the region around Tyre and Sidon. ⁹He told his disciples to have a boat ready for him because of the crowd, so that they would not crush him; ¹⁰for he had cured many, so that all who had diseases pressed upon him to touch him. ¹¹Whenever the unclean spirits saw him, they fell down before him and shouted, "You are the Son of God!" ¹²But he sternly ordered them not to make him known.

Romans and were thus despised by the contamination-conscious Pharisees who detested non-Jews and anyone who had dealings with them; Mark is thus saying that many Jews put aside even serious religious differences between sects to concentrate on the greater enemy, Jesus. There is a heavy irony here, since Jesus has just asked about taking away life on the Sabbath, yet here the legalists are plotting death on the Sabbath.

V7. *departed*: Jesus leaves public doings for a while in order to choose and instruct his disciples.

V8. *Judea*: the southern province of Palestine where Jerusalem was; *Idumea*: a mountainous area south of Judea; this is the Greek word for the Jewish area called Edom, showing that Mark wrote primarily for Greek speakers; *beyond the Jordan*: what is now the kingdom of Jordan, to the east across the Jordan River; *Tyre and Sidon*: Phoenician towns on the Mediterranean coast where Jews were outnumbered by non-Jews. Equivalent to: "from north, east, south, and west." This passage shows Jesus' interest in people outside Palestine and even outside Judaism, as well as showing how word of him was spreading.

V9. *a boat*: Three more times in his gospel, Mark has Jesus speaking to crowds from a boat. Sound carries far better across open water.

V10. *touch him*: The same urge today presses crowds to touch celebrities.

V11. *Son of God*: The diabolic spirits give testimony to the reality of Jesus, which ordinary folk are still incapable of seeing or acknowledging.

V12. *not to make him known*: Again maintaining Mark's structural device of the Messianic Secret.

Note that Mark acts as an omniscient narrator, one who knows truths that the actors in the story are ignorant of—except for the demons who have a subtler awareness. Two controlling themes are emerging: the power of Jesus' words and actions and the first movements of growing antagonism against him. The strongest note, however, is at the segment's end: "the Son of God."

¹³He went up the mountain and called to him those whom he wanted, and they came to him. ¹⁴And he appointed twelve, whom he also named apostles, to be with him, and to be sent out to proclaim the message, ¹⁵and to have authority to cast out demons.

¹⁶So he appointed the twelve: Simon (to whom he gave the name Peter); ¹⁷James son of Zebedee and John the brother of James (to whom he gave the name Boanerges, that is, Sons of Thunder); ¹⁸and Andrew, and Philip, and Bartholomew, and

Choosing the Twelve: VV13-19

V13. *up the mountain*: There is an obvious allusion to Moses ascending Mount Sinai to accept the law for the people; *those whom he wanted*: This is a special call, beyond the call to the kingdom. Note that, judging from their unsophisticated backgrounds and from their later consistent misunderstandings and cowardice, the Twelve were not chosen because of their ideal qualities; *came to him*: As with the preceding miracles, Jesus offers, but the individual must respond before the offer can be fulfilled.

V14. *he appointed*: Literally "he made"; it is the word used in the Hebrew scriptures for the official appointment of priests and of Moses and Aaron as Yahweh's emissaries; *twelve*: Again, an allusion to the twelve tribes of Israel, named for the sons of Jacob, whose name was changed to Israel. Here, again, Jesus is founding a new Israel—making severance with Judaism, with patching old cloaks, with putting new wine into old bottles. The lists of the Twelve in the four gospels are basically the same and yet not exact parallels. [See a larger commentary for details.]; *to be with him*: This is Mark's definition of the Christian disciple, being with Jesus in spreading the Good News (*proclaim*) and healing (*cast out*). Mark uses "be with" five times at the Last Supper. The Latin root of "companions" is those who break bread together. Therefore, Christian discipleship has two *melded* aspects: "being with," the person-to-Person connection that is the root of "religion," and healing, apostolic action.

V15. *demons*: These are, in fact, the powers of the Messiah, which Jesus confers on his companions. St. Paul develops this similarly when he describes the members of the church as the embodiment of the powers of Christ.

V16. *Simon . . . Peter*: In all gospel lists of the apostles, Simon is always named first; Mark is the only one to say Jesus changed his name this early; as Peter is characterized by Jesus' nickname for him, "Rocky," so James and John are characterized by *Boanerges* = hot-tempered hell-raisers. Just as Jacob's name was changed to Israel, so with the leaders of the New Israel.

V18. *Andrew . . . Philip*: Oddly, both Greek names, suggesting the breadth of the kingdom's reach. Andrew is Simon's brother; in John 1:43, Philip introduces Nathanael to Jesus; *Bartholomew:* has no other role in the gospels;

Matthew, and Thomas, and James son of Alphaeus, and Thaddaeus, and Simon the Cananaean, [19]and Judas Iscariot, who betrayed him.

Then he went home; [20]and the crowd came together again, so that they could not even eat. [21]When his family heard it, they went out to restrain him, for people were saying, "He has gone out of his mind." [22]And the scribes who came down from Jerusalem said, "He has Beelzebul, and by the ruler of the demons he casts out demons."

Matthew: whom Mark has previously identified as "Levi"; *Thomas*: "The Twin," best known for skepticism about Jesus' resurrection (John 20:28); *James son of Alphaeus*: appears only in apostolic lists in the four gospels; *Thaddaeus*: Again, has no explicit role in the NT. Scholars are not agreed that this is the "Judas son of James" in Luke's list (6:16), commonly linked with "St. Jude, patron of hopeless cases." Possibly, Mark uses "Thaddaeus" to differentiate this man from the traitor, Judas; *Simon the Cananaean*: Differentiating him from Simon Peter, "Cananaean" is probably a Greek transliteration of the Aramaic for "zealous." The politically revolutionary Zealots, however, did not exist until the Jewish War (AD 66–73), so it might be a character trait: "hothead" or "eager."

V19. *Judas Iscariot*: Last in every list of the Twelve. Several apt meanings are offered for "Iscariot": "false one," from the Hebrew for "hand over," from the village of Kerioth, or from *Sicarii* or "Daggermen," a radical group of Jewish assassins; *home*: Presumably to Capernaum.

Nearly all we believe we "know" about the apostles (like all we know about Matthew's wise men) is legend, unsubstantiated by any of the four gospels or Acts. The internet has plenty of them, though most of those assertions are as untrustworthy as tales of Paul Bunyan and his great blue ox.

Misunderstandings about Jesus: VV20-35

This is two episodes embedded in one another—the accusation of diabolic influence in Jesus, bookended in a story about his family's doubts about him.

V20. *could not even eat*: That is, break bread, be alone together.

VV21-22. *his family*: If the early churches were propagating a hoax, surely they would have suppressed such an accusation from their hero's own relatives; *to restrain him*: Jesus was becoming an embarrassment to his hardworking, scandal-conscious peasant relatives; *gone out of his mind*: Equivalently, "possessed," which is echoed by *the scribes . . . down from Jerusalem*: Jerusalem is seventy-five miles to the south, which shows his fame is spreading. "Down" means not "from the North" but "from the big city"; *Beelzebul*: named for Baal, the fertility god of the ancient Philistines; St. Jerome translated it "Beelzebub," which William Golding took as the title of his novel *Lord of the Flies*.

[23]And he called them to him, and spoke to them in parables, "How can Satan cast out Satan? [24]If a kingdom is divided against itself, that kingdom cannot stand. [25]And if a house is divided against itself, that house will not be able to stand. [26]And if Satan has risen up against himself and is divided, he cannot stand, but his end has come. [27]But no one can enter a strong man's house and plunder his property without first tying up the strong man; then indeed the house can be plundered.

[28]"Truly I tell you, people will be forgiven for their sins and whatever blasphemies they utter; [29]but whoever blasphemes against the Holy Spirit can never have forgiveness, but is guilty of an eternal sin"— [30]for they had said, "He has an unclean spirit."

[31]Then his mother and his brothers came; and standing outside, they sent to him and called him. [32]A crowd was sitting around him; and they said to him, "Your mother and your brothers and sisters are

---

V23. *Satan cast out Satan?*: How can the Adversary destroy the Adversary? Why would Satan destroy his own? There must be some opposite, counter power here.

V27. *a strong man's house:* The image here shifts from internal division to attack from without. Satan is "the strong man," but Jesus has already proven himself stronger; he has entered Satan's house—the World—and has begun to take it away from Satan, who is now *"tied up."*

VV28-29. *"Truly I tell you"*: A stock phrase from the OT signaling a statement authorized by God; *forgiven for their sins*: There is no sin whatever that God cannot forgive; *blasphemes against the Holy Spirit*: This seems to contradict the previous verse and the fact that the church believes anyone can repent of sin up until death—and even after. The most likely explanation is that this sin is precisely what Jesus' accusers have just done: accusing the Spirit of doing evil, seeing goodness as wicked and therefore shunning it, effectively blocking God's Spirit. How can they be forgiven if they reject the Source of forgiveness? They charge him with blasphemy, and he countercharges them of blasphemy. (For Catholic doctrine, see *Catechism*, 1834.)

V31. *his mother and his brothers*: Resumes the narrative interrupted at V21. Quite likely the same embarrassed relatives mentioned above. Matthew 13:55 mentions four brothers (James, Joseph, Simon, Judas). There is no need to take this literally. Some reputable scholars from ancient to modern times suggest these were natural children of Joseph and Mary born after Jesus (See Matt 1:25: "no marital relations with her until she had borne a son.") Others work around it by saying they were Joseph's children by a previous marriage. Still others call them "cousins," since families were more tightly knit then. Even if there were no definition of the Virgin Birth, had Jesus had blood brothers, it would be remarkable they would never be mentioned anywhere else in the gospels or early traditions. There is no mention of a "father."

outside, asking for you." [33]And he replied, "Who are my mother and my brothers?" [34]And looking at those who sat around him, he said, "Here are my mother and my brothers! [35]Whoever does the will of God is my brother and sister and mother."

V33. *Who are my mother . . . ?*: Like Jesus' reply to his mother in Luke (2:49), when he is discovered with the priests, this seems at first a very unfeeling remark. Rather than demeaning his kin, however, Jesus is raising his companions to the same relationship with him as his blood relatives (verses 34-35). After all, we have already seen that they themselves have left their own families behind. What's more, his relatives—in trying to abort his mission—are refusing to join it: "Whoever is not with me is against me" (Matt 12:30). Remember, too, that at the time Mark wrote, Christians were being turned in by their relatives to the synagogues and to Roman authorities as followers of Christ.

V35. *"Whoever does the will of God"*: But what *is* this "will of God"? Jesus answers that: "I am the way, and the truth, and the life" (John 14:6). In former times, religious orders had a questionable custom called "the living rule," in which a particular novice fulfilled the order's rule so exactly that, if the written rule were destroyed, one could rewrite the entire body of rules just following that person around and writing down what he or she said and did. However unwise such a custom with fallible humans, it is precisely correct about being Christian: allowing for radical differences in places, times, and customs, thinking and acting as Jesus did. What did he do? He went around *freeing* people—from illness, from guilt, from false notions of human value.

A major question throughout the gospels is: How could the officials of Jewish religion be so hard-hearted and judgmental of someone who others believe is doing only good? Nowadays, however, not a few of us are skeptical about televangelists who draw huge crowds (and huge bank accounts), believing they are *completely* unacceptable.

Note: "Whoever does the will of God" belongs to Jesus' family. He says nothing about ritual baptism or purity of doctrine.

Review Questions for Chapter 3

1. Jesus becomes angry in this chapter, and the cause is "hardness of heart." Show how this is true not only of the scribes and Pharisees but even of his own relatives, and yet—ironically—it is not true of the actual demons Jesus encounters.
2. What does the unity of purpose between such traditional antagonists as the Pharisees and the Herodians show about the opposition to Jesus? Why are

they so put out over what Jesus preaches that they are willing to overlook their longstanding opposition to one another's political and religious doctrines? What's so special about Jesus' "new sect"?

3. Since Jesus is doing nothing but good—healing—why would the teachers of the law from Jerusalem accuse him of being in league with the devil? Try to get inside their skins and describe Jesus as he looks from *their* point of view.

4. Even Jesus' own relatives think there is something wrong with him. List some latter-day prophets whose closest friends found them burdensome: Thomas More, Martin Luther King, opponents of modern wars.

5. List the places in the chapter that reemphasize the fact that, although everyone is invited into the kingdom, there has to be some kind of personal response to the invitation in order for it to be effective. In that same regard, explain the statement: "Many born Catholics have been baptized but never converted."

6. Explain verses 14-15. Precisely *what* is a Christian missioned to preach? Scaling down the metaphor of "demons" to our own less dramatic lives, what does it mean that a present-day Christian must "drive out demons"?

For Reflection

(1) *Verse 5.* Jesus was at one and the same time angry at those trying to trip him up and sorry for them. That is a difficult combination for most people to muster. There is a great difference between anger motivated by frustration or hurt feelings and anger motivated by love. The one is self-enclosed around its own hurt; the other is hurt not only for the self but for the loved offender who is also hurting him- or herself. The difference, of course, is that strangers or mere acquaintances can provoke anger, but only those we love can provoke anger and compassion in the same act.

Are too many people in your life still just strangers and mere acquaintances? How could you rectify that? There is no doubt that the more friends you love the more likely you are to suffer. But isn't it worth it?

(2) *Verse 8.* Jesus drew crowds, like a present-day celebrity; everybody wants to get a look at him so they can say, "I saw Whatshisname!" But it seems clear that Jesus didn't shun the crowds, nor did the fact that they had upset his own plans to instruct the disciples seem to shake his composure. One of the major patterns in Jesus' life—and therefore in the life of anyone who follows him—is not only that he healed and forgave sinners but also that he was not afraid of crowds or of intrusions on his well-made plans.

Elsewhere (Matt 10:27), Jesus says that he expects us to shout what we have heard—the Good News of healing and forgiveness—from the house tops. No need to take that literally, but are you too shy about your ordination to preach the gospel?

(3) *Verses 13-14.* For reasons known only to him—and not for their eminent qualifications!—Jesus chooses the ones he wants and sends them out to preach and to heal. From the outcome, you can see Christians were not and still are not chosen for their promise or merits: One of them betrayed Jesus to the police; another denied ever having known him; when the first sign of genuine threat arose, they all hiked up their skirts and skedaddled. Yet from that unpromising gaggle of cowards has arisen a church that has lasted two thousand years.

Do you ever say to yourself, "Oh, I'm nobody"? Most often that turns into a self-fulfilling prophecy: you do in fact and in deed become a nobody, of no use whatever in spreading the kingdom. Perhaps you are not extraordinarily gifted; neither were the first ones chosen. But you are in the hands of a Master who can work miracles with materials no more promising than mud and spittle. Is it possible that your self-defensive claims to be nobody are hindering God's ability to use you? That your shyness is tying the hands of an omnipotent God?

(4) *Verses 24-25.* If a nation or family is divided against itself, it is destined for collapse. But the Christian kingdom is painfully divided against itself, and often over doctrines so abstract and subtle that they could make no sense or difference to the ordinary Christian man or woman. What's more, even within the Roman Catholic segment of Christians there are strongly felt antagonisms: between liberals and conservatives, between women and the official church, between American Catholics and the Vatican. Have we forgotten something? What?

Is it possible that your silence has contributed to the divisions in the Body of Christ? As Eldridge Cleaver says, "If you're not part of the solution, you're part of the problem."

(5) *Verses 34-35.* Like the mythic story of God asking Abraham to sacrifice his beloved son Isaac, Jesus seems to be asking too much: that we reject the very people who love us. But both stories have a different—but just as harsh—question to pose: are those who love you and whom you love *more* important to you than the will of God? In an extreme case, if your sibling or child were selling drugs and refused to stop, would you call the police to protect the victims; is the safety of one of your own more important than the lives he or she is ruining? More realistically for the reader of these pages, do you make excuses in your mind for those you love rather than confronting them and asking them to change? Are your feelings more important than what you claim to believe?

4 ¹Again he began to teach beside the sea. Such a very large crowd gathered around him that he got into a boat on the sea and sat there, while the whole crowd was beside the sea on the land. ²He began to teach them many things in parables, and in his teaching he said to them: ³"Listen! A sower went out to sow. ⁴And as he sowed, some seed fell on the path, and the birds came and ate it up. ⁵Other seed fell on rocky ground, where it did not have much soil, and it sprang up quickly, since it had no depth of soil. ⁶And when the sun rose, it was scorched; and since it had no root, it withered away. ⁷Other seed fell among thorns, and the thorns grew up and choked it, and it yielded no grain. ⁸Other seed fell into good soil and brought forth grain, growing up and increasing and yielding thirty and sixty and a hundred-

---

The Sower: VV1-20

V1. *Again*: There is no concern, as there is for modern historians, with perfect historical accuracy of dates. The good news is far more important. The sayings and parables of Jesus have come to Mark through a long line of word-of-mouth sources. He pieces them together and adds explanations like any other commentator trying not only to tell a news story but also—and more important—to find its meaning, its effect on the life and behavior of the believer.

V2. *parables*: The Greek word for "parable" means not only a symbolic story but also a riddle to provoke thought. It is also the root of the word "parabola," a curved line on a graph: a roundabout way to an answer. Even though this story begins without introduction, as with all Jesus' parables, it is an explanation of the reign of God—which Jesus' audience did not understand—in terms of things they did understand.

VV4-7. *as he sowed:* The farmer flung the seed as he walked, thus some of the seed was bound to be lost; *path . . . rocky ground . . . thorns*: The focus of the parable is that, no matter what the setbacks (the hardness of heart we saw in chap. 3), the harvest—the kingdom of God—will come to fruition. One critic suggests the "rocky ground" is a sly dig at Peter, "Rocky." Later (8:33), Jesus will snap "Satan!" (V15 here) at him when Peter refuses to accept that Jesus must go to Jerusalem, even if it means his death. Also John 12:24 uses the same seed metaphor to capture the same unpalatable message: "Unless a grain of wheat falls into the earth and dies, it remains just a single grain."

V8. *a hundred*: A farmer's normal expectation was that he would get his investment of seed back plus a 20 percent "profit." Jesus' figures seem exorbitant, but think of beginning with only twelve fully committed companions and ending with a church today of global scope, one that continues to grow after two thousand years, despite attacks from without and corruption within.

fold." [9]And he said, "Let anyone with ears to hear listen!"

[10]When he was alone, those who were around him along with the twelve asked him about the parables. [11]And he said to them, "To you has been given the secret of the kingdom of God, but for those outside, everything comes in parables; [12]in order that

'they may indeed look, but not
   perceive,
and may indeed listen, but not
   understand;
so that they may not turn again
   and be forgiven.' "

[13]And he said to them, "Do you not understand this parable? Then how will you

---

V10. *was alone*: This stylistic device gives Mark a chance to explain this first parable and, in so doing, explain why Jesus spoke indirectly, through parables, rather than straightforwardly, like a philosophy or theology professor; *with the twelve*: The men and women designated elsewhere as "the disciples," as distinguished from the apostles, who had left everything to travel with Jesus and learn from him. Together, they make up the New Israel, the kingdom of God, separate from "*those outside*," the Israel left behind—because they refused to come along; *asked him*: Note that, as usual, the inner circle is still as clueless as the outsiders. There are sixty-three parables in Matthew, Mark, and Luke, and Jesus explains forty-one of them—but rarely to non-disciples, which he seems to do here.

V11. *the secret of the kingdom of God*: The Messianic Secret, that God has entered history in the form of Jesus, the hidden Messiah, and the kingdom of God has begun. As the parable of the sower shows, however, it will have mixed acceptance because of the receptivities of those to whom the word comes. Even the apostles and disciples will at times have "their fingers in their ears," like "*those outside*," including his own family; *everything comes in parables*: To understand, consider those who say, "All that religion stuff is a bunch of bull!"

V12. *look, but not perceive:* Any classroom gives evidence of these "talents"; *so that they may not turn again*: This is the most roundly debated verse in the entire NT. It sounds as if Jesus were deliberately talking in riddles to prevent the conversion of "those outside," and there certainly was a Jewish tradition that Yahweh withholds his revelation from sinners. But this interpretation seems to be ruled out by Mark's clear assertion in verse 10 that the innermost "in group" doesn't get it either. It becomes even less acceptable when we remember that, even after the stunning experience of the transfiguration (9:2), the innermost threesome (Peter, James, and John) were *still* in the dark. Parable expert Joachim Jeremias believes the Aramaic conjunction, *dilema*, can be understood not only as "lest" but "*unless* they repent." It is clear, however, that the parables are not meant to elicit faith from the unwilling but to

understand all the parables? [14]The sower sows the word. [15]These are the ones on the path where the word is sown: when they hear, Satan immediately comes and takes away the word that is sown in them. [16]And these are the ones sown on rocky ground: when they hear the word, they immediately receive it with joy. [17]But they have no root, and endure only for a while; then, when trouble or persecution arises on account of the word, immediately they fall away. [18]And others are those sown among the thorns: these are the ones who hear the word, [19]but the cares of the world, and the lure of wealth, and the desire for other things come in and choke the word, and it yields nothing. [20]And these are the ones sown on the good soil: they hear the word and accept it and bear fruit, thirty and sixty and a hundredfold."

---

clarify the object of the faith: the kingdom of God. To those without the willingness to believe, the parables remain simply senseless riddles. They refuse to admit the "curveball" was a fair pitch.

V15. *the word*: This word appears eight times in the passage and is, like "the good news," a catchword to stand for the whole Christian message. The Greek style, vocabulary, and method of explaining the parable (verses 13-20) are distinctively non-Hebrew, which suggests the interpretation is a meditation on the story by the early church rather than by Jesus. What's more, the interpretation changes the focus of Jesus' original story from the eventual triumph of the sower to the obstacles people put in the sower's way, and thus changes the whole point of the original story from "the kingdom of God will be an abundant harvest, no matter how many setbacks the sower encounters" to a judgment on people who have been invited into the kingdom but fail because of shallow hearts, hard hearts, rootlessness, greed, and so forth. This again echoes the hardness of heart in the Jewish officials and Jesus' relatives in the previous chapter. However, the interpretation is certainly very early, since Mark wrote his gospel around the year AD 65.

V17. *persecution arises*: This is a concrete example familiar with Mark's audience of persecuted Christians whose devotion to the *"the word"* is life-threatening.

V19. *the lure of wealth*: This should not be used (as some do) to condemn those who have achieved a comfortable material life. It is merely a warning that "the cares of the world" can be a severe distraction from what is truly important. Faith often has to struggle against prosperity as much as against hardship.

Proverbs and Parables: VV21-34

V21. *under a bushel basket*: The companions of Jesus are not to keep "the word"—the mystery of the kingdom of God—a secret from those who will

²¹He said to them, "Is a lamp brought in to be put under the bushel basket, or under the bed, and not on the lampstand? ²²For there is nothing hidden, except to be disclosed; nor is anything secret, except to come to light. ²³Let anyone with ears to hear listen!" ²⁴And he said to them, "Pay attention to what you hear; the measure you give will be the measure you get, and still more will be given you. ²⁵For to those who have, more will be given; and from those who have nothing, even what they have will be taken away."

²⁶He also said, "The kingdom of God is as if someone would scatter seed on the ground, ²⁷and would sleep and rise night and day, and the seed would sprout and grow, he does not know how. ²⁸The earth produces of itself, first the stalk, then the head, then the full grain in the head. ²⁹But when the grain is ripe, at once he goes in with his sickle, because the harvest has come."

³⁰He also said, "With what can we compare the kingdom of God, or what parable will we use for it? ³¹It is like a mustard seed, which, when sown upon the ground, is the smallest of all the seeds on earth; ³²yet when it is sown it grows up and becomes the greatest of all shrubs, and puts

---

listen with open hearts, which is echoed in **V24**: *the measure you give will be the measure you get*.

V22. *to be disclosed*: The concealment—the secret—is only temporary. The goal is to put the light on the lampstand after the resurrection validates the Good News. Jesus' power is, for now, as hidden as the life-power within a seed. Any private instruction is for future revelation.

V25. *more will be given*: Neither half of this verse should be taken materially, as if it were saying, "The rich get richer, and the poor get poorer." It is talking—as is the whole passage —of largeness of heart: the more love you give, the more you are able to love; the deadened heart is hardly likely to come alive. This echoes the bountiful harvest in verse 20.

V27. *the seed . . . grow*: The seed of the kingdom of God has already been planted: Jesus is among us. But we are not to fret that it has not reached fulfillment yet; as St. Paul said, "I planted, Apollos watered, but God gave the growth" (1 Cor 3:6)—in God's own good time. The kingdom of God is a revolution, but only in terms of gradual conversion, not in terms of forceful intervention like a blitzkrieg. On the other hand, real faith cannot remain inert but keeps growing.

V29. *with his sickle*: The phrase comes from the OT book of Joel 3:13.

V31. *smallest of all the seeds*: Actually, it is not, but that does not change the point of the comparison. Unlike, for instance, the parable that says, "The kingdom of God is like finding a treasure in a field," Jesus "de-compacts" this metaphor himself. Looking at a tiny seed, one cannot imagine the enormous reality lurking inside it; so too with the tiny group of apostles and disciples that became a church of hundreds of millions over two thousand years. Also, mus-

forth large branches, so that the birds of the air can make nests in its shade." ³³With many such parables he spoke the word to them, as they were able to hear it; ³⁴he did not speak to them except in parables, but he explained everything in private to his disciples.

³⁵On that day, when evening had come, he said to them, "Let us go across to the other side." ³⁶And leaving the crowd behind, they took him with them in the boat, just as he was. Other boats were with him. ³⁷A great windstorm arose, and the waves beat into the boat, so that the boat was already being swamped. ³⁸But he was in the stern, asleep on the cushion; and they woke him up and said to him, "Teacher, do you not care that we are perishing?"

---

tard bushes tend to "take over" where they are not especially welcome. Not a great cedar but a weed!

V34. *them*: Throughout this section, Mark is typically careless about point of view; at times Jesus is talking privately to the disciples, then suddenly the focus switches to "those outside."

The Storm at Sea: VV35-41

V35. *"Let us go across"*: From this point on, Jesus is on the move. Here, they cross the symbolic barrier between the western (Jewish) side and the eastern (Gentile) side.

V36. *boat*: The frequency with which Jesus and his companions are found in a boat has led to the use of a boat as a symbol for the storm-threatened church, e.g., The Barque of Peter. (For a picture, Google "Jesus Boat Project," the so-called Kinneret boat. About twenty-six feet long and eight feet wide, able to hold twelve to fifteen people.); ***just as he was***: Jesus was already in the boat (4:1), and the disciples left the crowd and joined him; ***Other boats***: Thus, likely not just the Twelve.

V37. *A great windstorm arose*: Echoes of Jonah (1:4): "A mighty storm came upon the sea." Like Jonah, Jesus is also asleep. The Sea of Galilee is 680 feet below sea level; the hills on its west bank are 2,000 feet high. Such sudden storms are common there, resulting from hot moist air from the Mediterranean colliding with cool, dry mountain air. Note Psalm 107:23-32, which is almost an outline sketch for the episode, which equates Jesus' powers with God's. The fact that at least four of those in the boat were professional fishermen on this same lake testifies that this storm was worse than usual.

V38. *cushion*: Probably the cushion of the helmsman's seat; ***do you not care***: Despite the high-toned translation, the statement implies the rather snotty tone of a spoiled child. It could, however, echo the very real cries of Mark's audience who were perishing in Nero's arenas.

³⁹He woke up and rebuked the wind, and said to the sea, "Peace! Be still!" Then the wind ceased, and there was a dead calm. ⁴⁰He said to them, "Why are you afraid? Have you still no faith?" ⁴¹And they were filled with great awe and said to one another, "Who then is this, that even the wind and the sea obey him?"

V39. *rebuked the wind*: The same act of authority as Jesus uses against demons; and note that he uses the same words as he has used before: ***Peace!***: literally "be muzzled!"; ***Be still!***: "lie down flat." In Jewish folklore, the sea could be the home of evil monsters. In the face of either demons or rebellious nature, Jesus acts with the calm authority of a father or elder brother.

V40. *no faith*: Since this event occurred before the resurrection, it cannot mean faith in Jesus as divine—and therefore indestructible. Rather, Jesus is rebuking his disciples (even those specially selected) for their lack of faith in God, who has proven, through the experiences they have already shared with Jesus, that a minor obstacle like a squall at sea is not going to interfere with God's plans for Jesus. Also, one critic holds that the opposite of faith for Mark is not doubt but fear. First John 4:18 says: "There is no fear in love, but perfect love casts out fear."

V41. *Who then is this?*: The question that occurs throughout Mark, which is answered by the high priest at Jesus' trial and by the centurion at Jesus' death; ***obey***: In a very real sense, they have answered their own question: Jesus has the powers of God; however, their suspicions about the answer to the riddle of Jesus will not be put to rest till the resurrection. The use of the present tense, "obey," shows that hostile forces yield to the power of Jesus not only in this one event but universally. Remember that, at the time Mark was writing, the church—like the boat—was being assaulted from all sides, both by Jews who considered Christian converts blasphemous and heretical and by Romans who considered them a threat to the peace of the state.

Review Questions for Chapter 4

1. Why would Jesus teach in parables—stories—rather than "straight out," like a present-day preacher or religion teacher? What advantages do stories give a speaker when he or she is talking to an audience that cannot—or do not want to—hear the message?

2. De-compact the metaphor that compares the infant church to a seed. What can you say about seed that is also true of the church from its beginning to today?

3. Why is there so much emphasis in Mark's gospel on hardness of heart? What kind of resistances to the message—the seed—would Mark have met in his own audience? What kind of resistances to the message would he find in today's audience?
4. List the varied ways in which Jesus encounters resistance from the Antagonist in this chapter. What does his overcoming them each time say about the ultimate success of the Christian kingdom?

For Reflection

(1) *Verses 3-8.* Human beings are born not fully human but only human*izable*; as infants, we are like animal cubs, only with a remarkable difference: We have the *potential* to break out into ever-wider fields of knowing and loving—or to remain unevolved, little better than high-level animals. Some of our brothers and sisters brought that human potential into shallow, parched, choking families and neighborhoods, so that they grew up twisted, bitter, belligerent, or passive, fearful, shy, or even mentally ill.

When you feel resentment for others, do you ever stop and wonder what *caused* the person you resent to become that way? Each of us is responsible for our own personalities and our own actions, but only insofar as we take the personality formed in us by others when we were children and try to control it, shape it, forge it into a character. What factors went into making this individual so irritatingly unpunctual? Why is that other one such a maddening fault-finder? Is it perhaps that no one has found a kindly, tactful way to point out how twisted they've allowed themselves to be grown?

(2) *Verse 21.* We are the light of the world; we cannot hide our lights under a bushel or a bed, behind a mask of shyness or in a flurry of busyness. Just as good people, not bad people go to confession, so good people, not bad people, are reading this text. But our goodness can be hidden (even from ourselves) out of a sense of misguided humility. "I don't want to look like a do-gooder; it's a kinder thing just to keep quiet and take it; they'll all think I'm trying to take over." With tragic irony, such a posture—which seems so laudably humble—is actually a twisted form of self-centeredness: self-defensiveness. What Jesus wants is that we *forget* ourselves and shine! In the measure you give joy you will receive joy.

(3) *Verse 27.* Farmers don't know how their seed grows, nor do we know how our children—or we ourselves—continue to grow. But whether it is our crops, or our faith, or our adulthood as Christians, growing anything is not as simple as Mark's treatment might suggest. We can't just plant a crop or a child or a

self, go to sleep, and let a provident God and the forces of nature work their magic. It takes hoeing, pruning, weeding away natural undergrowth to make the crop or child or self grow larger and more abundantly than it would have without prodding. And human growth is almost always painful. Do you resist the challenge to get out of halfhearted habits, halfway ways of doing things, cutting corners, avoiding pruning?

(4) *Verse 31.* A mustard seed is the smallest seed in the world according to Mark (bit of hyperbole again). But the point is still true: God can make somebodies of nobodies—provided only that the so-called nobodies aren't afraid. Martin Luther King Jr. was just a nobody preacher in a nowhere church; Lech Walesa was just a nobody miner in an unpronounceable Polish city; Mother Teresa was just a nobody nun in a Calcutta slum. And yet each of those nobodies won the Nobel Peace Prize. They started with just one meeting, one protest, one leper. You may not win a Nobel Prize, but you can make a difference. How?

(5) *Verse 39.* Jesus merely shouts, "Be still!" and the storm limps away like a whipped cur. Unfortunately, we haven't the power to shout, "Be still!" to the storms that rage around us at times. But we can shout it at the storms that rage within us at times: anger, shame, grudges, guilt. They're all curable, at our hands but at a price: distracting ourselves from anger, confessing shame, forgiving the offender, turning guilt into responsibility, and making amends.

Are you the victim of your moods, the weather, the wounds inflicted by the people around you? No one can demean you without your cooperation. When do you stop cooperating?

5 ¹They came to the other side of the sea, to the country of the Gerasenes. ²And when he had stepped out of the boat, immediately a man out of the tombs with an unclean spirit met him. ³He lived among the tombs; and no one could restrain him any more, even with a chain; ⁴for he had often been restrained with shackles and chains, but the chains he wrenched apart, and the shackles he broke in pieces; and no one had the strength to subdue him. ⁵Night and day among the tombs and on the mountains he was always howling and bruising himself with stones. ⁶When he saw Jesus from a distance, he ran and bowed down before him; ⁷and he shouted at the top of his voice, "What have you to do with me, Jesus, Son of the Most High God? I adjure you by God, do not torment me." ⁸For he had said to him, "Come out of the man, you unclean spirit!" ⁹Then Jesus asked him, "What is your name?"

A Man Possessed: VV1-20

V1. *Gerasenes*: Gerasa is thirty-three miles southeast of the Sea of Galilee and outside Jewish Palestine; therefore, the people in the story are not Jews but Gentile pagans, and the presence of pigs (abhorrent to Jews) is not unusual. Jesus' first miracle among Jews was the cure of a demoniac (1:23); so is his first miracle among Gentiles. From now on, Jesus will cross from one to the other side repeatedly.

V3. *among the tombs*: The detail gives an eerie chill to the story. See Isaiah 52, where the prophet speaks for God to pagans who live in tombs, practicing vile rites, and eating the flesh of swine. Like contact with swine, living among tombs was contaminating for pious Jews. Mark's Gentile readers might not be sensitive to the wallow of ritual impurity (demon, tombs, swine) into which Jesus fearlessly moves. The details enhance the maniac's strength and therefore Jesus' triumph.

VV3-4. *no one . . . subdue him*: Detail upon detail mounts up showing the intractability of this particular victim as a challenge to the power of Jesus.

V5. *howling and bruising himself*: This whole segment is one of the most detailed descriptions in the gospels.

V7. *What have you to do*: Nearly a repetition of the words in Jesus' first miracle (1:24); *Son of the Most High God*: As with previous cases of exorcism, he recognizes Jesus' true role, and it is clear the man is himself Satanic territory, divided against itself, fearing conquest by Jesus yet yearning for it—as is evident in some nondemonic part of him shouting: *I adjure you by God, do not torment me*: Jesus' very presence is a condemnation of everything the demon is. The two are as incompatible as blazing light and utter darkness. The "demons" use the plural; the goodness within the victim uses the singular.

V9. *What is your name?*: As before, 1:24, knowing another's name gave one power over him or her; just as the demon knows Jesus' name, Jesus demands

He replied, "My name is Legion; for we are many." [10]He begged him earnestly not to send them out of the country. [11]Now there on the hillside a great herd of swine was feeding; [12]and the unclean spirits begged him, "Send us into the swine; let us enter them." [13]So he gave them permission. And the unclean spirits came out and entered the swine; and the herd, numbering about two thousand, rushed down the steep bank into the sea, and were drowned in the sea.

[14]The swineherds ran off and told it in the city and in the country. Then people came to see what it was that had happened.

[15]They came to Jesus and saw the demoniac sitting there, clothed and in his right mind, the very man who had had the legion; and they were afraid. [16]Those who had seen what had happened to the demoniac and to the swine reported it. [17]Then they began to beg Jesus to leave their neighborhood. [18]As he was getting into the boat, the man who had been possessed by demons begged him that he might be with him. [19]But Jesus refused, and said to him, "Go home to your friends, and tell them how much the Lord has done for you, and what mercy he has shown you." [20]And he

---

the same of it. As with the storm, Jesus is extraordinarily calm and confident. *Legion*: Again, as in 1:24, the infestation is multiple, and here the metaphor is military, aggressive. The term used for "herd" was used for a gaggle of new army recruits; Jesus "dismisses" them, and they "charge" into the sea.

V13. *he gave them permission*: Jesus shows himself humane even to his Antagonist; *unclean spirits . . . entered the swine*: This is a difficult story to explain as literal and historical. First, the number of pigs—two thousand—is enormous; second, although it is hardly the point of the story, it shows Jesus as somewhat insensitive to other people's property; third, it seems to have no logical connection with the exorcism. What is more likely is that the exorcism itself was a historical event and, as Matthew uses "special effects" to heighten the meaning of the crucifixion, here some pre-Mark source used the massive stampede to show that Jesus' encounter with evil made a profound effect on people *outside* Judaism; *drowned in the sea*: As one critic observes, since the Sea of Tiberias was thirty-three miles away, this gallop was "a bit of a stretch, even for a miracle." Mark's geographical inaccuracy is hardly a challenging matter here.

V15. *clothed*: The detail not only stands in quiet contrast to the raving maniac but also shows Jesus' compassion; the only ones who could have clothed the man were the disciples; *they were afraid*: Or "awestruck," the same verb used of the disciples when Jesus calmed the storm.

V17. *beg Jesus to leave*: Having such a powerful man around is unnerving.

V18. *might be with him*: Be-with is the same verb as in the call of the apostles (3:14).

V19. *refused*: Any attempt to guess Jesus' reason for denying the man's request to become a disciple would be pure speculation, but perhaps one reason

went away and began to proclaim in the Decapolis how much Jesus had done for him; and everyone was amazed.

²¹When Jesus had crossed again in the boat to the other side, a great crowd gathered around him; and he was by the sea.

---

might have been that Jesus did not want such a choice to be made on the surge of emotion but rather only after thought in peace; *Go home*: Like the cured leper, this man has been totally outcast. Now, as in the sacrament of reconciliation, he is reunited; *tell them*: Unlike cures among the Jews, Jesus here explicitly asks the one cured to spread the word. Freed of his infestation, the man now becomes a missionary to his fellow Gentiles. He has called Jesus "Son of the Most High God," but notice that Jesus does not enjoin silence on this Gentile as he has done before with Jews. Jews were so rigidly monotheistic that they could not even conceive of God being more complex than they had always imagined—as will become evident at Jesus' trial. Pagans were not that inflexible about how far beyond rigid categories the divine power of gods could be; *the Lord*: Obviously the victim would understand "Lord" to mean God—though not necessarily the Yahweh of the Jews. Only later, after the resurrection, would the disciples understand that "the Lord" was Jesus himself.

V20. *the Decapolis*: A federation of ten towns in the areas of Gilead and Bashan; the detail shows that the good news of Jesus' power is spreading among non-Jews.

Do not be distracted by skepticism about demons and exorcisms. Even in a world accustomed to psychiatry as a commonplace, we still find little puzzlement when told that someone is "wrestling with his demons." Such inner agonies cause the same kind of alienation and isolation as this more dramatic story embodies.

Despite the Halloween aura surrounding the notion of exorcism because of films that depict it with "fright-night" giddiness, there have been reliable testimonies of all the occurrences in the film *The Exorcist* (except, of course, the impossible 360-degree head turn). M. Scott Peck, a Christian who was nonetheless quite skeptical of the idea, served as one of the now-required professional psychiatrists on two exorcisms and said that, in both cases, at the end of the ritual, "a presence" departed the victim and the room (see *People of the Lie*.)

Also as John R. Donahue and Daniel J. Harrington write, "liberation *from* evil is liberation *for* mission" (see *The Gospel of Mark*, Sacra Pagina Series, 171).

Healing Two Women: VV. 21-43

V21. *other side*: Back to the Palestine (mostly Jewish) side of the Sea of Galilee.

²²Then one of the leaders of the synagogue named Jairus came and, when he saw him, fell at his feet ²³and begged him repeatedly, "My little daughter is at the point of death. Come and lay your hands on her, so that she may be made well, and live." ²⁴So he went with him.

And a large crowd followed him and pressed in on him. ²⁵Now there was a woman who had been suffering from hemorrhages for twelve years. ²⁶She had endured much under many physicians, and had spent all that she had; and she was no better, but rather grew worse. ²⁷She had heard about Jesus, and came up behind him in the crowd and touched his cloak, ²⁸for she said, "If I but touch his clothes, I will be made well." ²⁹Immediately her hemorrhage stopped; and she felt in her body that she was healed of her disease. ³⁰Immediately aware that power had gone forth from him, Jesus turned about in the crowd and

---

V22. *fell at his feet*: Strong contrast between the humility of Jairus and the other synagogue officials Jesus has encountered; also, this is a man used to *being* asked favors, not begging, and he does not send a servant but humbles himself to plead.

V23. *lay your hands on her*: The point of both of these two bookended and intertwined stories is that mere physical contact with Jesus is healing; restoring and rejuvenating. As with all healing stories, the verbs used connote healing not only of the body but also of the soul.

VV25-26. *hemorrhages*: During their menstrual periods, Jewish women were ritually unclean; this woman, because of a continued uterine bleeding, could never attend religious services; further, she was incapable of childbearing and subject to legal divorce; she is, equivalently, ritually "dead"; *twelve years*: There must be some hyperbole here because, if the woman hemorrhaged uninterrupted that long, she would have died; *many physicians:* It seems obvious many doctors were mystified but prescribed anyway, only making her worse; *spent all that she had*: As with the Gerasene maniac, the futility of other attempts underscores Jesus' authority.

V28. *If I but touch his clothes*: As in every case so far, in order for the victim to be healed, he or she must meet Jesus halfway, with faith in him. Since she is ritually unclean, her touch "defiles" Jesus. Nonetheless, she is steadfast and gutsy.

V29. *her hemorrhage stopped*: Literally "the flow of her blood dried up." Just like that. No ritual, no words, no action by Jesus. In contrast to her doctors, he is charged with power.

V30. *Who touched my clothes?*: Mark has already noted, 5:24, that the crowd was large and "crowding" Jesus; the point is that Jesus was aware that someone had reached out to him and that his power had reached back.

said, "Who touched my clothes?" [31]And his disciples said to him, "You see the crowd pressing in on you; how can you say, 'Who touched me?' " [32]He looked all around to see who had done it. [33]But the woman, knowing what had happened to her, came in fear and trembling, fell down before him, and told him the whole truth. [34]He said to her, "Daughter, your faith has made you well; go in peace, and be healed of your disease."

[35]While he was still speaking, some people came from the leader's house to say, "Your daughter is dead. Why trouble the teacher any further?" [36]But overhearing what they said, Jesus said to the leader of the synagogue, "Do not fear, only believe." [37]He allowed no one to follow him except

---

V31. *how can you say, 'Who touched me?'*: Even after their experience of calming the storm and the demoniac, the disciples still do not get it.

V33. *in fear and trembling*: St. Paul makes this phrase, "fear and trembling," nearly a cliché to describe the awe one feels at accepting salvation (Phil 2:12). In his masterwork on the soul, *The Idea of the Holy*, Rudolf Otto describes encounter with the divine as the *Mysterium Tremendum et Facinans*, experience of the transcendent in the immanent, not terror so much as profound awe that—in the same instant—humbles and exalts. "Fear of the Lord" hardly captures it. The "victim" is not "fearful." Rather, the Presence is "fearsome." (Google: "numinous.")

V34. *He said to her:* A male talking to a female stranger in public would be shocking; *Daughter*: Recall 3:33-35. Anyone who "does the will of God" is his family; *your faith*: In contrast to his own disciples. It is not the contact that healed her, nor is it magic, but her trust in God. As before (2:5), Mark is writing after the resurrection, when faith in Jesus meant faith in him as the embodiment of God; here, however, it can mean only faith in God and faith in Jesus as his agent; *be healed of your disease*: Since Mark has said the woman's physical problem is already cured, Jesus means here a more profound healing of the searching soul.

V35. *While he was still speaking*: Here Mark resumes the interrupted story of Jairus. The declaration of the little girl's death, once again, boosts the obstacles against Jesus.

V36. *fear . . . believe*: Yet again, the obstacle is not rational doubt but faintheartedness.

V37. *Peter, James, and John*: These three are frequently singled out from the rest (the exaltation of the transfiguration and the abasement of the agony in the garden); here they are given a privileged insight into the extent of Jesus' power. One purpose is to show that, despite their special experiences, they still remain resolutely clueless.

Peter, James, and John, the brother of James. ³⁸When they came to the house of the leader of the synagogue, he saw a commotion, people weeping and wailing loudly. ³⁹When he had entered, he said to them, "Why do you make a commotion and weep? The child is not dead but sleeping." ⁴⁰And they laughed at him. Then he put them all outside, and took the child's father and mother and those who were with him, and went in where the child was. ⁴¹He took her by the hand and said to her, "Talitha cum," which means, "Little girl, get up!" ⁴²And immediately the girl got up and began to walk about (she was twelve years of age). At this they were overcome with amazement. ⁴³He strictly ordered them that no one should know this, and told them to give her something to eat.

V38. *commotion*: People of the Middle East and Asia make a great din at the time of death to show the depth of their loss; Jesus uses this occasion to show how wrong they are—that death is not the end, merely a "sleep." Quite likely, many of the mourners were hired.

V39. *The child is not dead*: The child *is*, of course, literally dead; the funeral rites have already begun. Simply from the words he used, it is impossible to tell whether Jesus is speaking literally (that the girl is not actually dead) or theologically (that every death is actual only to us but merely a passing phase in the eyes of God), but Mark's viewpoint from after the resurrection makes obvious what meaning he intended. Belief in resurrection is an automatic assertion that death is, in fact, only apparent.

V40. *laughed at him*: It is difficult to blame them. What Jesus is suggesting is clearly preposterous from their limited, this-world point of view. But for Mark's community, with their steadfast-unto-death belief in the resurrection, such mourning was to be laughed at.

V41. *took her by the hand:* Touching a corpse was the severest of impurities; *Talitha cum*: Literally "Little lamb, arise"; *which means*: Since Mark always translates, it is obvious his audience did not know Hebrew or the Aramaic dialect of it; *get up*: As in 1:31, this word meant to the early Christian communities far more than a mere physical act of rising but had connotations of the resurrection.

V42. *got up*: Again, the Greek word goes beyond physical action; fifteen times in the NT it is used for Jesus' resurrection. Jesus defies nature, demons, sickness, and death; *amazement*: The Greek is more closely "ecstatic." Note: the miracles are a *result* of faith; they do not seem to have provoked belief in the scornful mourners, merely amazement at a newsworthy event. People have not changed in two thousand years.

V43. *no one should know this*: Besides Jesus and the girl, there are only five witnesses to this stunning event, and Jesus enjoins them to keep the Messianic Secret; *something to eat*: Such homely details have a ring of authenticity to them and show Jesus' everyday solicitousness.

Review Questions for Chapter 5

1. Jesus released the demons from the madman into the pigs. If he is that lenient with souls of the self-damned, what does that suggest of his way of dealing with lesser sinners like ourselves?
2. How does Jesus' dealings with Gentiles in this chapter fit in with his dealings with the scribes and Pharisees in previous chapters? What are his actions with them tacitly "saying"?
3. List all the healings in the chapter. What do they all have in common, despite their surface differences? How does each subtly indicate that Jesus is healing not merely torments of the body?
4. Where in the chapter does Mark resurface a common theme in the gospel: the differences between our limited this-world ideas of what is possible and God's ideas of what is possible?
5. Go back over the last four chapters and, concentrating only on references to Jesus silencing people, trace how the Messianic Secret is gradually coming more and more to light.

For Reflection

(1) *Verse 5.* The afflicted man roamed the tombs day and night, punishing his body with stones. The scene is dramatic enough for a horror movie and has to be scaled down to fit into the more commonplace scope of most of our own ordinary lives. But there are people all around us punishing themselves—often in ways far in excess of the misperceived causes. Young people savage themselves for failing to live up to (often imagined) expectations of their parents; sensitive consciences of all ages torment themselves over sexual weaknesses that could be healed if they could only bring them out of the tombs and into the open, talk with somebody; cold wars continue to break apart families and inwardly devour all concerned because no one is willing to sit down and clear the air once and for all. Do you know someone like that who needs someone to lure them into the Light? Perhaps even yourself?

(2) *Verse 9.* The infestation within the tormented man says that its name is "Mob" or "Legion," because there are so many demons there. Many of us, when the number of mistakes and gaffes we make seem worthy of *The Guinness Book of World Records*, sometimes feel the same way: there are simply too many weaknesses inside us for a single person to cope with. We want to turn in this faulty model of a self and get another; some even resort to suicide attempts.

What will heal that? Prayer. Not "saying prayers," but finding a quiet place alone, relaxing (it will take a strong act of the will), emptying yourself to let God come in and put things into perspective. But we balk at that; it seems a sign of weakness: "I should be able to handle this myself." That reluctance is another sign of the animal self-centeredness with which we were born. We are weak; that's an objective fact. Until we acknowledge it, we'll never ask for help.

(3) *Verse 20.* Jesus wouldn't let the freed man become a disciple. Perhaps because of what he had been through, he didn't need the kind of wearing down of resistance that the muddleheaded apostles needed. Instead, Jesus sent him out to declare "how much the Lord had done for [him]."

Often when we are embroiled in problems, we pray for light; we beg for a miracle. But then, in those times when the light does break through, like the nine lepers, we go our way, filled with the exhilaration of liberation. But how few of us that liberation turns into apostles. We've seen too many embarrassing fundamentalists carrying signs that say, "Jesus saves!" We keep our redemption to ourselves. Why?

(4) *Verse 33*. When the woman was healed, she came to Jesus "with fear and trembling." Most likely because what had happened to her, after all those years of fruitless attempts for a cure, was simply too good to be believed. Those of us who have been "blessed" with good health and relatively few serious problems can become unconsciously smug, almost as if our uprightness had given us some right to believe we deserved good fortune. A visit to a hospital or nursing home will often cure us of that.

On the contrary, no need to wallow in neurotic "fear and trembling," sure that, because things have gone so very well for us, we'll sooner or later have to "pay." One reason God calls on some to be "poor" might be to arouse our compassion and our ability to heal or at least share their burdens. One reason God makes some "rich" might be so that we have the serenity and confidence to believe that we can, in fact, help.

(5) *Verse 42.* The core message of the gospel is that Jesus died in *order* to rise—to prove to us concretely that we need not fear annihilation at death. But also he showed us that the only way to rebirth, even in this life, is through a countless number of "little deaths." Suffering can always be an invitation to a more profound way of living than we had planned. As in Jesus' own life, every betrayal is a painful invitation to a deeper compassion and forgiveness; every setback is an opportunity to find an even stronger resolve; every mockery is a chance to free ourselves even more from our need to validate ourselves by the approval of others. There is only One whose approval we need.

6 ¹He left that place and came to his hometown, and his disciples followed him. ²On the sabbath he began to teach in the synagogue, and many who heard him were astounded. They said, "Where did this man get all this? What is this wisdom that has been given to him? What deeds of power are being done by his hands! ³Is not this the carpenter, the son of Mary and brother of James and Joses and Judas and

---

Rejection in Nazareth: VV1-6

V1. *his hometown*: Even though Capernaum has been his "home base," the mention of Jesus' relatives as villagers points to Nazareth; and his rejection here will be symbolic of his eventual rejection by all Judaism.

V2. *teach*: If invited, any Jewish layman could address the synagogue. As before, Mark says nothing of the content, but Jesus does not appear in the synagogue merely as a learned and pious layman, offering his personal comments on the scriptures; he "teaches." This time, however, the response of his fellow townspeople degenerates from amazement to skepticism, to opposition, and finally to outright rejection; *astounded*: Whatever their feelings about the speaker, what Jesus said seems to have made a stunning impression on them. All five questions pose the theme question of Mark's entire gospel: Who are you?

V3. *Is not this the carpenter?*: The Greek word is *tekton*, which could be any kind of skilled craftsman, like a stone mason. In none of the gospels is Jesus ever pictured actually working as a carpenter. Whatever his occupation, he was not penniless, nor well-to-do. As he gradually discloses who he truly is, he encounters more and more refusal to reassess old ways of thinking. There is a certain resentment when a "local boy" makes good: the instant rock star, the Pulitzer Prize winner: "Hell, I went to school with that guy"—which means that the speakers not only aggrandize themselves by association but also snarl that they didn't have the same "luck"; *the son of Mary*: Ordinarily, in the male-dominated society, a man is designated as the son of his father; this is an insult, like boys mocking "your mother." The other three gospels identify Jesus by his supposed father, Joseph; Jesus' mother has the same name as the sister of Moses, the Liberator; *brothers . . . sisters*: Again, this need not be taken literally; no one knows who the people designated were—which argues that they could not have been blood brothers and sisters of Jesus, or they would have been celebrated. Some argue that the "James" mentioned (distinguished from the two apostles of that name) became a figure in the early churches (Gal 1:19); *they took offense at him*: They found Jesus too much for them, which says it all: Jesus was and is a challenge to all of our preconceptions of what is possible. We would rather deny who he is than reassess our unquestionable convictions.

Simon, and are not his sisters here with us?" And they took offense at him. ⁴Then Jesus said to them, "Prophets are not without honor, except in their hometown, and among their own kin, and in their own house." ⁵And he could do no deed of power there, except that he laid his hands on a few sick people and cured them. ⁶And he was amazed at their unbelief.

Then he went about among the villages teaching. ⁷He called the twelve and began to send them out two by two, and gave them authority over the unclean spirits. ⁸He ordered them to take nothing for their journey except a staff; no bread, no bag, no money in their belts; ⁹but to wear sandals and not to put on two tunics. ¹⁰He said to them, "Wherever you enter a house,

---

The Greek philosopher Socrates faced the same treatment and the same condemnation, and the Suffering Servant of Isaiah (a model for the future Messiah) "was despised and rejected by others" (53:3). In fact, many in Mark's own reading audience had been scorned by their non-Christian neighbors.

V5. *he could do no deed of power there*: The Nazarenes wanted to be dazzled, like the crowds at the crucifixion: "Come down from the cross now, so that we may see and believe" (15:32). Consistently, there can be no miracle to elicit faith, only in response to it; the Nazarenes had no faith in someone they "knew so well." Smugness ties even the hands of God. Again consistent: we must meet Jesus halfway. Jesus will not—in fact *cannot*—compel acceptance. Having been rejected by most of the people of his native province, Jesus now moves out into Palestine, and the Christian community starts its march toward a worldwide mission.

V6. *he was amazed*: See chapter 4, "Jesus' Consciousness of His Divinity." It would be very difficult for anyone with full use of the divine knowledge to be "surprised" by anything whatever. The rejection by this synagogue is symbolic of the rejection of Jesus by official Judaism. For the rest of Mark's gospel, Jesus never enters a synagogue again.

First Mission of the Twelve: VV7-13

V7. *the twelve*: Nowhere does Mark suggest the prestigious roles of the twelve in the kingdom, as Matthew does (19:28); *two by two*: Deuteronomy 19:15: "A single witness shall not suffice"; *authority over the unclean spirits*: That is, the powers of the Messiah against evil, in any form; this mission "bookends" the death of the Baptist.

V8. *to take nothing*: Symbolizing their total reliance on God; as with Jesus, whatever the Twelve accomplish will be done by God; they are only instruments in his hands. God will provide for them, through the charity of others. They are not paid entertainers. They themselves will gain nothing but their "daily

stay there until you leave the place. ¹¹If any place will not welcome you and they refuse to hear you, as you leave, shake off the dust that is on your feet as a testimony against them." ¹²So they went out and proclaimed that all should repent. ¹³They cast out many demons, and anointed with oil many who were sick and cured them.

¹⁴King Herod heard of it, for Jesus' name had become known. Some were saying, "John the baptizer has been raised from the dead; and for this reason these powers

---

bread." Socrates also said, "My poverty is sufficient witness of the truth of what I say"; *staff*: This is possibly the scriptural justification of the crosier—the shepherd's staff—that bishops carry. It would be a stretch to suggest that Jesus here uses the staff as a symbol of elevated authority; it is merely a useful tool to dissuade unfriendly dogs. Unfortunately, overemphasis on this symbolism can reduce the ordinary lay Christian to the role of a passive sheep, which humans are not meant to be.

V11. *shake off the dust*: As a symbol that, in rejecting the Twelve and their message, they are rejecting the kingdom of God—and are thus themselves rejected. Matthew and Luke clarify here that such inhospitable towns will fare worse on Judgment Day than Sodom and Gomorrah.

V12. *repent*: Not merely a regret for past sins but a conversion—a complete turnabout in their expectations of what life is for, who God can be, what death means.

V13. *cast out many demons*: This is the first stage of Jesus' passing on his power and mission to the church: preaching the good news of forgiveness and expelling demons. Again, no reason to restrict this empowerment to *literal* demons; *anointed with oil*: The church sees in this the scriptural foundation for the sacrament of anointing the sick. Their powers come not from themselves but from their "connection" to Jesus.

The Execution of John: VV14-29

V14. *King Herod*: Herod Antipas (4 BC–AD 39), one of three sons of Herod the Great, who had been king at Jesus' birth. Antipas was not quite a "king," like his father, but a tetrarch ("ruler of one quarter" of his father's kingdom). Moreover, he "ruled" merely under toleration of the Roman occupation. At his death, Herod's three sons divided Palestine, and Herod Antipas ruled Galilee in the north. He was conceited, indolent, crafty, and corrupt— well-satirized in *Jesus Christ Superstar*. In Luke (13:32) Jesus calls this Herod "that fox!" Mark has his history wrong here: Herod Antipas divorced his wife for Herodias, the wife not of his brother Philip, but of his half brother, also

are at work in him." [15]But others said, "It is Elijah." And others said, "It is a prophet, like one of the prophets of old." [16]But when Herod heard of it, he said, "John, whom I beheaded, has been raised."

[17]For Herod himself had sent men who arrested John, bound him, and put him in prison on account of Herodias, his brother Philip's wife, because Herod had married her. [18]For John had been telling Herod, "It is not lawful for you to have your brother's wife." [19]And Herodias had a grudge against him, and wanted to kill him. But she could not, [20]for Herod feared John, knowing that he was a righteous and holy man, and he protected him. When he

---

named Herod; *Jesus' name*: Not just the name but the reputation; *John . . . from the dead*: Note the escalating quality of the power attributed to Jesus: he is the reincarnation of John, of the great Elijah, and finally equal to any of the great prophets.

V15. *Elijah*: The definitive symbol of a prophet in conflict with a king. He reputedly did not die but ascended to heaven in a fiery chariot (2 Kgs 2:11) and would return to point out the Messiah. Moses (the law) and Elijah (the prophets) appear in testimony to Jesus at his transfiguration (9:4). A place for Elijah is always set at the annual Passover table. Since John was presumed dead in verses 14-16, the rest of the section is a flashback to how John met his end. Although it is possible that an eyewitness actually heard Herod say something like these words and somehow the words got to Mark, it is more likely that Mark is fictionalizing here and saying what Herod *possibly* thought.

V17. *in prison*: According to the contemporary non-Christian historian, Josephus, Herod imprisoned John in the fortress of Machaerus, many miles south on the northeastern end of the Dead Sea—well outside his domain. In Mark's account, the prison is close enough for John's head to be brought almost immediately; *Herodias*: Just as the infamous Jezebel (2 Kgs) plotted to kill Elijah, John's OT counterpart, this wicked queen connived to kill John. The Herod family had no apparent scruples about multiple (or incestuous) marriages.

V18. *It is not lawful*: According to Jewish law (Lev 18:16), marrying one's sister-in-law constituted incest when the brother was still alive; Herod executed John not only in angry response to the criticism but also to prevent a rebellion on the part of John's followers. St. Thomas More (1477–1535) was executed by Henry VIII for exactly the same reason.

V19. *had a grudge*: Literally "had it in for."

V20. *Herod feared John*: Given the reason in the next clause—*"righteous and holy man"*—perhaps a better translation is "stood in awe of John"; as with the Gerasene demoniac, evil is never comfortable in the presence of confident goodness.

heard him, he was greatly perplexed; and yet he liked to listen to him. ²¹But an opportunity came when Herod on his birthday gave a banquet for his courtiers and officers and for the leaders of Galilee. ²²When his daughter Herodias came in and danced, she pleased Herod and his guests; and the king said to the girl, "Ask me for whatever you wish, and I will give it." ²³And he solemnly swore to her, "Whatever you ask me, I will give you, even half of my kingdom." ²⁴She went out and said to her mother, "What should I ask for?" She replied, "The head of John the baptizer." ²⁵Immediately she rushed back to the king and requested, "I want you to give me at once the head of John the Baptist on a platter." ²⁶The king was deeply grieved; yet out of regard for his oaths and for the guests, he did not want to refuse her. ²⁷Immediately the king sent a soldier of the guard with orders to bring John's head. He went and beheaded him in the prison, ²⁸brought his head on a platter, and gave it to the girl. Then the girl gave it to her mother. ²⁹When his disciples heard about

V21. *birthday . . . banquet*: There are many verbal parallels in Mark's version of this story to the OT book of Esther 1–2 in which the Persian king, Xerxes (Ahasuerus), gave a great banquet. Since Xerxes was an occupier of Palestine, the negative connotations are transferred to Herod, who was a collaborator with the Romans.

V22. *his daughter Herodias*: Here, the same name as her mother. Most modern translations other than the NRSV translate this "the daughter *of* Herodias." Nowhere in the NT is she explicitly named "Salome," any more than Matthew's wise men are identified as "Caspar, Melchior, and Balthasar." There is no evidence either that this dance is sexually seductive as it has been in films and opera. The name comes from Josephus, who says (against Mark in verse 22) she was Herod's *step*daughter; *pleased*: There are no sexual overtones in the Greek verb.

V23. *solemnly swore*: For a Jew, a solemn oath was very serious business. This is further evidence that this Herod has fallen victim to Greco-Roman customs, just as Ahab had become seduced by Canaanite fertility gods and married Jezebel, a pagan; *Whatever . . . kingdom*: An expanded repetition of the oath in verse 22, strong evidence of a thoroughly unqualified ruler.

V26. *for the guests*: Just as Herod is cornered into killing John against his will, so also Pontius Pilate was cowed into condemning Jesus (15:14). His reputation is more important than the life of a prophet he formerly admired.

Feeding Five Thousand: VV30-44

V30. *The apostles*: The only place in Mark where the Twelve are given this name; the word means simply "those sent out"; at the time Mark was writing,

it, they came and took his body, and laid it in a tomb.

³⁰The apostles gathered around Jesus, and told him all that they had done and taught. ³¹He said to them, "Come away to a deserted place all by yourselves and rest a while." For many were coming and going, and they had no leisure even to eat. ³²And they went away in the boat to a deserted place by themselves. ³³Now many saw them going and recognized them, and they hurried there on foot from all the towns and arrived ahead of them. ³⁴As he went ashore, he saw a great crowd; and he had compassion for them, because they were like sheep without a shepherd; and he began to teach them many things. ³⁵When it grew late, his disciples came to him and said, "This is a deserted place, and the hour is now very late; ³⁶send them away so that they may go into the surrounding country and villages and buy something for themselves to eat." ³⁷But he answered them, "You give them something to eat."

---

the term had a more technical meaning, designating an official position in the community and a validation to testify to Jesus from personal experience; ***all that they had done and taught***: Matthew and Luke are probably closer to accuracy here than Mark. The Twelve had been sent out to preach repentance and to heal, not to teach—that is, to explain the gospel, which Mark repeatedly stresses the Twelve did not even understand themselves and were thus incapable of explaining. Mark here reads back into his narrative the role apostles had in the postresurrection community.

V31. *all by yourselves*: Not only to escape the crowds but to escape the same fate as John the Baptizer; ***rest a while***: In the OT, the word "rest" is often associated with the Israelites finally attaining the Promised Land, thus echoing the parallel between the new and the old Israel; "rest" is also used often for Yahweh's protection of Israel, his flock, which emerges here in verse 34 with Jesus as the Good Shepherd.

V34. *compassion for them*: Consider a famous entertainer and his or her family trying to get off alone for a picnic. Highly doubtful he or she would be gently compassionate as Jesus is on five thousand intruders. Just as healing scenes in the gospel deal with not only physical but also spiritual healing, so Jesus pities not only the crowd's physical but also their spiritual hunger; ***shepherd***: See Ezekiel 34 for thirty-one verses fiercely criticizing the exclusive self-interest of the shepherds of Israel, as fierce as Jesus' attacks on the temple officials of his own time.

V35. *a deserted place*: Another reference to the New Israel in the desert, without food, which Yahweh miraculously supplied with manna and quail.

V36. *send them away*: The verb is pretty bossy from the disciples: "Get *rid* of 'em!"

V37. *You give them something*: Jesus cannot be naive enough to believe these few have brought along enough to feed five thousand people. He must

They said to him, "Are we to go and buy two hundred denarii worth of bread, and give it to them to eat?" ³⁸And he said to them, "How many loaves have you? Go and see." When they had found out, they said, "Five, and two fish." ³⁹Then he ordered them to get all the people to sit down in groups on the green grass. ⁴⁰So they sat down in groups of hundreds and of fifties. ⁴¹Taking the five loaves and the two fish, he looked up to heaven, and blessed and broke the loaves, and gave them to his disciples to set before the people; and he divided the two fish among them all. ⁴²And all ate and were filled; ⁴³and they took up twelve baskets full of broken pieces and of the fish. ⁴⁴Those who had eaten the loaves numbered five thousand men.

---

have a different meaning; *two hundred denarii*: A *denarius* was a day's wages for a laborer, therefore, seven *months'* wages.

V39. *in groups*: An allusion to the OT book of Exodus (18:25) where Moses divides the first Israelites into such groups; *on the green grass*: An allusion to Psalm 23, "He makes me lie down in green pastures"—which continues the theme of the Good Shepherd.

V41. *Taking the five loaves*: This section of feeding the five thousand will be paralleled exactly in Mark's chapter 8: feeding, crossing back over the lake, argument with the Pharisees, dialogue about bread, and a cure; *blessed . . . broke . . . gave*: Clearly a foreshadowing of the Eucharist.

V42. *ate and were filled*: Allusion to the OT formula describing the manna in the desert ("They ate and were well filled"; Ps 78:29) and to the abundance the Israelites would enjoy at the coming of the Messiah ("They shall not hunger or thirst"; Isa 49:10). Throughout this story, it is clear again and again that Jesus is revealing—indirectly through symbols and OT allusions—the Messianic Secret. Oddly, there is no expression of wonder from the crowd. Note also that this is in sharp contrast to Herod's upper-class and raucous banquet.

V43. *twelve baskets*: The overabundant caring of God for the people; allusion again to the twelve tribes of Israel. One could well ask where these baskets came from. The *kophinos* (the word used here) had a cord handle by which it could be carried on the back, a "provision basket," on journeys. About two gallons, like a small picnic basket.

V44. *five thousand men*: The Greek is *andres*, i.e., explicitly males, probably as heads of households—which would imply a hugely more impressive number fed.

Origen (AD 185–254), an early father of the church, wrote, "Scripture interweaves the imaginative with the historical, sometimes introducing what is utterly impossible, sometimes what is possible but never occurred." One nonacademic, commonsense, but nonetheless persuasive explanation for this abundant feeding is simply this: No mother—surely no Jewish mother—would

⁴⁵Immediately he made his disciples get into the boat and go on ahead to the other side, to Bethsaida, while he dismissed the crowd. ⁴⁶After saying farewell to them, he went up on the mountain to pray.

⁴⁷When evening came, the boat was out on the sea, and he was alone on the land. ⁴⁸When he saw that they were straining at the oars against an adverse wind, he came towards them early in the morning, walking on the sea. He intended to pass them by. ⁴⁹But when they saw him walking on the sea, they thought it was a ghost and cried out; ⁵⁰for they all saw him and were

---

take her brood out into a "deserted place" *without* bringing food, and Jesus preached so persuasively that they produced a true miracle: they gave away some of their children's food to strangers. (In contrast, see 7:27). Scholars may reject the explanation, but it helps ordinary believers. This episode reflects backward to the equally improbable feeding of the Hebrews with quail and manna in the desert (Exod 16) and looks forward to the multiplication of the Body of Christ in the Eucharist and in the church.

Jesus Walks on the Sea: VV45-56

V45. *Bethsaida*: A slip for Mark; Bethsaida was on the eastern shore of the Sea of Galilee where they already are.

V46. *up on the mountain to pray*: Jesus' motive for insisting that the disciples leave him behind. It is suggested that, as in the desert temptations in Matthew and Luke, the exertion of such power in the multiplication of the loaves was not only exhausting but also a temptation to Jesus—"If you are the Son of God, turn these stones into bread"—resulting in hundreds of conversions, both automatic and by that very fact a temptation to "buy" acceptance with food.

V47. *When evening came*: "The fourth watch of the night," between three and six in the morning, a Roman rather than a Jewish measuring of time.

V48. *against an adverse wind*: None of the accounts mentions a storm; *intended to pass them by*: An allusion to God's appearance to Moses (Exod 33:19) in which he "passes before" his eyes, since no one can look on the face of God and live. Also, Job 9:8, Yahweh "who alone stretched out the heavens and trampled the waves of the Sea." Mark gives subtle hints as to who Jesus really is.

V49. *a ghost*: No wonder, since someone walking on the water was no more common in the apostles' day than in our own. But there is also a foreshadowing of the resurrection here. These very men will say the same thing when the women say they've seen Jesus.

V50. *it is I*: A formula no Jew could use, since it is the unspeakable name of Yahweh: "I am who am"; later, when the high priest asks Jesus if he is the

terrified. But immediately he spoke to them and said, "Take heart, it is I; do not be afraid." [51]Then he got into the boat with them and the wind ceased. And they were utterly astounded, [52]for they did not understand about the loaves, but their hearts were hardened.

[53]When they had crossed over, they came to land at Gennesaret and moored the boat. [54]When they got out of the boat, people at once recognized him, [55]and rushed about that whole region and began to bring the sick on mats to wherever they heard he was. [56]And wherever he went, into villages or cities or farms, they laid the sick in the marketplaces, and begged him that they might touch even the fringe of his cloak; and all who touched it were healed.

Christ, the Son of the Blessed, Jesus replies (and only in Mark): "I am," at which the high priest instantly reacts to what he believes is blasphemy; *do not be afraid*: Frequently in the OT, this formula is used after a sudden and terrifying appearance of Yahweh in the midst of the people; for instance, Exodus 20:20, where Moses' delivery of the Ten Commandments is accompanied by thunder, lightning, a trumpet blast, and a quaking mountain.

V52. *not understand about the loaves*: They themselves were the agents of that miracle, and they had seen Jesus command the sea before, but they are still too thick to grasp the power in Jesus. Had they understood, they would not have been so reluctant to believe that it was Jesus walking on the water; their minds were completely closed; *hearts were hardened*: They are not so much stubbornly doubtful as simply *bewildered*. Mark consistently stresses the disciples' inability to comprehend or accept the reality of who Jesus was, despite Jesus' veiled explanations through parables, the fulfillment of so many predictions from the OT, and the overwhelming power displayed in Jesus' miracles. Remember that Jews were unyielding monotheists; how would it be possible for them even to conceive that God could be so uncomplicated and yet so complex? If they could not understand this miracle "of the loaves," how would they cope with the Eucharist? If someone next to you had shouted to a windstorm to be quiet—and it actually happened—it would hardly be "hard-heartedness" that made you ask, "Do you mean to say you really *did* that yourself?" The disciples are unarguable proof that miracles cannot *cause* faith. They are still asking the focal Markan question: "Who *are* you?"

V53. *Gennesaret*: On the western side, where they started out. Possible that the adverse winds had driven them back.

V55. *rushed about*: In that brief passage there is a subtle suggestion that Jesus is trying to avoid the crowds. His reason could have been continuing fear of being arrested as John had been, fatigue, or any number of others.

Review Questions for Chapter 6

1. Try to put yourself into the skins of the people of Jesus' hometown, Nazareth. They have watched this boy grow up, perhaps a touch jealous of his abilities. Try to describe what would go on in your mind if someone you knew all your life suddenly had powers that you never expected he or she might have. Is it possible that someone you thought you knew so well could "pull off" what Jesus did?

2. For Mark, the story of Herod and John is uncharacteristically long, detailed, and well-structured. Probably he got it as a "whole piece of goods" from one of his sources. But, considering what we have seen so far of Mark's gospel version and its recurring themes—healing, the Messianic Secret, the hardening of hearts—what does this story add to the theme Mark has been building?

3. The feeding sections of the gospel have some relationship with the healing sections. What is that connection?

4. When Jesus walks on the water, Mark says that "He intended to pass them by." In a literal story, that wouldn't make any sense. What motive would Jesus have had? More important, what motive would Mark have had for putting in that seemingly unimportant sentence?

5. Explain verse 52: "they did not understand about the loaves." What does that miracle have to do with the apostles struggling against the storm? What does it say about the power of Jesus? What does it say about our limited space-time expectations of what God is capable of doing?

6. Explain: God is so uncomplicated, and yet God is so complex.

For Reflection

(1) *Verse 4.* A prophet is a welcome diversion when he or she comes from out of town, but the same person can be a bit of an embarrassment at home. Prophets tend to stand out, make waves, draw attention to themselves and away from the "truly important" things in the lives of the locals. Does that ever bother you? Or perhaps even immobilize you? In a herd of sheep, anyone with confidence is going to look arrogant. But our confidence comes not from ourselves but from the One who bids us speak. The root of the word "confidence" is *fides*, "faith." Is your faith strong enough that you can speak out without fear of your everyday neighbors' yearning for nothing better than "peace and quiet"? All that's needed for the triumph of evil is that good men and women be silent.

(2) *Verse 26.* Herod is caught in a corner. He has promised his daughter anything she wanted, and now she demands something the king doesn't want to give. But, like Pilate, he backs down out of fear of the crowd. History is filled with

such tragic self-absorption: The charge of the Light Brigade, for instance, was clearly doomed from the start, and yet the commander had given the order and refused to admit his mistake, for which men lost the only lives they would ever have. In the smaller scope of your own life, do you have both the self-esteem and the confidence to admit your own mistakes? Do you have the Christian generosity—to yourself—to laugh at them?

(3) *Verse 41.* Here as at the Last Supper, Jesus took bread, gave thanks, and broke the bread to pass it around and feed people. In a very real sense, that eucharistic action is a symbol for the Christian life. Jesus asks us to break ourselves up and pass around the pieces for the aliveness of those around us— and the more we give away of ourselves, the more there is left to give!

Often we hesitate to give of ourselves because of fear—fear of intruding, fear of embarrassment, fear of rejection, and, worst of all, fear that we are offering an inferior gift when we offer ourselves. If, like the apostles, we have been chosen and sent by an all-wise God, the fear comes only from ourselves, not God. And every time you stand up to be counted, the exhilaration takes away a bit more of the fear. Risking enriches us.

(4) *Verse 49.* In Matthew's version, not only does Jesus walk on the water, but he bids Peter to come out onto the water too. The point of the passage is not to ask the reader's belief that Jesus and Peter literally walked on the water but that, in the hands of God, any of us can do what we believed in our self-doubt we were incapable of doing. Peter could do what he thought impossible as long as he kept his eyes only on Jesus, but as soon as he pulled the focus of his attention back onto himself and his own capabilities, he began to sink. When Jesus calls us to self-forgetful service, he asks us to forget even our shortcomings. Perhaps Peter didn't literally walk on water, but the craven coward of Good Friday went forward to die an agonizing death upside down on a cross rather than forswear his belief in Jesus. That's a miracle indeed.

(5) *Verse 56.* "And all . . . were healed." At times we believe that is what we are called to do as Christians: to heal everyone we attempt to heal, and on the first attempt at that. We allow ourselves to forget that we are not the Messiah but only his rather fumbling agents. Many of the problems we genuinely and generously attempt to heal have been building for years: defenses against intrusion and hurt, unfounded anxieties, neuroses. Even Jesus could not heal without the victim's faith—yielding, the desire to be made well. No power in earth or heaven can heal an alcoholic who doesn't want to be healed or refuses to admit he or she has a problem.

Are you willing to make peace with merely *striving* to heal, very often without the satisfaction of achieving it?

7 ¹Now when the Pharisees and some of the scribes who had come from Jerusalem gathered around him, ²they noticed that some of his disciples were eating with defiled hands, that is, without washing them. ³(For the Pharisees, and all the Jews, do not eat unless they thoroughly wash their hands, thus observing the tradition of the elders; ⁴and they do not eat anything from the market unless they wash it; and there are also many other traditions that they observe, the washing of cups, pots, and bronze kettles.) ⁵So the Pharisees and the scribes asked him, "Why do your disciples not live according to the tradition of the elders, but eat with defiled hands?" ⁶He

---

Clean and Unclean: VV1-23

V1. *Pharisees:* This section, along with the one that preceded it and the one that follows, concentrates on two doctrines of the Pharisees with which Jesus is strongly in conflict: (1) their finicky attention to details of the law and (2) their immovable opposition to non-Jews. These men came all the way from Jerusalem. This is no longer investigation by the local synagogue authorities; Jesus' reputation has now brought him to the attention and suspicions of national religious authorities.

V2. *eating:* Some translations insert "their food" or "loaves of bread"; *defiled hands*: Such rules were not written until the Mishnah (AD 200; the first published version of rabbinic customs), but this episode suggests it was already an oral tradition centuries earlier.

V3. *all the Jews*: Writing for non-Jews, Mark inserts a long explanation of customs unfamiliar to people living in Rome.

V4. *many other traditions*: The Pharisees considered these nonscriptural interpretations of the law just as binding as the law of Moses itself (the Torah). Anyone who has seen the musical *Fiddler on the Roof* is aware of how intimately traditions were woven into every nook and cranny of ordinary Jewish life—especially when they were trying to preserve their separate identity from the intrusions of a dominant culture enveloping them. Conversion to Christianity was a painful tearing of this purpose-giving fabric of their former lives. To understand in terms of Christian doctrine, think of all the statements of the fathers of the church or of a group of parish pastors having as much binding force as the words of Jesus himself.

V5. *your disciples*: The petty tone here reminds one of small-minded catty neighbors trying to belittle parents by calling attention to the bad manners of their children or pets.

V6. *hypocrites*: The Greek word *hypokrites* was a word for "actor," one who "plays a part." Jesus does not even bother with the charge but goes to the core—and minces no words about it: the Pharisees are pious on the outside and dead to compassion on the inside.

said to them, "Isaiah prophesied rightly about you hypocrites, as it is written,

'This people honors me with their lips,

but their hearts are far from me;

⁷in vain do they worship me,

teaching human precepts as doctrines.'

⁸You abandon the commandment of God and hold to human tradition."

⁹Then he said to them, "You have a fine way of rejecting the commandment of God in order to keep your tradition! ¹⁰For Moses said, 'Honor your father and your mother'; and, 'Whoever speaks evil of father or mother must surely die.' ¹¹But you say that if anyone tells father or mother, 'Whatever support you might have had from me is Corban' (that is, an offering to God)—¹²then you no longer permit doing anything for a father or mother, ¹³thus making void the word of God through your tradition that you have handed on. And you do many things like this."

V7. human precepts as doctrines: That is, investing purely human insights about upright behavior with divine authority—where there is no indication that such conduct is clearly the will of God. For instance, some Christian sects have a difficult time supporting their belief that God's will forbids use of alcoholic beverages when the gospels report that Jesus himself was criticized for being "a glutton and a drunkard" (Matt 11:19; Luke 7:34).

V9. You have a fine way: Heavily ironic.

V10. Moses said: Jesus accepts the authority of Moses, but not the authority of every interpreter of Moses. He does not deny the law but rather its misuse.

V11. Corban: The individual "dedicates" his property to God and therefore weasels out of giving any of it to his own parents.

V13. making void the word of God: A human being dares to displace his own Creator. The tradition blinds its followers to the actual will of God. Nor was the infant church free from the same blindness. Despite Jesus' obvious disdain for rule-mongering, a segment of Jewish Christian converts in Mark's time insisted that non-Jewish male converts be circumcised and follow all the strictures of the Jewish dietary laws; in effect, become Jews before they could become real Christians. Peter himself, the first pope, chosen by Jesus himself, submitted only after a vision in which he was told—*three times!*—"What God has made clean, you must not call profane" (Acts 10:15). That later controversy, from the time of Mark rather than the time of Jesus, could suggest Mark reads the problem back into the life of Jesus and attributes to him the solution arrived at by the early churches. There is much to justify that view: If Jesus had been as remarkably forceful and concrete as Mark pictures him here, why would the issue arise so strongly as it does in Acts, 1 Corinthians, and Romans?

V14. called the crowd: Here he widens his scope to the crowd, in defiance of the Pharisees, and speaks authoritatively.

¹⁴Then he called the crowd again and said to them, "Listen to me, all of you, and understand: ¹⁵there is nothing outside a person that by going in can defile, but the things that come out are what defile." [16]

¹⁷When he had left the crowd and entered the house, his disciples asked him about the parable. ¹⁸He said to them, "Then do you also fail to understand? Do you not see that whatever goes into a person from outside cannot defile, ¹⁹since it enters, not the heart but the stomach, and goes out into the sewer?" (Thus he declared all foods clean.) ²⁰And he said, "It is what comes out of a person that defiles. ²¹For it is from within, from the human heart, that evil intentions come: fornication, theft, murder, ²²adultery, avarice, wickedness, deceit, licentiousness, envy, slander, pride, folly. ²³All these evil things come from within, and they defile a person."

V15. *nothing . . . defile*: There are no forbidden foods whatever. St. Paul wrote, "I know and am persuaded in the Lord Jesus that nothing is unclean in itself" (Rom 14:14). Despite this direct saying of Jesus, the Jewish Christian converts mentioned in **V13** above tried to second-guess him. Consider, too, that God freely chose to have his Son born in a drafty stable and to grow up relatively poor and inconspicuous. Well-intentioned Christians have gone into those places, however, and covered them with marble and gold, the way God would have done, had God known better; *the things that come out*: this means not merely human waste but the words and deeds one performs. This is an indirect attack on the actions and hardened hearts of the Pharisees.

[**V16.** Note that the verse has been omitted as inauthentic in the NRSV. It hardly seems even worth omission, since it said merely: "Let anyone with ears to hear listen."]

V17. *left the crowd*: Mark continues the theme of a slow revelation of the Messianic Secret to the inner group and its total reversal of their previous expectations, values, and customs.

V18. *Do you not see?*: Just as they could not understand about the loaves (6:52).

V19. *not the heart*: In biblical thought, the "heart" was the center of one's life: the self of modern psychology; *into the sewer*: Let no one declare that Jesus avoided concreteness.

VV21-22. *evil intentions:* Note that the list of moral flaws that issue from twisted human hearts are all sins against other individuals rather than directly against God; *folly:* The other vices Jesus lists are well known and obvious, but this climactic one undergirds them all: small-mindedness combined with a heart like a clenched fist.

From here, Jesus is going to venture back into Gentile territory, where "unclean" is supposedly everywhere he turns.

[24]From there he set out and went away to the region of Tyre. He entered a house and did not want anyone to know he was there. Yet he could not escape notice, [25]but a woman whose little daughter had an unclean spirit immediately heard about him, and she came and bowed down at his feet. [26]Now the woman was a Gentile, of Syrophoenician origin. She begged him to cast the demon out of her daughter. [27]He said to her, "Let the children be fed first, for it is not fair to take the children's food and

---

Also, it is wise to recall that it would be unfairly simplistic to speak of Jesus as taking a stance against "Judaism." At his time, there were multiple "Judaisms"—Pharisees, Sadducees, Essenes, followers of John—varying interpretations of the Hebrew scriptures and of centuries of reflection on its contents.

Jesus Heals Two Gentiles: VV24-37

V24. *Tyre*: Phoenician town on the Mediterranean coast, a new field of operations, this time among non-Jews. Tyre juts out from the coast of the Mediterranean Sea fifty miles south of Beirut, Lebanon; ***could not escape notice***: Nor will he very often escape it again.

V25. *unclean spirit*: Once again, this is not in contrast to sexual purity. Rather, it is the opposite of "holy" or "godly."

V26. *Syrophoenician*: To distinguish from Phoenician emigrants to Africa. This episode is a fish bone in the throats of literalists who, lacking any sense of humor, read Jesus as being nasty to this obviously sincere woman rather than teasing—because (as the episode proves) he guesses just by looking at her that she has the wit to engage in verbal byplay. Even the bizarre Gerasene demoniac was not treated nastily; then why would anyone think Jesus had radically changed?

V27. *fed first*: Which leaves open the possibility of others fed later. In fact, this is exactly how the gospel spread, first to Jews, then out to Gentiles; ***the children's food***: Again, the word is "loaves" and it connects this story, too, to the multiplication story before. The "children" are the Jewish chosen people, and ordinary Jews called all non-Jews "dogs"; ***dogs***: Actually, here Jesus uses the gentler word "puppies." Dogs were not usually allowed inside Jewish homes, although Gentiles enjoyed them. Jesus is echoing what had always been the misguided Jewish tradition: the Messiah was theirs alone. But since the Jews refused the Messiah—the offered food—when he came, he now turns to the Gentiles. Unlike the restrictive community of the Pharisees, the community of Jesus will be universal. Jesus is tantalizing the woman, testing her.

throw it to the dogs." ²⁸But she answered him, "Sir, even the dogs under the table eat the children's crumbs." ²⁹Then he said to her, "For saying that, you may go—the demon has left your daughter." ³⁰So she went home, found the child lying on the bed, and the demon gone.

³¹Then he returned from the region of Tyre, and went by way of Sidon towards the Sea of Galilee, in the region of the Decapolis. ³²They brought to him a deaf man who had an impediment in his speech; and they begged him to lay his hand on him. ³³He took him aside in private, away from the crowd, and put his fingers into his ears, and he spat and touched his tongue. ³⁴Then looking up to heaven, he sighed and said to him, "Eph-

---

V28. *dogs under the table*: The woman is clever enough to snag Jesus' own metaphor about dogs and turn it to her own advantage in a very homely way, which also suggests her experience as a mother when her children slip food they don't like under the table. She slyly says that, if the children of the family reject the food, then it should go to those who are eager for it. She is respectful but not cringing. In all the gospels, she's the only one who "bests" Jesus.

V29. *For saying that*: Her belief has worked the miracle; *the demon has left*: Implied in the verb tense is the adverb "already." One cannot help but guess Jesus admired the spunk of this lady; no other miracle reported in Mark is dispatched so quickly. Moreover, it offers concrete support to Jesus' refusal to let the written rule shackle his compassion. He "should" have rejected this petitioner because she was not only a female but also a pagan.

V31. *the Decapolis*: Jesus is still in Gentile territory. Tyre is forty miles north of Capernaum; Sidon is up the Mediterranean coast another twenty miles. This is the long way back to the lake.

V32. *impediment in his speech*: Many deaf people are incapable of speaking clearly since they can only approximate the lip movements of people who can hear; Isaiah 35:5: "Then the eyes of the blind shall be opened, the ears of the deaf unstopped."

V33. *took . . . crowd*: Certainly redundant: "aside," "private," "away"; *he spat*: Even today biologists recognize the healing powers of spittle.

V34. *looking up to heaven*: As he had done before blessing and multiplying the loaves, 6:41, acknowledging the Source of his power; *a groan*: Some scholars believe this is the transcendent, divine reality within Jesus, straining against human limitation. Others suggest it was part of a magician's "routine," as today when a shot-putter or tennis player grunts to explode energy. Hardly likely, since Mark has been extra careful to stress this miracle was private and there was no one there to hear but a man who couldn't; *Ephphatha*: Which Mark translates for his non-Jewish readers.

phatha," that is, "Be opened." ³⁵And immediately his ears were opened, his tongue
was released, and he spoke plainly. ³⁶Then
Jesus ordered them to tell no one; but the
more he ordered them, the more zealously
they proclaimed it. ³⁷They were astounded
beyond measure, saying, "He has done
everything well; he even makes the deaf
to hear and the mute to speak."

V36. *to tell no one*: Although Jesus could keep the performance of the
miracle private, he could not do the same with the obvious change in the boy;
the more zealously they proclaimed it: the Greek word is used almost exclusively in the early church for proclamation of Jesus as Messiah. Taken with the
reference from Isaiah 35, the whole purpose of this story is one more step
toward revealing that.

V37. *astounded beyond measure*: These pagans are in dramatic contrast
to the Nazareth neighbors of Jesus and his own disciples.

Review Questions for Chapter 7

1. What evidence does the chapter give to indicate Jesus was not "into" an
   abundance of rules? When he accuses the Pharisees of hypocrisy, he is not
   as thorough as Matthew (chap. 23), but this speech is all the more powerful
   for its brevity. Unlike Matthew, Mark does not accuse Pharisees of imposing
   burdens they themselves do not carry. Precisely what aspect of their directions to people is Mark criticizing?
2. Explain what Jesus means when he says there is nothing that goes into a
   person from the outside that can make him ritually unclean. Rather, it is
   what comes out of a person that makes him unclean. How is that in direct
   opposition to the Pharisees' doctrine?
3. How does the story of Jesus with the Gentile Phoenician woman show Jesus'
   sense of playfulness?
4. List the evidence in this chapter that shows Jesus is turning more and more
   away from Israel and outward to the non-Jews.

For Reflection

(1) *Verse 5.* Traditions give a tribe or nation or family a symbolic sense of
coherence with one another and with a past that gives a sense of meaning, a
sense of a continuing story. But often traditions can harden into harnesses not
only to creativity and spontaneity but to kindness and compassion. Think of

the scene in *Fiddler on the Roof* where Tevye refuses to embrace his daughter, even though they may never see one another again, even though it's breaking both their hearts, because she has defied tradition and married a Gentile.

That doesn't seem to be a difficulty for us today. We have perhaps even gone too far to the opposite extreme: an erosion of traditions and meaning-giving symbols and an assimilation into "just like everybody else." Are there any Christian symbols you personally still find meaningful, that give you the sense that you "belong" to a tradition that not only stretches all over the earth but backward in time for two thousand years? Ashes? Palms? Religious medals?

(2) *Verse 6.* It is worth noting that in the whole New Testament Jesus never bawls out anyone except the clergy—the officials of Judaism and his own stubborn seminarians. Despite the fact Jesus was not a sinner himself, he shows a startling empathy for those who sin out of weakness: the adulterous woman, the prodigal son, the disciples when they fell asleep during his agony in the garden, even Peter when cowardice overcame him. But he seems to have little sympathy for those who sin from their strength and self-inflation: the Pharisees with their pretensions to righteousness and the apostles with their pretensions to the first places in the kingdom.

We can't overlook our sins of weakness, but is it possible that you might overstress them? Consider the vastness of the universe; don't your petty faults look smaller judged against that background? Surely the Artist who created the hairy-nosed wombat and the giraffe and sex can't be entirely without a sense of humor. Is it possible that you take yourself more seriously than God does?

(3) *Verses 20-22.* Unlike the Pharisees, Jesus was not picky about what or when or how anyone ate. He was interested in more substantial matters: what came out of a person's heart and mouth—evil ideas that lead us to degrade others and ourselves. It's doubtful many robbers, killers, or adulterers are reading these pages. Our sins tend to be far pettier, the ones Jesus mentions at the end of verse 22: the little white lies that get us out of tight scrapes, the dirty thoughts we allow to entertain us too long, the envious yearning to cut the more gifted down to our own size, the self-absorption that forbids us the liberating grace of laughing at ourselves, our silly self-importance that magnifies our problems to world-class catastrophes. True?

(4) *Verse 27.* Pious people who believed Jesus humorless surely have no sensitivity to the playfulness of this segment. Jesus never refuses the requests of Gentiles anywhere else in the scripture. Neither suffering nor faith are exclusive to Jews. But the gospel writers—who were not eyewitnesses—were limited to reports from those who had been there, here most likely Peter. But only the

best storytellers think to say that the speaker grinned or winked at the particular moment —which changes the whole tone of the story itself and the statement Jesus makes.

It is obvious, from the whole gospel and from our experience of God, that God and Jesus, God's embodiment, don't really take too seriously many aspects of life that are very important to us. Evolution shows that God is not too hung up on efficiency, as we are; if God had been, why did he dally for so many centuries with trilobites and dinosaurs, only to let them die out? He is not too concerned with perfectionism, as we often are; if he were, why would he give freedom to an inadequately evolved tribe of apes? And Jesus seems not to be as concerned about "making restitution" as we are; no sinner Jesus forgave had to do a penance. Is it possible that we are guilty of anthropomorphism—reading our attitudes and concerns *into* God's mind?

(5) *Verse 34.* Jesus is as brusque and forthright with this man's ears as he was with the storm at sea: "Open up! Shut up!" When he means yes, he says, "Yes," and when he means no, he says, "No." We, on the other hand, tend to pussyfoot, play with words, use euphemisms rather than calling an attitude or an action by its right name. Think of the agonies some people go through to find words that will "fool" the priest in confession, vague words like, "I did bad things" or "I was mean" or "I cheated on my girlfriend" rather than "I masturbated five times" or "I called my sister a moron" or "I had sex with a near-stranger." The first step toward wisdom—and freedom—is to call a thing by its right name: not "stretching the truth" but out-and-out "lying," not "making love" but "using another person as a sex object, in a way I wouldn't even use an animal." Do you say what you mean and mean what you say? Always?

8 ¹In those days when there was again a great crowd without anything to eat, he called his disciples and said to them, ²"I have compassion for the crowd, because they have been with me now for three days and have nothing to eat. ³If I send them away hungry to their homes, they will faint on the way—and some of them have come from a great distance." ⁴His disciples replied, "How can one feed these people with bread here in the desert?" ⁵He asked them, "How many loaves do you have?" They said, "Seven." ⁶Then he ordered the crowd to sit down on the ground; and he took the seven loaves, and after giving thanks he broke them and gave them to his disciples to distribute; and they distributed them to the crowd. ⁷They had also a few small fish; and after blessing them, he ordered that these too should be

---

Feeding Gentiles: VV1-13

V1. *a great crowd*: Working from reported sources, Mark could quite likely be giving a second version of the same historical incident of multiplying the loaves. Note the consistent parallels and repetitions from the previous story. This story, however, has one major difference: it is a feeding of non-Jews, since Jesus is still in the pagan territory of the Ten Towns. Here, too, the emphasis is not so much on the spiritual hunger of the people, as before, but on Jesus' genuine compassion for their physical hunger. And yet, as Gentiles, they "have come from a great distance."

V2. *three days*: No commentary I could find dealt in any meaningful way with this puzzling detail. Why have they been with Jesus so long? What have they eaten meanwhile? One point for sure: There is no chance here of explaining this miracle by Jesus' persuasiveness moving them to share. They would have had nothing left.

V4. *How can one feed*: Another argument for the repetition of the same story from a different source: these are the same disciples who actually have *already* witnessed Jesus do what they say here is impossible. Think of a reporter coming to a historical description of a man's life thirty years after the events he or she is describing. How would the reporter determine whether one source or the other merely got the wrong vague number?

V5. *seven*: Whereas the previous multiplication had five loaves, two fishes, twelve hampers, this has seven and seven, which is stylistically less sophisticated. Why? Why would (ironically) a lack of stylistic sophistication argue to the truthfulness of the deposition?

V6. *giving thanks*: The Greek is *eucharistesas*, a reference to the multiplication of Christ in the Eucharist. The essentials of this description are taken almost verbatim from a non-Palestinian account of the action at the Last Supper (1 Cor 11:24); *distributed them*: The same words used for deacons handing

distributed. ⁸They ate and were filled; and they took up the broken pieces left over, seven baskets full. ⁹Now there were about four thousand people. And he sent them away. ¹⁰And immediately he got into the boat with his disciples and went to the district of Dalmanutha.

¹¹The Pharisees came and began to argue with him, asking him for a sign from heaven, to test him. ¹²And he sighed deeply in his spirit and said, "Why does this generation ask for a sign? Truly I tell you, no sign will be given to this generation." ¹³And he left them, and getting into

---

out the Eucharist, consecrated by the bishop, in the early communities. Note that the bread here gets far more attention than the "few fish." Why?

V8. baskets: Unlike the word in 6:43 (*kophinos*), the word used here (*spyris*) is the same word used when Paul is lowered down the wall in Damascus (Acts 9:25), therefore considerably larger. If nothing else, this particular episode gives Jesus' ideas about eating with Gentiles.

V9. he sent them away: This echoes the earlier verse, 8:3, "If I send them away," and also echoes the old ending of the eucharistic meal: *Ite, missa est*, "Go, the Mass is complete."

V10. Dalmanutha: A place scholars cannot identify. Matthew calls it "Magadan" (15:39).

V11. Pharisees: Jesus and his disciples are now deep in Gentile territory. Either Mark has sandwiched in this encounter incautiously, or these Pharisees have really gone out of their way to track him down; **a sign**: This draws attention to a difference between Jewish and Greek thinking. "Knowing, proof, authentication" for a Jew came "from the gut," experientially, as in "He knew his wife" in a sexual commitment. For the Greek world of Plato, Socrates, and Aristotle, "knowing" came from step-by-step logical analysis. St. Paul called attention to that different mind-set: "For Jews demand signs and Greeks desire wisdom" (1 Cor 1:22); **to test him**: Even the wonders Jesus has worked without a request for secrecy should have been enough to convince the most cynical, one would guess. And yet, even his own disciples "did not understand." From the beginning of OT history to our own day, the potential believer wants to have "proof," an ironclad guarantee before taking a "risk." But, consistently, Jesus refuses to give a sign in order to *buy* faith, only in response to faith.

V12. sighed deeply: This fatigue and anguish makes Jesus very human; so few of the people he has met before—even his own companions—are willing to take the risk of trusting in him, even after what they have seen; **this generation**: In the NT, this term means all those who are skeptical, demanding certitude, and yet the term could be used for any age since then; **I tell you**: Usually translated, "Amen, amen, I say to you," indicating that Jesus is speaking with utmost seriousness, since what they ask—unarguable certitude—is impossible.

the boat again, he went across to the other side.

¹⁴Now the disciples had forgotten to bring any bread; and they had only one loaf with them in the boat. ¹⁵And he cautioned them, saying, "Watch out—beware of the yeast of the Pharisees and the yeast of Herod." ¹⁶They said to one another, "It is because we have no bread." ¹⁷And becoming aware of it, Jesus said to them, "Why are you talking about having no bread? Do you still not perceive or understand? Are

----

The abruptness of his leaving underscores his anger. The verbal construction suggests that what Jesus is saying is equivalent to "I'll be damned if I give you a sign." Matthew (12:39) and Luke (11:29) add that the only sign Jesus will give will be "the sign of Jonah," i.e., resurrecting, as Jonah survived the belly of the big fish.

Truth Blindness: VV14-26

V14. *forgotten to bring any bread*: The inexorable recurrence of bread in these passages cannot be accidental. Over and over Jesus keeps harping on bread. Why?

V15. *yeast*: The fungus that induces fermentation in beer and that makes bread rise. Obviously, it is a good symbol for the heart and soul, which are the life-source of the human person, and if one's yeast/soul is corrupt, so will everything one does be corrupt; *the yeast of the Pharisees*: Legalism. An inner urge to "save" oneself, by one's own quantifiable good deeds, according to the law. Their "yeast" is blindness, refusal to rethink; the disciples' blindness is not a lack of good will but a lack of insight; *the yeast of Herod*: Materialism. Sheer self-indulgence and political machinations. The disciples could be infected by that yeast too: materialism and ambition. Their last question to Jesus, even after the crucifixion and resurrection, was, "Lord, is this the time when you will restore the [literal] kingdom to Israel?" (Acts 1:6). Is it possible twelve people could so miss Jesus' point? On the other hand, do we also miss his point, simply because it is too contrary to our own desires to be "acceptable"?

V16. *because we have no bread*: With almost unimprovable thickheadedness, the disciples miss the whole point; they are not the ideal disciples, just the usual ones. Like ourselves, they have become so used to miracles that they take them for granted. Can you almost hear the bruised-ego tone in their voices? We can empathize too: "We don't have *enough!*"

V17. *Do you still not perceive or understand?*: What Jesus has done is self-evident. Again, this is the Hebrew sense of "understanding," meaning a grasp of the experientially undeniable (all Jesus has already done) versus the Greek "understanding" arrived at by painstaking intellectual analysis. Any

your hearts hardened? [18]Do you have eyes, and fail to see? Do you have ears, and fail to hear? And do you not remember? [19]When I broke the five loaves for the five thousand, how many baskets full of broken pieces did you collect?" They said to him, "Twelve." [20]"And the seven for the four thousand, how many baskets full of broken pieces did you collect?" And they said to

him, "Seven." [21]Then he said to them, "Do you not yet understand?"

[22]They came to Bethsaida. Some people brought a blind man to him and begged him to touch him. [23]He took the blind man by the hand and led him out of the village; and when he had put saliva on his eyes and laid his hands on him, he asked him, "Can you see anything?" [24]And the man looked

---

hardworking teacher knows exactly the feelings inside Jesus at that moment. You go over the same thing, again and again, and they still give the same stupid answers when you ask, "What did I just say?" Anyone who believes Jesus never lost his temper has never read this passage, or has never tried to teach. At the end of all his questions, shoving their faces into their own recent—and quite stunning—experiences, he rasps, "Can you possibly be that dense?" And, looking around at their faces, in one's imagination, the answer is painfully obvious. There is hope, then, for all of us.

V18. *eyes . . . ears*: A direct quote from Jeremiah 5:21. Natural enough for any Jewish speaker or listener, since the Hebrew scriptures were their only book.

V21. *not yet understand*: As if it were necessary again to underscore the fact that the disciples he himself chose were not rocket scientists and brain surgeons. If they are this obtuse about Jesus' ability to supply bread, after two astounding miracles in which he did precisely that, imagine how long it will take them to cope with the Eucharist.

V22. *Bethsaida*: On the northeast shore of the Lake of Galilee, about four miles away from Capernaum, probably the hometown of Peter and Andrew.

V23. *out of the village*: A strong parallel to the cure of the mute earlier, and another attempt to hold back the Messianic Secret. Note that, untypically, there is no mention of faith asked for this miracle; *put saliva on his eyes*: Jesus can use even the most unlikely means—not merely spittle, but his thickheaded companions—to work miracles. Jesus doesn't merely mix spittle with something else; here he actually spits on the man's eyes; **Can you see anything?**: Unlike all other miracles in the gospels, this one takes place not instantaneously but in stages; it occurs only in Mark and is omitted by Matthew and Luke possibly because the use of spittle and laying on of hands was a pagan practice, rendering the episode doubtful in their eyes.

V24. *like trees, walking*: A fine detail; if the man knows what trees look like, he has probably been sighted and gone blind. This cure is gradual—the

up and said, "I can see people, but they look like trees, walking." ²⁵Then Jesus laid his hands on his eyes again; and he looked intently and his sight was restored, and he saw everything clearly. ²⁶Then he sent him away to his home, saying, "Do not even go into the village."

²⁷Jesus went on with his disciples to the villages of Caesarea Philippi; and on the way he asked his disciples, "Who do people say that I am?" ²⁸And they answered him, "John the Baptist; and others, Elijah; and still others, one of the prophets." ²⁹He asked them, "But who do you say that

man has begun to regain his sight, but not fully yet. Taken with the previous parallel of healing the mute, this fulfills the prophecy of Isaiah that, at the coming of Yahweh, the blind will see and the deaf will hear. It is also preparation for the disciples' finally seeing and hearing—in the next chapters—that Jesus is, indeed, the Messiah.

V25. *clearly*: The miracle is complete.

V26. *Do not . . . village*: Consistent with Jesus' attempt to reveal himself only gradually, but that is becoming less and less possible, if Jesus can't resist the need of people for healing.

Peter Sees . . . To a Point: 8:27–9:1

V27. *Caesarea Philippi*: A town twenty-five miles northeast of the lake; *on the way*: This begins their journey from the northernmost point in Israel down to the fatal entrance into Jerusalem; *Who do people say that I am?*: "People" here means "those outside." This question is the whole focus of Mark's gospel: the gradual revelation of who Jesus truly is. Here, there is a dramatic shift in Mark's treatment; Jesus is becoming more open in his attempts to clarify the Messianic Secret.

V28. *John . . . Elijah . . . prophets*: These associations have been made before in Mark's gospel and rejected as inadequate. Note: No one is said to suspect he is *The* Messiah.

V29. *But who do you say?*: There is a strong contrast between the disciples and "those outside"; the disciples have been entrusted with the Secret. It has been a hazy awareness; now Peter changes that. And Jesus asks that question of each of us; *You are the Messiah*: Peter is the first human being to confess, openly—besides those possessed by demons—that Jesus is "the One who is to come." It is an admission that Jesus is the Messiah, though not yet an act of faith in Jesus' divinity, which was still—for a monotheistic Jew—unthinkable. Up to this point, the disciples surely had some intuition Jesus was "special"; otherwise, they would not have left all and followed him. But here Peter makes

I am?" Peter answered him, "You are the Messiah." [30]And he sternly ordered them not to tell anyone about him.

[31]Then he began to teach them that the Son of Man must undergo great suffering, and be rejected by the elders, the chief

---

a definite—if long overdue—commitment, even though he still sees Jesus only inadequately, like the blind man seeing people as walking trees. Some critics mention here the fact that, in Greek drama, the turning point of the play is the instant the protagonist sees the truth—which overturns all his previous convictions (the climax or turning point). That is only remotely true here, since Jesus' fierce reaction a few moments later shows clearly that Peter had only part of the truth. This is *a* turning point, but hardly *the* turning point. In Matthew's expanded version (16:13-20) of this moment, Jesus praises Simon for his intuition and faith, and uses the occasion to change his name to Peter and promises him the keys of the kingdom. Oddly, Mark—one of whose major sources was allegedly Peter's own recollections—omits that.

V30. *not to tell anyone*: The reason for this prohibition is not that others could not accept Jesus as Messiah (far short of any divine identification) but that the disciples themselves do not yet fully comprehend what "Messiah" means. In the following section, Jesus sets about correcting the false notions the contemporary Jews—including his disciples—had about a gallant and warlike Messiah, like David, who would set the Jews free from foreign oppression using military power. Such a small-*m* messiah would indeed be a threat to the status quo for the Roman occupiers and their toadies. One did not require the divine intelligence to foresee almost inevitable deadly opposition.

V31. *the Son of Man*: Jesus has switched titles: not "Messiah," but something far more powerful. The first use of this term in Mark. An allusion to the OT book of Daniel in which "one like a human being" is summoned into the presence of "the Ancient One" (Yahweh) and given sovereignty over the whole earth (7:13): *The* Messiah, not a momentary reprieve from invaders. In Jewish thought, the Son of Man was associated with the judge who would appear on the Day of the Lord to judge the world; *undergo great suffering*: Jesus is now specifying a kind of Messiah his disciples aren't ready for. The Messiah had to suffer (see chap. 5); it was necessary that he identify himself utterly with suffering humanity and bring victory out of his sheer impotence. He thus completely reverses the current expectation of the Son of Man as a military conqueror and judge, whom the Jews hoped for. Rather, the Son of Man is the Suffering Servant of Yahweh in Isaiah (Isa 52:13–53:12): "disfigured . . . without beauty or majesty . . . despised . . . crushed for our sins . . . like a lamb led to slaughter." Thus, Mark's Jesus has fused the independent OT ideas

105

priests, and the scribes, and be killed, and after three days rise again. ³²He said all this quite openly. And Peter took him aside and began to rebuke him. ³³But turning and looking at his disciples, he rebuked Peter and said, "Get behind me, Satan! For you are setting your mind not on divine things but on human things."

³⁴He called the crowd with his disciples, and said to them, "If any want to become my followers, let them deny themselves and take up their cross and follow me. ³⁵For those who want to save their life will lose it, and those who lose their life for my sake, and for the sake of the gospel, will save it. ³⁶For what will it profit them

---

of the Son of Man (whom Daniel does not picture as suffering) and the Suffering Servant (whom Isaiah does show as a liberator who undergoes agonies); *rejected . . . killed . . . rise*: Jesus focuses the image of the Suffering Servant into his own life and time; *the elders, the chief priests, and the scribes*: a major component of the Antagonist. The elders are probably the Sanhedrin council, lay and rabbinical representatives of the people—the men who will try Jesus (Mark 15). Chief priests had authority over all functions in the temple, especially animal sacrifice—their curtailed authority somewhat similar to the German bishops under the Nazis. Scribes were "teachers of the law," intellectuals rather than mere secretaries; *after three days*: Whether Jesus actually specified like this at the time is unimportant. It surely was the experience of the early witnesses. This is the first of three predictions of the passion in each of the Synoptic Gospels.

V32. *quite openly*: Jesus now departs from veiled hints, allusions to the OT, and parables; *Peter . . . rebuke him*: Proof again that, although Peter believes Jesus is the Messiah, he has no notion whatever what that really means. Even if this new understanding of the Messiah comes from Jesus, even if it is the truth, Peter does not want it to be the truth. "Oh no, Jesus!" One critic insists Peter rebuked Jesus only because according to the scriptures the Messiah was not "supposed" to suffer, rather than because he loved Jesus. Such scholars should not impose their own intellectual chill on simple, loving men.

V33. *turning . . . looking*: The two details are most graphic; one can almost see the scowl and hear the scorn: *Get behind me, Satan*: "Satan" = "Tempter." One of the most chilling sentences in the gospel. For all his fumbling goodwill, Peter is unwittingly playing Satan's part here. He is in league with the Antagonist; he wants the Messiah to be his image of what a Messiah should be. In this, as always, Peter is the model disciple, not the ideal disciple, but the usual one; *setting your mind*: Peter limits God's perspective to a cramped human perspective; in trying to change the truth about the Messiah, Peter is aligning himself with "those outside." It is a cliché that "God's ways are not man's ways," but it is probably the easiest of all clichés to forget.

to gain the whole world and forfeit their life? [37]Indeed, what can they give in return for their life? [38]Those who are ashamed of me and of my words in this adulterous and sinful generation, of them the Son of Man will also be ashamed when he comes in the glory of his Father with the holy angels."

V34. *If any want*: Discipleship is entirely free; no one can legitimately be compelled; *become my followers*: Jesus has just told Peter to "get behind me"; now he tells him, the disciples, and the crowd what commitment to be his companion and disciple really means; *deny themselves*: It is a question of staking one's whole life—losing focus on self in order truly to discover the self. A modern equivalent might be "Surrender center stage; stop acting as if you are the Lead"; *take up their cross*: The phrasing may be, again, Mark reading word choice back into his material, since crucifixion was not common among non-Roman people. It was a custom, however, to sign the forehead with oil or water as a symbol of repentance (the cross mark being an ancient form of the Hebrew T or Greek *tau*), like a "brand" showing one belonged to God again. Scholars believe Jesus' original statement might have been something like: "Whoever does not mark himself with the cross mark of dedication-wholly-to-God cannot come with me."

V35. *save . . . lose*: This translation says "life"; the Greek, however, is *psyche*, "soul," the self, the inner core of everything an individual is. To enter the reign of God, one must put "self" aside—the one reality most of us are most concerned with. Paradox is constant in the gospel: God's ways and expectations are most often quite the opposite of our own. Here is the central focus of the "turnabout" good news: You are not the focus of reality; God is. Once you submit to that truth, everything else will fall into place. By "lose their life" Jesus does not mean exclusively martyrs. He means all men and women who genuinely set others' needs before their own. This, of course, is in direct contrast to Peter's idea—and quite likely our own—of how things "should be." Jesus can bestow sight on the literally blind, but not insight into Peter.

V36. *forfeit their life*: Again, "life" is really "their soul," the essence of who the individual is. Jesus is saying that if one does not stop staring into the mirror—whether at one's beauty or one's shortcomings—he or she will be blinded to the whole purpose of life. His or her life will be, ultimately, meaningless.

V38. *ashamed of me*: Embarrassed at the seeming naiveté of becoming vulnerable, unselfish, willing to be used, forgiving debts without repayment. There are some cynics who believe that, if Jesus had not risen from the dead, his disciples could have "made up" the gospel, out of self-interest. If they did, they surely did not come up with an immediately appealing "product." Anyone who "invented" Jesus and his message would surely have eliminated verses 31-38 of this chapter and fabricated a Jesus more along the lines of Peter's expectations.

Mark's whole gospel tries to explain what kind of Messiah Jesus really is.

9:1. *see that the kingdom of God has come:* Not that they will be aware at the moment it occurs (presumably, the resurrection), but that the kingdom had become real without their being explicitly aware of it, like an event when one was sleeping.

Review Questions for Chapter 8

1. How does Jesus' concern to provide bread for the crowd relate to our modern concern to "mind your own business"?
2. Jesus speaks of "yeast" as a metaphor for whatever is at the focus of our lives, what gives them meaning and drive. The "yeast" of the Pharisees is different from the "yeast" of Herod. What did that mean in Jesus' time, and what does it mean in our own time?
3. The healing of the blind man at Bethsaida takes place more slowly than most other healings in the gospel. Why is this healing more like healings in our own lives than the nearly instantaneous healings elsewhere?
4. List the details in this chapter that show that Jesus is becoming less and less secretive about who he really is.
5. Advertising has convinced us that we must avoid even inconvenience. How does that differ from Jesus' insistence that following him means carrying a cross? How is advertising the voice of the Antagonist?

For Reflection

(1) *Verse 12.* We keep thinking that a miracle would be enough to prop up our sagging faith. Hardly. Just suppose that tonight, while you're watching television, the tube goes suddenly blank and a deep voice comes from it speaking your name. "This is God. To put all your doubts to rest, I'm going to lift this enslaving machine in the air, turn it around, and set it down again." And it happens! Right before your very own eyes! My hunch is the question of belief or disbelief in God would vanish, not because it was solved but because your mind would be filled with a quite different problem: disbelief in your sanity! Is somebody pulling a trick? Martians, maybe?

The same happens when we pray that God will change his mind. That mind-set treats God as if he were a genie in a bottle, ready to be uncorked every time we want a wish fulfilled. Do you often pray to God like a pouty child at the supermarket asking her mother to buy her bubble gum and ice cream and dolls?

(2) *Verse 23*. Here we see the "stuff" Jesus uses to perform his miracles: not whirlwinds of exploding lights, but spittle. Perhaps one of the reasons we expect space-age special effects when God is present is caused by what the church has done to the simplicity of the gospel. When Jesus first came among us, he came quietly to a man and woman in a stable in the midst of the dung smell. But as early as Matthew's gospel, we have to hoke it up with skies ablaze with angelic choirs. We have taken that unpretentious cave and walled it with marble and hung it with gold lamps—the way God would have done from the start, had God known better. When God chose his agents on earth, he didn't choose from professors or physicians or lawyers. He chose eleven unschooled fishermen and a tax collector. Now we give exaggerated deference to churchmen, as if ordination in some way automatically changes the man on whom it is conferred.

Do you expect the work of the kingdom to be done in our day only by those who have been trained and are "qualified"? God is waiting for permission to use someone far less pretentious: you.

(3) *Verse 24.* At first, when his sight is just beginning to return, the blind man sees people "like trees, walking." In the reality that God inhabits—free of time and space—we are all "blind." We brush up against God every day and are as unaware of who God is—or even that God is there—as Helen Keller was before her liberating encounter at the pump. At times we get intriguing hints that there is a "strange presence" near us: seeing a mountain at sunset, a star-strewn sky, a baby.

It is only after a conversion—a complete turnaround of our expectations of what is important (or even truly real)—that we begin to see God lurking under the surfaces of everything, sending us hints and pleas for help in eyes we had never really looked into before. Are you yourself too busy with "more pressing" matters to be susceptible to that conversion?

(4) *Verses 32-33.* More than any other human being who ever existed, Jesus was aware of the reality that God inhabits among us right now, what Gerard Manley Hopkins called "the dearest freshness deep-down things," and what Dietrich Bonhoeffer called "the Beyond in our midst." It would be months after the resurrection before Peter became aware of it. Jesus' perspective on the relative values of things is God's perspective; Peter's perspective is cramped down to what is important to him—which he then automatically transfers into the mind of God.

There is no argument against the existence of an all-powerful and benevolent God more persuasive than the problem of evil: babies born horribly deformed, children starving all across the planet and in our own streets, people who have led the best lives they could stricken with slow and agonizing diseases. "Why doesn't a good God step in and do something about those tragedies?" But God did step in and do something about them: God made you.

(5) *Verse 35*. What does it honestly mean "to save one's soul"? Surely it doesn't mean merely the childish notion that we are somehow saving our souls from a future hell after we die, just managing to get a toenail-hold on the rim of heaven. In fact, what does one's soul even mean? Your soul is your self, your who-I-am, the immortal spark of the divine within you. Jesus has taken care of saving our souls from the annihilation of death, but only we control whether our souls will die—or even come alive!—before we suffer physical death.

Our bodies quicken without any cooperation on our part, but the human soul is not a command. It is an invitation to rise above the animal in us, an invitation no animal receives. We are capable of compassion even for our enemies; we are capable of pangs of conscience no tiger or shark endures; we are capable of offering forgiveness to those who have wronged us. Or we are free to leave that capability unactualized. If we do, we have lost our souls long before we die.

9 [1]And he said to them, "Truly I tell you, there are some standing here who will not taste death until they see that the kingdom of God has come with power."

[2]Six days later, Jesus took with him Peter and James and John, and led them up a high mountain apart, by themselves. And he was transfigured before them, [3]and his

---

The Transfiguration: VV2-13

V2. *Six days later*: A reminder of the six days one has to wait for the Sabbath, but also the six days Moses had to wait (Exod 24:15-16) on the mountain for his theophany (experience of God in the here-and-now); *Peter and James and John*: Again, these three are selected out as special witnesses. Their choice also links this episode back to the daughter of Jairus and forward to the later episode of the agony in the garden—its direct opposite, which they alone witnessed also; *high mountain*: an allusion to Moses (Exod 24:16) whose encounter with God on Sinai is mirrored in many of the details of this event: the mountain, the cloud, Moses, the tents, fear, brilliant clothing; *he was transfigured*: A metamorphosis, like a cocoon suddenly revealing a butterfly, which is a symbol of the true life after resurrection. Like the butterfly "within" the caterpillar, the reality has been there all the time. Paul says (Phil 2) that at the incarnation, the Son "emptied himself." The true nature of Jesus is a reality their limited minds were incapable of accepting—or unwilling to accept. At this moment, the divinity of Jesus momentarily burns away the mere surface appearances that we—with our tunnel vision—believe to be the limits of reality. Although the event has been embellished by apocalyptic (ultimate, visionary, grandiose) symbols, it could be based on some factual occurrence—even a post-Easter event—when the disciples really did comprehend Jesus' role as Messiah, not only the deliverer but also the glorious Son of Man. Accepting that this transfiguration understanding was read back into Mark's book would explain the scarcely credible *disbelief* and disloyalty these three privileged witnesses will show for the rest of the story: James and John jockey for privilege (10:35) and Peter apostatizes almost immediately after his ordination and first Communion (14:66-72). How could anyone who had beheld this shattering event have "forgotten" it? Surely as Mark was writing, it was a confirmed postresurrectional belief.

V3. *dazzling white*: Throughout scripture, gleaming white garments—like fire—are a symbol of the presence of God: the Ancient of Days on his throne, angels, men in white. The source of the whiteness would be impossible to any earthly cause. When Moses came from speaking to God (Exod 34:29), his face was so radiant he had to wear a veil.

clothes became dazzling white, such as no one on earth could bleach them. [4]And there appeared to them Elijah with Moses, who were talking with Jesus. [5]Then Peter said to Jesus, "Rabbi, it is good for us to be here; let us make three dwellings, one for you, one for Moses, and one for Elijah." [6]He did not know what to say, for they were terrified. [7]Then a cloud overshadowed them, and from the cloud there came a voice, "This is my Son, the Beloved; listen to him!" [8]Suddenly when they looked around, they saw no one with them any more, but only Jesus.

V4. *Elijah . . . Moses*: Elijah is the symbol of all the prophets, and Moses is the symbol of the law. The Jews referred to the OT as "The Law and the Prophets"; thus, at this moment the whole Hebrew scriptures give testimony to Jesus as Lord. Further, since both Elijah and Moses were closely connected with Mount Sinai, this event on a mountain becomes a new covenant relationship with God. No clue how the three disciples would know who these two figures were; *appeared*: The same Greek verb Paul uses four times for Christ's appearance after death.

V5. *Rabbi*: The term was used for teachers during Mark's time, but it was only beginning to be used in the time of Jesus; *three dwellings*: Such small huts were set up at the harvest feast of Tabernacles or Tents, *Sukkoth*, the oldest of Hebrew feasts, which is also called the feast of Yahweh. Peter—with typical clumsy, inappropriate fervor—is trying to prolong the experience.

V6. *did not know what to say*: Typically, even when he is rendered "speechless," Peter still *must* say something; *terrified*: As before, closer to being astounded than horrified .

V7. *a cloud*: Another OT symbol for the presence of God, as with the pillar of cloud that went before the Israelites by day (Exod 13:21). In a parched land where life really depended on rain from October to April, a cloud was a sign of hope; *overshadowed*: Recall that in Luke the angel tells Mary that the Holy Spirit will "overshadow" her. This, then, is a symbol of a kind of spiritual "impregnation." The three apostles are not mere spectators of this event but have somehow been themselves transformed by it; *a voice*: As at Jesus' baptism, this need not be taken literally. Note that, unlike that previous divine speech that was expressed to Jesus ("you"), this utterance is in the third person ("This is"), addressed to the three witnesses. It is a symbolic attempt to grasp a real but nonphysical awareness within the apostles; *my Son, the Beloved*: The words used by the voice at Jesus' baptism, symbolizing his realization of his divinity. Here, the apostles, in some remote way, attain that same realization about Jesus: He is more glorious than Moses or Elijah. In the overall structure of Mark's book, a divine revelation of Jesus' relationship to God began his mission in Galilee and here begins his mission to Jerusalem; *listen to him*: Jesus is now

⁹As they were coming down the mountain, he ordered them to tell no one about what they had seen, until after the Son of Man had risen from the dead. ¹⁰So they kept the matter to themselves, questioning what this rising from the dead could mean. ¹¹Then they asked him, "Why do the scribes say that Elijah must come first?"

¹²He said to them, "Elijah is indeed coming first to restore all things. How then is it written about the Son of Man, that he is to go through many sufferings and be treated with contempt? ¹³But I tell you that Elijah has come, and they did to him whatever they pleased, as it is written about him."

---

the prophet and lawgiver, like Elijah and Moses, who vanish, leaving only Jesus.

V9. *tell no one*: Although the Messianic Secret is gradually being revealed, the three are not to tell even the other apostles; ***risen from the dead*:** This jarring note invites the reader to cope with this glorious revelation of Jesus, uneasily fused with the Suffering Servant he has also identified himself with, when he rebuked Peter immediately before this (8:31-38).

V10. *what rising from the dead could mean*: Yet these three privileged men have seen the daughter of Jairus dead and then alive again. In fact, in this very experience, they witnessed Moses and Elijah raised! Immediately before this, Jesus has predicted his own resurrection (8:31)! In their day, however, explanations of life-after-death (accepted by the Pharisees but not by the priestly Sadducees) considered resurrection not in terms of individuals but in terms of a collective arising. Moreover, it would not occur until the end time. Therefore, their puzzlement might arise from contemplating Jesus rising, singly, within their own lifetimes—something old hat to modern Christians but a first-time confusion for these unlearned men.

V11. *the scribes say*: The official, trained interpreters of scripture at the time; ***Elijah must come first*:** The prophet Malachi writes: "Lo, I will send you the prophet Elijah before the great and terrible day" (4:5). How can this Son of Man arise before Elijah comes? Of course, as Mark has shown, Elijah already has come, in John the Baptizer.

V12. *treated with contempt*: No OT source directly connects the explicit term "Son of Man" with suffering. But among the many references to the future Messiah is Isaiah's Suffering Servant (Isa 53). Reading that chapter, written seven hundred years before Jesus, a modern Christian could easily believe it was a quotation from the *New* Testament. Jewish scholars read the "Servant" to be the millennial sufferings of the entire Hebrew nation.

V13. *whatever they pleased*: As they imprisoned and executed Elijah/John, so will they imprison and execute the Son of Man, the Suffering Servant.

¹⁴When they came to the disciples, they saw a great crowd around them, and some scribes arguing with them. ¹⁵When the whole crowd saw him, they were immediately overcome with awe, and they ran forward to greet him. ¹⁶He asked them, "What are you arguing about with them?" ¹⁷Someone from the crowd answered him, "Teacher, I brought you my son; he has a spirit that makes him unable to speak; ¹⁸and whenever it seizes him, it dashes him down; and he foams and grinds his teeth and becomes rigid; and I asked your disciples to cast it out, but they could not do so." ¹⁹He answered them, "You faithless generation, how much longer must I be among you? How much longer must I put up with you? Bring him to me." ²⁰And they brought the boy to him. When the spirit saw him, immediately it convulsed the boy, and he fell on the ground and rolled about, foaming at the mouth. ²¹Jesus asked the father, "How long has this been happening to him?" And he said, "From child-

---

A Possessed Boy: VV 14-29

V14. *a great crowd*: Unlike the miracles so far, which took place very often in private, Jesus is now less wary of showing his Messianic power; *arguing with them*: Unclear whether the scribes are arguing with the crowd or with the disciples who had been left behind.

V16. *them . . . them*: Again unclear. It seems Jesus is asking the disciples ("them") what they were arguing about with the scribes ("them")—though the scribes are not mentioned again, and the answer to his question comes from the disappointed father in the crowd.

V17. *a spirit*: Judging from the symptoms, he is quite likely an epileptic. Matthew (17:15) does diagnose these vividly described symptoms that way: "moonstruck." Unlike the two previous exorcisms, neither the spirit nor its victim here is able to speak.

V18. *asked your disciples*: A justified expectation, since Jesus had sent them out (6:7) with authority over unclean spirits. This episode suggests they need something more than merely ordination as exorcists—which is explained in the final verse of this section.

V19. *You faithless generation*: Religious instruction is never easy, even for the Son of Man. It does show there is no sin in being exasperated.

V20. *convulsed the boy*: Although pitiful, the boy is a secondary character in this conflict; the battle is between Jesus and the power of evil, in its broadest sense, encompassing both moral evil and physical suffering—just as the conflict has been since Jesus' temptations in the desert.

V21. *How long*: Mark uses this not because Jesus needs the information but to underline the father's distress and the long-standing nature of the illness.

hood. ²²It has often cast him into the fire and into the water, to destroy him; but if you are able to do anything, have pity on us and help us." ²³Jesus said to him, "If you are able!—All things can be done for the one who believes." ²⁴Immediately the father of the child cried out, "I believe; help my unbelief!" ²⁵When Jesus saw that a crowd came running together, he rebuked the unclean spirit, saying to it, "You spirit that keeps this boy from speaking and hearing, I command you, come out of him, and never enter him again!" ²⁶After crying out and convulsing him terribly, it came out, and the boy was like a corpse, so that most of them said, "He is dead." ²⁷But Jesus took him by the hand and lifted him up, and he was able to stand. ²⁸When he had entered the house, his disciples asked him privately, "Why could we not cast it out?" ²⁹He said to them, "This kind can come out only through prayer."

VV22-23. *If you are able*: With some scorn, Jesus repeats the father's words, implying "If you didn't think I could, why did you come?" Or "Hasn't the word gotten round that I *can*?" The father came with hope in the healer, but Jesus is helpless (as his disciples were) without the father's accepting trust in God. The moment shows the recognizable difference between hope and faith. Hope has its fingers crossed; faith says, "I accept whatever God chooses for me."

V24. *help my unbelief*: The father is profoundly honest. Like so many, he truly wants to believe, but there is always that itch of doubt holding one back. Nonetheless, the *desire* to believe is clearly enough for Jesus.

V25. *rebuked*: In Greek, the same word Jesus used with the demoniac (1:25); *I command you*: A clear demonstration of authority *beyond* the designation by ordination. The unflinching confidence and power to confront such an Antagonist takes more than mere delegation. Against all evidence to the contrary, a simpler age believed holy orders automatically *made* a man holy.

V26. *like a corpse*: Mark intends this episode to be a symbol for Jesus' death and resurrection, which has been the subject of the previous episodes. This symbolism is continued in the following sentence: he "lifted him up"— from what everyone thought was terminal, just as with Jairus's daughter (6:35-43).

V29. *only through prayer*: Casting out evil cannot be merely a matter of ritual formulas and intense good will. One needs a profound union with God even to attempt it. At least for now, the disciples obviously lack that. Notice that Jesus doesn't criticize their lack of faith here.

This is the same Jesus whose stupefying transcendence the favored threesome has just witnessed, bringing that power to bear through commonplace human means—and faith.

[30]They went on from there and passed through Galilee. He did not want anyone to know it; [31]for he was teaching his disciples, saying to them, "The Son of Man is to be betrayed into human hands, and they will kill him, and three days after being killed, he will rise again." [32]But they did not understand what he was saying and were afraid to ask him.

[33]Then they came to Capernaum; and when he was in the house he asked them, "What were you arguing about on the way?" [34]But they were silent, for on the way they had argued with one another who was the greatest. [35]He sat down, called the twelve, and said to them, "Whoever wants to be first must be last of all and servant of all." [36]Then he took a little child and put

---

Private Instructions: VV30-50

V30. *did not want anyone to know*: For a time, Jesus wants to get away from the crowds and instruct the disciples, to prepare them to take his place. Again, his message is that he will be put to death and rise, and again they fail to understand.

V31. *the Son of Man*: In all three passion predictions—8:31, here, and 10:33—Jesus uses this apocalyptic term from the climactic Day of the Lord.

V32. *afraid to ask*: Possibly because of Jesus' fierce response to Peter's objection the first time Jesus mentioned this. Also, they could well have been thinking, "You mean us too?"

V34. *they were silent:* Again, like trapped boys, shrugging, "Oh, uh, nothing!"; *who was the greatest*: Like adolescent boys sneering about which one can lift the most deadweight. Throughout church history, however, men have been tempted to judge their capacities by the color of their cassocks. Even today unbalanced liberalism and conservatism battle in the churches over which has the powerful inside track to the will of God. *Plus ça change, plus la même chose.*

V35. *called the twelve*: Presumably out from among the other disciples, perhaps because their privileged association with Jesus would make them more likely candidates for complacency and arrogance about rank and status; **Whoever wants to be first**: This critical doctrine of Jesus is 180 degrees in the opposite direction from what we consider "natural": getting ahead. On the contrary, Jesus says that, to claim to be Christian, one must put the needs of all the others ahead of one's own needs. In order to be useful, one must be willing to be used.

V36. *took a little child*: Chosen not for innocence so much as for a child's utter lack of rank and stature in that society, totally dependent, a social nobody. Unlike our own society, these men listening to Jesus would be shocked. This child is less important than a slave and should not even be with men discussing serious matters without the "inferior" women.

it among them; and taking it in his arms, he said to them, [37]"Whoever welcomes one such child in my name welcomes me, and whoever welcomes me welcomes not me but the one who sent me."

[38]John said to him, "Teacher, we saw someone casting out demons in your name, and we tried to stop him, because he was not following us." [39]But Jesus said, "Do not stop him; for no one who does a deed of power in my name will be able soon afterward to speak evil of me. [40]Whoever is not against us is for us. [41]For truly I tell you, whoever gives you a cup of water to drink because you bear the name of Christ will by no means lose the reward.

[42]"If any of you put a stumbling block before one of these little ones who believe

---

V37. *Whoever welcomes one such child*: The Christian disciple must welcome everyone he or she meets as confidently, trustingly, and lovingly as one would welcome a child; *who sent me*: Yahweh. This echoes the episode in Matthew (25) on the Last Judgment: whoever welcomes the needy welcomes God. The sole question to determine our value is our kindness.

V38. *in your name*: This problem came up in the early church, but Jesus could have faced the same problem earlier. What do the disciples do when those who "don't belong to our group" use Jesus' name? Clearly, Jesus was not given to the sectarianism—or even extreme clericalism—that claims that only "our" people can do good in the name of Christ. The disciples tried to prevent someone else from doing what they were incapable of doing; *not following us*: Perhaps a trivial point, but John says "us" and not "you," misplacing the source of power.

V39. *Do not stop him*: Another small bit of evidence that the early church did not "make up" the gospels, since they themselves were frequently intolerant of non-Christians invoking the name of Jesus (See Acts 8:18; 13:6; 19:13). Their objections could have been motivated, however, by some non-Christian who attempted black magic using Jesus' name. But it does seem that a non-disciple has succeeded in exorcizing in Jesus' name where his own have failed.

V40. *Whoever is not against us*: A remarkable plea for tolerance and perhaps even pluralism of religions? Interesting to ponder how Jesus would react to the mutual exclusions various Christian communities impose on one another.

V41. *whoever gives you a cup of water*: A man or woman need not be Christian in order to be good, or even a saint (cf. Gandhi). Here begins a collection of sayings of Jesus that probably occurred at different times but that Mark has linked together by catchwords that echo from one to another; e.g., the word "name" jumps from verse 37 to verse 38 to verse 41; also with "better," "scandal," "fire," "salt." This argues to oral transmission, as stand-up comics organize jokes for easier recall.

V42. *put a stumbling block*: On the other hand, anyone—even those "of our company"—who shakes another's faith in Christ is worse than a condemned

in me, it would be better for you if a great millstone were hung around your neck and you were thrown into the sea. ⁴³If your hand causes you to stumble, cut it off; it is better for you to enter life maimed than to have two hands and to go to hell, to the unquenchable fire. [44] ⁴⁵And if your foot causes you to stumble, cut it off; it is better for you to enter life lame than to have two feet and to be thrown into hell. [46] ⁴⁷And if your eye causes you to stumble, tear it out; it is better for you to enter the kingdom of God with one eye than to have two eyes and to be thrown into hell, ⁴⁸where their worm never dies, and the fire is never quenched.

⁴⁹"For everyone will be salted with fire. ⁵⁰Salt is good; but if salt has lost its saltiness, how can you season it? Have salt in yourselves, and be at peace with one another."

---

criminal or a suicide; *one of these little ones*: Not merely children, but all "nobody" believers. The resultant statement seems to say that anyone, of any position, who makes belief in Jesus more difficult is better off dead; *millstone*: In heavy contrast to the relatively smaller "stumbling block." In a landlocked farming community, the metaphor would mean what an anchor meant to seafarers.

V43. *hand . . . stumble*: Where the previous warning was against causing others to give up the quest, here the warning is against misleading oneself. It would be—and has often been—far too simplistic to restrict these falls solely to sexual sins; *cut it off:* Obviously, hyperbole. Many fundamentalists who insist that every word of Jesus must be taken absolutely literally are pulled up short on these verses since, being human, we have all been led by our hands and feet and eyes into "difficulties." Had Jesus meant these statements literally, all serious Christians would be crawling about handless, footless, and eyeless! Jesus used hyperbole to stress the seriousness of our need for vigilance against our own weakness. These words were especially meaningful for the Romans in Mark's audience, subject as they were to Nero's persecution (AD 54–68).

V45. *enter life*: The parallel in verse 47 substitutes "kingdom of God," suggesting an equivalence between truly living and the kingdom; *hell*: The word Jesus uses is *Gehenna*, a ravine southwest of Jerusalem where in ancient times human sacrifices had been made to the Canaanite gods and where in Jesus' time garbage was continuously burning. Despite its popularity with preachers over the centuries, there are remarkably few mentions of hell in the gospels—only thirteen, many of them repetitions: Mark (3); Matthew (7), Luke (3), John (0).

V48. *where their worm . . . never quenched*: The very last verse of Isaiah (66:24).

V49. *salted with fire*: Animals sacrificed in the OT were salted before being burned.

V50. *if salt . . . saltiness*: A shift in meaning here, enjoining the disciples not to become contaminated by the motivations of the world and lose their fervor, namely, the enlivening Spirit; *be at peace*: "Salt" used in a quite different application than in the first half of the verse. Mark ties this up with the dispute over positions that began this section. Rather than antagonisms, what should give zest to this community is the common pursuit of reconciliation.

Review Questions for Chapter 9

1. For a moment at the transfiguration, Jesus relents and shows the three disciples the kind of Messiah and kingdom they were hoping for. How many places in this and previous chapters indicate that anything less than a dramatic, this-world messiah is "not acceptable" to them?
2. When the father of the boy says he has faith, but what he feels is not enough faith, why doesn't Jesus reprimand him as he has the others in verse 19?
3. What symbols of the resurrection occur in the chapter?
4. The two touchstones of the Christian and the Christian community are healing and service. What elements of this chapter underline both those duties?
5. Pluralism is the peaceful coexistence of several quite different attitudes about the ways a common job should be done. What in the chapter shows Jesus is not opposed to pluralism?

For Reflection

(1) *Verse 2.* When Jesus was transfigured, all the godliness in him burned through the surfaces—surfaces that are all we are able to contact with our eyes and fingers, trapped as we are in space-time limitations. We become unwittingly arrogant, believing that, if God were present, we ought to be aware of him. But most realities that surround us—objectively there—are inaccessible to our senses and therefore to the usual ways we reason. We see only the tiniest band of the light spectrum; we can't see ultraviolet rays or gamma rays, although when we get a sunburn we know they are unarguably there. The chair you are sitting on is not really solid at all but aswarm with galaxies upon galaxies of particles moving so fast that they only seem to be at rest.

The only way we can contact the Really Real is not with our senses and our calculating intelligence but with that part of us that also transcends space and time, that spark of the divine in us: our souls.

(2) *Verse 23.* Statements by Jesus about the power of faith and prayer are always disconcerting. He at least seems to be saying that if we pray and our prayers are not answered, the fault must be with some weakness of faith or lack of diligence in prayer. But that clearly couldn't have been what Jesus meant, since

he himself—our model of faith—prayed in the garden to the point of shedding blood to be released from his commitment to death, and his prayers were *not* answered.

The key is in what Jesus said after that: "Yet not what I want, but what you want." Like Peter at the transfiguration, in moments of weakness Jesus too is hampered by his cramped, this-world, space-time human limitations. But even at such perilous times, Jesus still had enough grasp on God's perspective that he surrendered the decision on the matter to God.

Our Lady is a good model for praying. At the annunciation she used nearly the same words as Jesus in the garden and on the cross: "Be it done unto me according to your word." Later, at the wedding feast at Cana, she didn't approach Jesus and beg him to perform a miracle; she merely said, "They have no wine," only informing him of a need and leaving the rest to him.

(3) *Verse 34.* Twenty centuries of church art have left us with the unexamined impression that the apostles were larger than life, heroic figures on an epic canvas. Only recently have movies begun to show us who they really were: homespun men with scruffy beards who didn't bathe too often. But the evidence has been there in the gospels all along, despite our tendency to spruce them up. The apostles were as thickheaded as we, as self-centered, as fumbling. Here, once again, they misread everything Jesus has said about the kingdom, reading it with this-world eyes as a literal kingdom in which they would be the big shots, like small-time Mafiosi, hitching their fortunes to someone who looks like he might become the next big-time Don.

If your job in the kingdom is to lure others to conversion of their values from the world to the kingdom, take heart. The best Teacher who ever lived had no success at all until long after his students had left him. If you are just trying to conquer your own reward-conscious self, take heart too: the apostles were also total klutzes and look what Jesus made of them.

(4) *Verse 38.* Our parochial outlook is not limited to our blindness to the transcendent in our midst; it is also sometimes blind to the goodness in our midst. Since Vatican II, we have fortunately distanced ourselves from the smugness of the previous hundred years, which motivated Catholics to use disdainful words about other religions. Now we respect any man or woman's attempt to connect with God and to bring that awareness into our common environment. We no longer speak of non-Catholic Christians as "heretics" but as "our separated brethren."

But that welcome openness may have distracted us from the evident fact that we still reserve that same parochial outlook *within* the Catholic Church. Conservatives lob criticisms at liberals for not being "authentic Catholics" and the liberals hurl them back, heedless of the fact that both sides at least claim to be worshiping and serving the *same* God through the *same* Christ. Is there anyone "on our side" to whose sincerity you have not been quite fair?

(5) *Verse 50.* Any good cook tastes again and again. "It needs something. Oregano? Salt?" There just isn't the tang that there was the last time. A lot of us are too busy to "taste" our lives, to see if the tang has gone out of them. There are just too many things that should have been done yesterday. As a result, our lives turn into insipid endurance contests. As Macbeth says in his grim, existentialist soliloquy: "Tomorrow, and tomorrow, and tomorrow, creeps in this petty petty pace from day to day, to the last syllable of recorded time; and all our yesterdays have lighted fools their way to dusty death. Out, out brief candle! Life's but a walking shadow, a poor player that struts and frets his hour upon the stage and then is heard no more: it is a tale told by an idiot, full of sound and fury, signifying nothing."

Is it worth going aside awhile, pulling off the road, to find out where you're going?

10 ¹He left that place and went to the region of Judea and beyond the Jordan. And crowds again gathered around him; and, as was his custom, he again taught them.

²Some Pharisees came, and to test him they asked, "Is it lawful for a man to divorce his wife?" ³He answered them, "What did Moses command you?" ⁴They said, "Moses allowed a man to write a certificate of dismissal and to divorce her."

Marriage and Divorce: VV1-12

V1. *Judea . . . Jordan*: Jesus now moves beyond the river on his way south to Judea and Jerusalem, where his final encounter with evil awaits; ***taught***: No indication of the content.

V2. *Some Pharisees*: Likely the entire trip down the far side of Jordan has ended without note, and they have now crossed it back into Judea; ***to divorce his wife***: The only OT place that treats the topic (Deut 24:1-4) deals with a man who has *already* divorced his wife, who remarries, displeases her *second* husband—who also divorces her. Deuteronomy says the first husband may not *remarry* her. This whole passage reflects the profound male dominance over women in first-century Judaism. A man could put away his wife merely by handing her a piece of paper, because she "displeased" him or he found "something objectionable" about her. Those terms are so vague, experts delighted in debating them, as with Jesus here. No woman had the same recourse. On the other hand, the bill of divorcement did leave her free to marry any (Jewish) man she cared to. A sensitive reading of this apparently inflexible stance by Jesus reveals someone who is defending the inborn rights of women against the overwhelming social conviction that they had none.

V3. *What did Moses?*: Question for question. Jesus knew they themselves already had the answer for the question they asked him; ***command***: Deuteronomy *presumes* the acceptability of divorce. (Cf. the situation of Joseph and Mary in Matt 1:19.) There is no recorded "command" of Moses. There are also nonreligious, civil dangers here, though. After all, John the Baptist lost his head for criticizing Herod Antipas's marriage to his brother's former wife (6:17-19). Recall, too, that the Herodians had made an unusual conspiracy with the Pharisees to bring down Jesus (3:6).

V5. *your hardness of heart*: A recurring theme in the gospel. In Hebrew thinking, the heart was not only the seat of emotions but also the "location" of judgment and understanding. This is in real contrast to the Greek mind-set where legitimate conclusions could be sought only exclusively in the "head," what we know as the strict "scientific method," wherein anything smacking of emotion (loyalty, jealousy, selfishness, compassion, etc.) should be resolutely excluded from any decision worthy to be called "rational." Anything less rigidly restrictive

⁵But Jesus said to them, "Because of your hardness of heart he wrote this commandment for you. ⁶But from the beginning of creation, 'God made them male and female.' ⁷'For this reason a man shall leave his father and mother and be joined to his wife, ⁸and the two shall become one flesh.' So they are no longer two, but one flesh.

⁹Therefore what God has joined together, let no one separate."

¹⁰Then in the house the disciples asked him again about this matter. ¹¹He said to them, "Whoever divorces his wife and marries another commits adultery against her; ¹²and if she divorces her husband and marries another, she commits adultery."

---

would be clouded thinking, "womanish," unworthy of trust. Deuteronomy 24 was not a commandment but a concession to weakness. Clearly—again—"What does the law say?" is not always the same as "What does God say?" In first-century Judaism, marriage was very much a legal arrangement, not entirely unlike buying a cow. Most Jews in Jesus' time took divorce for granted.

V6. *from the beginning*: Jesus implies that every marriage should be as monogamous as Adam and Eve's. He overrides the flimsy Deuteronomy quote with the earlier scriptural example of the original marriage. No one, however, has yet explained satisfactorily where Cain's wife—or the wife of Seth, their third son—came from (Gen 5:4). Nor do many call into obvious question the innumerable examples of polygamy in the OT. Solomon alone had "seven hundred princesses and three hundred concubines" (1 Kgs 11:3). Best to leave sleeping dogs lie.

V8. *two shall become one flesh*: Just as Eve was to Adam "bone of my bones and flesh of my flesh," marriage is a "reunification" of those originally fused, then separated, elements. Any marriage is a union more organic even than the relationship with one's parents. This is the ideal.

V9. *let no one separate*: Not even Moses, whom Jesus corrects here.

V10. *in the house:* Apparently this is private instruction, away from the crowds.

V11. *whoever divorces . . . adultery*: Jesus' ideas on the indissoluble nature of marriage are without parallel in the writings of the rabbis; *against her*: Argues to at least some conviction that—despite the oppressive Hebrew customs—the wife could be illegitimately harmed as well. Unclear if the one against whom the man commits adultery is the first wife or the second.

V12. *if she divorces her husband*: Since a woman instituting divorce proceedings was not allowed in Palestine, Mark must be referring to customs in the wider Roman world. Matthew eases the stricture a bit by adding "except on the ground of unchastity" twice (5:32; 19:9). Paul concluded that it would fulfill Jesus' demand, at least in spirit, for a Christian whose non-Christian spouse had divorced him or her to remarry—a Christian.

¹³People were bringing little children to him in order that he might touch them; and the disciples spoke sternly to them. ¹⁴But when Jesus saw this, he was indignant and said to them, "Let the little children come to me; do not stop them; for it is to such as these that the kingdom of God belongs. ¹⁵Truly I tell you, whoever does not receive the kingdom of God as a little child will never enter it." ¹⁶And he took

---

Despite the apparently inflexible stance of this segment, one has to recall Jesus' own adaptiveness. Never once, in all the gospels, did Jesus ever chastise a sexual sinner—the woman known as a "sinner" (Luke 7:38) or the prodigal son (Luke 15). His light banter with the multiply united Samaritan woman at the well (John 4:7-42) makes no mention of her breaking off her current illegitimate union, and his response to the woman unarguably caught in adultery (John 7:53–8:11) shows him to be nearly casual on the subject: "Has no one condemned you? . . . Neither do I condemn you. Go your way, and from now on do not sin again." Practice > preach.

The function of the church is to heal, not to insist that matters go from bad to worse. It would be inconceivable, for instance, that Jesus would have demanded a battered woman and abused children should stay with a deranged husband. On the other hand, it would be a denial of our origin if the church allowed couples to give up a commitment too quickly or simply because it was not exciting or convenient anymore.

Jesus with Children: VV13-16

V13. *bringing little children*: It was customary to bring children to scribes on the Day of Atonement for a blessing. The disciples object, perhaps because the parents are treating Jesus as no better than a mere scribe; *disciples spoke sternly*: This is commonplace for an "entourage" of personally unimpressive underlings trying to exert an "importance" they don't themselves have.

V14. *was indignant*: The word suggests that there is something more important going on here. The children's parents understand what the Messiah is, far better than Jesus' own disciples. It is important to realize that Jesus never got angry except at the clergy—the temple adherents and his own seminarians-in-training; *kingdom of God belongs*: Because only children, incapable of sin, can call God "Abba" with total confidence. Unlike adults whom experience has made more wary, children are receptive and trusting. What's more, children still have the sense of wonder and awe that is essential even to suspect what a nonmaterialist kingdom might be worth. We must all become "small" before God in order to enter the kingdom. Some scholars consider this as a basis for

them up in his arms, laid his hands on them, and blessed them.

¹⁷As he was setting out on a journey, a man ran up and knelt before him, and asked him, "Good Teacher, what must I do to inherit eternal life?" ¹⁸Jesus said to him, "Why do you call me good? No one is good but God alone. ¹⁹You know the commandments: 'You shall not murder; You shall not commit adultery; You shall not steal; You shall not bear false witness; You shall not defraud; Honor your father and mother.' " ²⁰He said to him, "Teacher, I have kept all these since my youth." ²¹Jesus, looking at him, loved him and said, "You lack one thing; go, sell what

---

infant baptism. It is heavily ironic that in church practice innocent children may not receive the Eucharist; only those who have sinned (and repented).

Unlike today, where our society romanticizes children, in both the Hebrew and the Roman worlds children were very often used as pawns in a marriage game that would profit the families. As with his ideas on divorce, Jesus' ideas on the value of children stood in stark opposition to his society's. Jesus takes the rights of both women and children seriously.

The Seduction of Wealth: VV17-31

V17. *setting out*: Jesus now has his face set resolutely for the encounter in Jerusalem; *eternal life*: Not only in the next world but the enlivening of the Spirit in this life that comes from accepting the new reign of God. Like the word "perfect," it meant wholeness, fulfillment.

V18. *Why do you call me good?*: Puzzling that Jesus seems to take offense at what seems not flattery but a sincere salutation; *No one is good but God alone*: Obviously a figure of speech, or else the word "good" would be meaningless. "God saw everything that he had made, and indeed, it was very good" (Gen 1:31). This puzzling statement stresses that, compared to the goodness of God, all other goods fade to near nothingness.

V19. *defraud*: There is no such commandment in the OT. Mark makes an error that both Matthew and Luke correct by omitting the word when they copy this story.

V21. *Jesus, looking at him, loved him*: Keeping the commandments is enough, whether one keeps them as a Jew or as a Christian. (Cf. C. S. Lewis, *The Abolition of Man*, Appendix, "Illustrations of the Tao," which exemplifies how the Ten Commandments are not an exclusively Hebrew or Christian preserve but are echoed verbally in nearly all world philosophies of life. Similarly, the Golden Rule ["Do unto others . . ."] is also not a matter of Christianity but of human survival.) As Jesus says later in a similar situation (12:34), anyone who lives up to the principles expressed in the Judeo-Christian Decalogue, no

you own, and give the money to the poor, and you will have treasure in heaven; then come, follow me." ²²When he heard this, he was shocked and went away grieving, for he had many possessions.

²³Then Jesus looked around and said to his disciples, "How hard it will be for those who have wealth to enter the kingdom of God!" ²⁴And the disciples were perplexed at these words. But Jesus said to them again, "Children, how hard it is to enter the kingdom of God! ²⁵It is easier for a camel to go through the eye of a needle than for someone who is rich to enter the

---

matter what their religious affiliation, is "not far from the kingdom of God"; *sell what you own*: This invitation goes well beyond the invitation to be a good human being or even a good Christian. It is, in fact, the same invitation given to the apostles: a vocation. Jesus is inviting him to the dependency of the children he spoke of immediately before.

V22. *grieving*: The intensity of the language here does not justify any assertion that the man is less worthy because he is incapable of going further. After all, Jesus already "loved him."

V23. *How hard it will be for those who have wealth*: One cannot read this verse in isolation from the rest of the gospel. Jesus had well-to-do friends—Martha, Mary, Lazarus, Joseph of Arimathea—all of whom seem to have understood and accepted the Good News, and yet had money. The Good Samaritan would have been of little use for the victim in the ditch without money. If those who have "left all" are directed by Jesus to depend on the charity of others (6:8-10), then some members of the community have to retain the means to provide for them. The point of this story is not that riches are evil but that they can shield one from the challenges to the more demanding and fulfilling life Jesus has just offered. The rich are not unwelcome, just more easily diverted. Clearly also, Jesus is not offering poverty merely as some ideal of Spartan self-denial as an end in itself but as a means of streamlining one's life, shedding anything that impedes adaptability for the apostolic mission.

V24. *disciples were perplexed*: They are baffled because the rabbis consistently taught that wealth was a sign of God's favor for a life well lived (Deut 28:1-14)—to say nothing of his disciples' own hopes for this promising "kingdom." They are so brainwashed by what the authorities in their lives have told them that they can't even remember the immediately preceding episode of the children as the only ones who can appreciate the kingdom; *Children*: Even if these disciples have not remotely suspected what Jesus is about, they have truly shown the simplicity and gullibility of children to leave all and follow this stranger.

V25. *for a camel*: No need to look for some gate into Jerusalem called "The Eye of the Needle"; there was none. Jesus is again using both hyperbole and

kingdom of God." ²⁶They were greatly astounded and said to one another, "Then who can be saved?" ²⁷Jesus looked at them and said, "For mortals it is impossible, but not for God; for God all things are possible."

²⁸Peter began to say to him, "Look, we have left everything and followed you."

²⁹Jesus said, "Truly I tell you, there is no one who has left house or brothers or sisters or mother or father or children or fields, for my sake and for the sake of the good news, ³⁰who will not receive a hundredfold now in this age—houses, brothers and sisters, mothers and children, and fields, with persecutions—and in the age

---

paradox to stress not that riches are evil but that they are an obstacle to freedom.

V26. *greatly astounded*: It seems that at this moment they are—momentarily—in danger of understanding just how directly Jesus' intentions conflict with their own intentions. The insight is only momentary; it won't prevent them from future misjudgments.

V27. *but not for God*: An allusion to Genesis 18:14, where barren old Sarah giggles when she overhears that she will have a child who will father a great nation. Just as God can render the barren fruitful, so he can make the rich susceptible to the gospel, as Jesus often did.

V28. *Peter began to say*: Consistently, Peter is the spokesman. Also consistently, he isn't the slightest bit cautious.

V29. *Truly I tell you*: Elsewhere translated as "Amen, I say unto you." Each time, it signals a solemn pronouncement from Jesus. These become more frequent in the latter half of Mark's gospel as we approach the climax and conclusion; ***who has left house***: This is the same kind of self-surrender Jesus spoke of before (8:35), the invitation he gave to the rich man who walked away disheartened.

V30. *a hundredfold*: Elsewhere, all other promises of reward are relegated to the future. As any religious who has given away all and come to follow Jesus knows, this promise, too, is taken literally only by fools. As with our expectations of the kingdom of God and the role of the Messiah, this promise defies our expectations of literal homes and families. It is a different kind of family that Jesus promises; ***brothers, etc.***: This is the "new family" Jesus spoke of when his own family considered him insane (3:35; 4:7, 20). Note that in this second list, "father" is lacking, possibly because there is now only one ultimate Father; ***with persecutions***: A quite unexpected intrusion among so many welcome promises. There is the kicker. Persecution is a reward. There is no stronger mode in which one could see that God's ways are not our ways. This was surely the "reward" Mark's contemporary community was reaping for accepting the kingdom.

to come eternal life. [31]But many who are first will be last, and the last will be first." [32]They were on the road, going up to Jerusalem, and Jesus was walking ahead of them; they were amazed, and those who followed were afraid. He took the twelve aside again and began to tell them what was to happen to him, [33]saying, "See, we are going up to Jerusalem, and the Son of Man will be handed over to the chief priests and the scribes, and they will con- demn him to death; then they will hand him over to the Gentiles; [34]they will mock him, and spit upon him, and flog him, and kill him; and after three days he will rise again."

[35]James and John, the sons of Zebedee, came forward to him and said to him, "Teacher, we want you to do for us what- ever we ask of you." [36]And he said to them, "What is it you want me to do for you?" [37]And they said to him, "Grant us to sit,

---

V31. *first will be last*: This paradox makes sense only if there are two races, each going in the opposite direction from one another: James Bond and Mother Teresa—whoever is first in one race is dead last in the other. The gospel does not ask one to be at the head of either race; it asks only in which direction one is running.

Just as Jesus upended the accepted evaluation of women and children, here—at the opposite end of the social spectrum—he overturns their unques- tioned acceptance of the primacy of wealth in evaluating personal value.

Third Passion Prediction vs. Self-Seeking: VV 32-45

V32. *up to Jerusalem*: Keeping the reader's focus on the ultimate goal; *ahead of them*: Rabbis usually walked ahead of their disciples. Since Jesus takes the Twelve aside, there are more disciples on the journey than merely the apostles; *amazed . . . afraid*: Jesus is saying that he is going up to Jerusalem in order to be crucified. That would cause as much wonderment in any modern Christian as in the apostles and disciples. If "Jerusalem" meant danger for Jesus, it took some courage to stay with him and risk the same fate.

V34. *flog him*: Such explicit details, more abundant than the last two predic- tions, show Mark is "reading back" into his narrative from what he knows after the resurrection, especially: *hand him over to the Gentiles* (V33). But there is no explicit mention of crucifixion, earlier or here. Note: At each of the three passion predictions in Mark, the disciples are resolutely clueless—in 8:31, Peter; in 9:31, the Twelve; here, James and John. The point could hardly be clearer.

V35. *whatever we ask of you*: Childishly, they ask for a "blank check." Their presumption is even more ludicrous, coming as it does immediately after Jesus' preceding speech.

V37. *Grant us to sit*: After all that we have read so far, it is difficult to imagine such "obtuse hearts," unless one is humble enough to admit his or her

one at your right hand and one at your left, in your glory." ³⁸But Jesus said to them, "You do not know what you are asking. Are you able to drink the cup that I drink, or be baptized with the baptism that I am baptized with?" ³⁹They replied, "We are able." Then Jesus said to them, "The cup that I drink you will drink; and with the baptism with which I am baptized, you will be baptized; ⁴⁰but to sit at my right hand or at my left is not mine to grant, but it is for those for whom it has been prepared."

⁴¹When the ten heard this, they began to be angry with James and John. ⁴²So Jesus called them and said to them, "You know that among the Gentiles those whom

---

own double-mindedness. Their thickheadedness is so embarrassing that Matthew blames their grasping for eminence on their mother. In other places, these two are presented specially with Peter. Perhaps he was not asked to come with them on this wheedling expedition because his position had already been established; *in your glory*: More likely they are hankering for a sooner, more tangible splendor than the celestial kingdom. However, such extravagant otherworldly ambitions are not unheard of.

V38. *Are you able to drink the cup?*: A paradoxical symbol: to drink the cup meant both to taste the ultimate bitterness and the ultimate joy; the two are inseparable. In Jesus' agony in the garden while he begged his Father to take away "this cup" (14:24), these men snored; *be baptized*: Again a paradox: to drown and to come back to life. In Romans 6:3, Paul says, "Do you not know that all of us who were baptized into Christ Jesus were baptized into his death?"

V39. *We are able*: It did not take divine insight to see how hollow this self-assurance was. Nevertheless, it is heartening to see what amazing tolerance Jesus has for arrogant foolishness.

V40. *is not mine to grant*: Similarly, in 13:32, Jesus says, "About that day or hour [of the end] no one knows, neither the angels in heaven, nor the Son, but only the Father." In order to be the model for all limited humans, Jesus divested himself of divine knowledge. (Cf. chap. 4, "Jesus' Consciousness of His Divinity.") All the Christian disciple can offer to God is the willingness to suffer for the gospel. Until one forgets about rewards and guarantees, he or she will never make the offering and thus never give God the chance to reward.

V41. *When the ten heard*: Since it is unlikely either the brothers or Jesus told them, it is difficult to see how they found out, unless of course they were given to eavesdropping; *angry*: Since they themselves (9:33-34) were previously arguing among themselves about precisely the same matter, their anger was probably caused not by raising the question but by the brothers beating them to the chance to ask.

V42. *lord it over*: In the Christian community, leadership means the example of service, not coercion or threat of punishment; the Messiah himself is

they recognize as their rulers lord it over them, and their great ones are tyrants over them. ⁴³But it is not so among you; but whoever wishes to become great among you must be your servant, ⁴⁴and whoever wishes to be first among you must be slave of all. ⁴⁵For the Son of Man came not to be served but to serve, and to give his life a ransom for many."

⁴⁶They came to Jericho. As he and his disciples and a large crowd were leaving Jericho, Bartimaeus son of Timaeus, a blind beggar, was sitting by the roadside. ⁴⁷When he heard that it was Jesus of Nazareth, he began to shout out and say, "Jesus, Son of David, have mercy on me!" ⁴⁸Many sternly ordered him to be quiet, but he cried out even more loudly, "Son of David, have mercy on me!" ⁴⁹Jesus stood still and said, "Call him here." And they called the blind man, saying to him, "Take heart; get up, he is calling you." ⁵⁰So throwing off

---

a voluntary servant. Jesus gives quite evident emphasis to this point. Thus, the pope is called "the servant of the servants of God."

V45. *ransom*: Jesus suffers in our place; this verse hearkens back to Isaiah 53: "He was pierced through for our faults . . . he offers his life in atonement." To read such passages as if God the Father were a vindictive banker, however, would be blasphemous. Certainly offering such economic metaphors to explain original sin as irreparable until the death of Jesus—suggesting that God, the Father of the prodigal son, could hold a grudge so long—is indefensible. This is, after all, the God Jesus revealed as demanding that we imperfect humans forgive seventy times seven times (Matt 18:22). Surely, we can expect at least as much from him. One might dare say that Jesus' death undergirds the sacrament of reconciliation, rather than the sacrament of baptism.

Blind Bartimaeus: VV46-52

V46. *Jericho*: About eighteen miles northeast of Jerusalem, in the Jordan Valley.

V47. *Son of David*: Several times in the OT, Yahweh promises David "a house," "a dynasty that will last forever." Jesus is the heir to that promise. They are nearing David's city where Jesus will be enthroned on a gibbet. Mark will mention the relationship again in 12:35-37.

V48. *cried out even more loudly*: Bartimaeus's persistence is evidence of his faith in Jesus, like the faith of Jairus, the Syrophoenician woman, and the men who pried open the roofing.

V50. *throwing off his cloak*: Such concrete specifics suggest testimony of an eyewitness. It also shows a carefree enthusiasm the rich man (10:22) was unable to muster.

his cloak, he sprang up and came to Jesus. ⁵¹Then Jesus said to him, "What do you want me to do for you?" The blind man said to him, "My teacher, let me see again." ⁵²Jesus said to him, "Go; your faith has made you well." Immediately he regained his sight and followed him on the way.

V51. *What do you want*: The same question Jesus asked of James and John when they were finagling for lofty positions—in sharp contrast to Bartimaeus's humble request; *let me see again*: As always, the miracle has not only a physical aspect but a spiritual one as well: Bartimaeus not only wants his physical sight back but also wants to understand the truth, as Yahweh sees truth. Isaiah consistently (29, 35, 61) points to healing the blind as an omen of the new age. It is difficult to avoid the contrast between the sight of this blind beggar and the obtuseness of his disciples.

V52. *followed him on the way*: That is, the road of discipleship; the fact that Mark names him (which we have rarely seen before in a miracle story) suggests Bartimaeus may have continued to be one of the disciples, though he is never mentioned again in the NT. The journey to Jerusalem begins (8:22) and ends (here) with the healing of a blind man. Now that Jesus has reached Jerusalem and the climax of Mark's story, the commands to be silent cease.

Review Questions for Chapter 10

1. How is Jesus' teaching on divorce different from the teaching of rabbis and the attitude of most Americans about divorce? His teaching may seem harsh, but what would be the result if Christians took Jesus' teaching very seriously *before* they got married?
2. For the second time Jesus uses children as models of what a Christian should be. What habitual attitudes do children have that most adolescents and adults feel are somehow "beneath" them?
3. What are Jesus' ideas on wealth? Don't answer too hastily or too one-sidedly.
4. How many occurrences in the last two chapters have echoed in some way the persistent theme of "the first shall be last"?
5. Where has the persistence of Bartimaeus occurred before in Mark's gospel? What does that thematic recurrence say about the attitudes of the ordinary Christian?

For Reflection

(1) *Verse 9.* There is no skirting the fact that Jesus was unyielding in his resistance to divorce. His exception-less insistence on the unbreakable marriage

bond is without any parallel in Jewish thought. But surely there are cases when, judging from the way Jesus handled other such problems, like the adulterous woman, forcing two people to remain in a mutually destructive marriage (not to mention the trauma to children) seems "cruel and unusual punishment." Must they face a lifetime of misery together or celibacy apart for a mistake committed by two young people whose judgment was weakened by blinding romance? The official church recognizes that and will grant annulments to those who, after long scrutiny, seem to be victims of a "marriage" that was not, strictly speaking, a marriage at all.

But today half of new marriages break up. Couples lined up for marriage licenses were asked if they thought this union would last "till death do us part"; 63 percent said no. Perhaps the way Mark quotes Jesus on divorce is too unbending—compared to Jesus' usual compassion. But it does give us pause to reflect on how a sense of commitment has eroded from our lives. What happens to any society when giving your word is relatively meaningless?

(2) *Verse 14.* Jesus says that the kingdom of God belongs to children. But, like the statement about rich people and the camel's eye, where does that leave those of us who are no longer children? What do children have that most of us have lost in the transition of puberty? Vulnerability, awe, dreaminess, wonder at the commonplace—all the things Holden Caulfield resisted surrendering in *Catcher in the Rye.* And children lack all the things Holden fought to avoid, even when he was beginning to drown in it: defensiveness, sophistication, world-weariness. In his word: phoniness.

How could you get back that sense of wonder, of the specialness of the commonplace? Would an occasional walk in the woods, away from the plastic and neon and trumpeting headlines, do some good? When?

(3) *Verse 21.* Many read the story of the rich young man as a kind of accusation, a slap on the wrists to anyone who has been materially successful. If they do, they haven't read it carefully enough. Notice that when the man said that he had obeyed all the commandments since he was a boy, "Jesus, looking at him, loved him." What the man had done was enough, no matter how rich or poor he was. But the man wanted more, so Jesus invited him to leave everything behind as the Twelve had done and become an apostle. This story is not an indictment of wealth; it is an invitation to a religious vocation. And because the man was unable to rise to the challenge, Jesus did not stop loving him.

Jesus had many wealthy friends: the Lazarus family, Nicodemus, Joseph of Arimathea, who did not leave everything and come out on the road with him. Yet Jesus' weeping at Lazarus's tomb proves that he loved them nonetheless.

Wealth is neither good nor bad in itself. What is important is where wealth fits into your scale of values.

(4) *Verse 39.* James and John answer so glibly when Jesus asks if they can drink the cup he is about to drink. Despite the fact that immediately before they make their request Jesus has told them precisely what that "cup" means: "they will mock him, and spit upon him, and flog him, and kill him." Either they weren't really listening to all that disheartening stuff or, with the bravado of youth, they believed they were up to any challenge. Jesus himself called them Boanerges, "Sons of Thunder" (Mark 3:17). Later events proved how hollow their resolve was: the moment a real challenge arose, James and John—who had witnessed the transfiguration—ran for their lives.

But after the enlightenment of Pentecost, when they broke through from this-world sight to the eternal perspective of God, they saw the true meaning of suffering and death: birth pains.

(5) *Verse 48.* Continued suffering either breaks the victim or gives him or her an indomitable courage. Blind Bartimaeus is such a man. The crowd around him try to hush up his embarrassing cries, but that further resistance only made him more resolute. What does he have to lose? What are their petty concerns about what's "acceptable" compared with what he's gone through?

Perhaps that is what Jesus meant when he said, "Blessed are those who mourn." Scar tissue is the toughest. Only those who have suffered know what they can endure. To quote Nietzsche, a source one doesn't often hear quoted favorably in scripture commentaries: "What doesn't kill me makes me stronger."

When you are enduring a challenge that seems unendurable, does that thought ever occur to you?

11 ¹When they were approaching Jerusalem, at Bethphage and Bethany, near the Mount of Olives, he sent two of his disciples ²and said to them, "Go into the village ahead of you, and immediately as you enter it, you will find tied there a colt that has never been ridden; untie it and bring it. ³If anyone says to you, 'Why are you doing this?' just say this, 'The Lord needs it and will send it back here immediately.' " ⁴They went away and found a colt tied near a door, outside in the street. As they were untying it, ⁵some of the bystanders said to them, "What are you doing, untying the colt?" ⁶They told them what Jesus had said; and they allowed

Entry into Jerusalem: VV1-11

V1. *Bethphage and Bethany*: Two villages on the slopes of the Mount of Olives, southeast of the city. Jesus is now closing in on Jerusalem and his destiny. Bethphage means "House of Green Figs." The Mount of Olives and the Temple Mount face each other directly across the Kidron Valley. They can be seen as two opposing fortresses, the Adversary and the Christ. Zechariah writes (14:3-4): "Then the LORD will go forth and fight. . . . On that day his feet shall stand on the Mount of Olives, which lies before Jerusalem on the east"; *olives*: The source of oil, which is used to anoint; "Christ" means "The Anointed One," the Messiah. For this final week, there will be only three backgrounds: the Lazarus home in Bethany, the city, and the Mount of Olives between those two.

V2. *you will find*: It is clear Jesus has prepared for this "triumphal" entry and that there is no longer any need to veil the Messianic Secret. Little mystery to Jesus' foreknowledge if he has made a prior arrangement unknown to the others; ***never been ridden***: Suggesting that, like unblemished animals for ritual sacrifice, it is destined for a religious purpose. The prophet Zechariah also wrote: "Lo, your king comes to you; triumphant and victorious is he, humble and riding on a donkey, on a colt, the foal of a donkey" (9:9). The allusions here to OT prophecy are more meaningful than belaboring the historicity of a certain donkey being on a certain street corner at a verifiable time two thousand years ago. This "Holy Week" will show what kind of messiah Jesus is. This "triumphal" entry—and his rage in the temple in the next episode—give reasons he was executed.

V3. *The Lord*: The Greek word is *kyrios*, a circumlocution for Yahweh, but here most likely Jesus means merely "the Master." If Mark intended that divine meaning, he is reading back into his material from after the resurrection; ***immediately***: Apparently, Jesus' reassurance is enough to settle any anxiety.

VV4-6. *near a door . . . street . . . take it*: Again, such concrete specifics in a narrative otherwise lacking in that kind of details at least suggests an eyewitness.

them to take it. ⁷Then they brought the colt to Jesus and threw their cloaks on it; and he sat on it. ⁸Many people spread their cloaks on the road, and others spread leafy branches that they had cut in the fields. ⁹Then those who went ahead and those who followed were shouting,

"Hosanna!
Blessed is the one who comes in the name of the Lord!
¹⁰Blessed is the coming kingdom of our ancestor David!
Hosanna in the highest heaven!"

V7. *cloaks on it*: In a clumsy, well-meaning way, making the mount something "special."

V8. *spread their cloaks*: An allusion to the OT. When Jehu was anointed king of Israel, the people spread their cloaks under him (2 Kgs 9:13); *spread leafy branches*: An allusion to Psalm 118:27 which exhorts the faithful to "Bind the festal procession with branches" at the approach of Yahweh during the feast of Tabernacles. It is intended to show this is a religious, not a political, occasion. The Romans were ultrasensitive to any hint of insurgence. Passover is a feast of liberation from slavery, thus the crowds were volatile. (Even without a cinematic mob, this is like Martin Luther King's march on Montgomery, Alabama.) Forty years later, just such an upsurge of nationalism brought an all-out war by the occupation forces, the ultimate leveling of the temple, and the dispersion of most Jews for twenty more centuries. It was in the best interests of both the religious and civil authorities to be vigilant against unrest.

V9. *those . . . shouting*: Biblical movies of this scene testify more to the director's budget to impress theater audiences than to the probable historical event. There were "many people," but hardly thousands. Had it been as large as the films show, the Romans would have been all over them before they'd gone ten yards. The size of this "crowd" probably made both civil and religious authorities edgy, but not serious enough to break it up by force; *Blessed is the one*: The word "Hosanna," says literally, "Save us, we pray," a liturgical cheer during the feast of Tabernacles, in homage to the approach of the Messiah to Jerusalem.

V10. *the coming kingdom . . . David*: This is equivalent to a proclamation of Jesus as the heir of David's throne. His idea of the nature of the new kingdom is quite different, however, from the idea of those in the crowd. This is a religious event, not a political one—which is further stressed by Jesus' entry into the temple. It is unclear how much Jesus tolerated such messianic outbursts, although the Messianic Secret is coming closer to the surface. The problem was that everyone concerned—not just the Jewish and Roman authorities but Jesus' own people—misunderstood completely Jesus' nonpolitical intentions. Dorothy Sayers, the scholar-playwright, suggests that this moment "turned"

¹¹Then he entered Jerusalem and went into the temple; and when he had looked around at everything, as it was already late, he went out to Bethany with the twelve.

Judas. She conjectures that Judas had been a Zealot, convinced that the Jews' only hope against the invaders was guerilla warfare. But, she suggests, Jesus completely turned him from political action, and yet here Jesus submits to all this false "majesty." As a result Judas turned Jesus in to the priests out of *love*— "to save him from himself."

V11. *into the temple*: The whole temple area was (roughly) one thousand feet on the north and south sides and fifteen hundred feet on east and west sides, thirty-five acres, larger than thirty football fields, capable of holding four hundred thousand people at festivals. The court of the Gentiles consisted of two huge areas on either side of the central temple enclosures, an island that bisected the temple acreage and was aligned east to west, with its doors opening to the east. This pair of large external courts was porched by marble pillars forty feet tall all around and open even to non-Jews (unlike the central temple). These areas were primarily bazaars, with vendors selling souvenirs, sacrificial animals, food, as well as exchanging Jewish coins for foreign ones (which had on them images of the emperor or of pagan gods). Some used the temple as their bank. The businesspeople crowding those courts were doing nothing *illegal*; the hierarchy were more than willing to offer easement to commercial operations that provided the wherewithal for sacrifices. From time immemorial, the world over, and in every religion, there has never been a lack of those who profiteered from the piety of their coreligionists. Some, in fact, have no religious pretensions themselves.

At its center stood the temple itself, each of whose inner courts was raised above the other by several steps. Within the temple was first a large court allowing females, within which was the court of Israelites for males only. Within that was the court of priests for sacrifices, within which was the innermost room, behind a huge curtain, sixty-five feet high and thirty-five feet wide, the holy of holies, ornamented with gold inside and out, which only the high priest entered, and that only once a year on Yom Kippur to offer sacrifice.

John has Jesus cleansing the temple at the outset of his book, with several other journeys from the countryside to the capital, with plenty of opportunities for opposition to ferment. Matthew and Luke follow Mark with having only one journey.

[12]On the following day, when they came from Bethany, he was hungry. [13]Seeing in the distance a fig tree in leaf, he went to see whether perhaps he would find anything on it. When he came to it, he found nothing but leaves, for it was not the season for figs. [14]He said to it, "May no one ever eat fruit from you again." And his disciples heard it.

[15]Then they came to Jerusalem. And he entered the temple and began to drive out those who were selling and those who

The Fig Tree and the Temple: VV12-19

V12. *the following day*: Presumably the party spent the night with the Lazarus family in Bethany.

V13. *a fig tree*: Fig trees are green at Passover (April), but a Palestinian native like Jesus would know the fruit would not appear until June (***not the season***). Therefore, this event has no real motivation unless taken figuratively—too strong a reaction. The prophets frequently compare Israel to a fig tree cultivated by Yahweh. Micah (7:1): "There is no first-ripe fig for which I hunger," where Yahweh searches for righteous Jews. Jesus is passing God's judgment on a sterile Israel. The point is reinforced by cleansing the temple. That "fig tree" will not nourish again.

V15. *entered the temple*: The prophet Malachi described the approach of Yahweh to a sinful Israel: "He will purify the descendants of Levi [the nation's

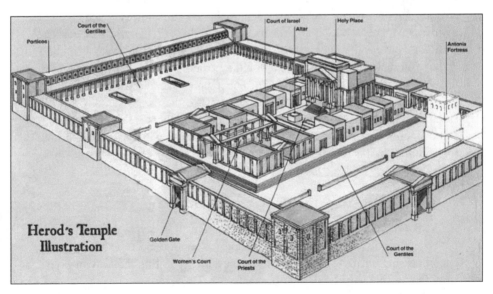

("Herod's Temple Illustration" from *New Interpreter's Bible*, vol. 8, ed. Leander E. Keck [Nashville, TN: Abingdon Press, 1995], 662.)

were buying in the temple, and he overturned the tables of the money changers and the seats of those who sold doves; [16]and he would not allow anyone to carry anything through the temple. [17]He was teaching and saying, "Is it not written,

'My house shall be called a house
of prayer for all the nations'?
But you have made it a den of
robbers."

[18]And when the chief priests and the scribes heard it, they kept looking for a way to kill him; for they were afraid of him, because the whole crowd was spellbound by his teaching. [19]And when evening came, Jesus and his disciples went out of the city.

[20]In the morning as they passed by, they saw the fig tree withered away to its roots. [21]Then Peter remembered and said to him,

---

priests] . . . until they present offerings to the LORD in righteousness" (3:3); **began to drive out**: Hosea writes, "I will drive them out of my house" (9:15). This is an exercise of Messianic authority. The Jesus of this passage is certainly not Jesus meek and mild. There are times when one cannot turn the other cheek; **doves**: For those incapable of purchasing more expensive animals. One can imagine the chaos.

V17. *for all the nations*: Jesus quotes Isaiah 56:7 in which Yahweh promises to welcome foreigners—non-Jews—"for my house shall be called a house of prayer for all peoples." Since Mark was written for Gentiles, and since the episodes of cursing the fig tree and cleansing the temple are a clear rejection of Jerusalem, Jesus is declaring the new kingdom of God to be universal, open to anyone; **den of robbers**: The prophet Jeremiah: "Has this house, which is called by my name, become a den of robbers in your sight?" (7:11). Mark repeats the word *lestes* ironically later at Jesus' arrest (14:48, "as though I were a bandit") and at his crucifixion (15:27, "with him they crucified two bandits").

V18. *looking for a way to kill him*: The temple officials now; **his teaching**: Not merely his commonsense talk, in contrast to the establishment, but his stunning example in regard to their profiting from others' religion. Odd they waited to move, except that in such a vast area, clogged with Passover pilgrims, the commotion may not have been as dramatic as we imagine.

The Third Day: VV20-25

V20. *the fig tree withered*: The tree has not just lost a year of bearing fruit but is dead to the roots. "The Chosen People" is about to become a much more encompassing term. At Jesus' death, the curtain separating the holy of holies from the outside world will be torn open.

V21. *Peter remembered*: A hint that perhaps the disciples are beginning to have some less vague understanding.

"Rabbi, look! The fig tree that you cursed has withered." [22]Jesus answered them, "Have faith in God. [23]Truly I tell you, if you say to this mountain, 'Be taken up and thrown into the sea,' and if you do not doubt in your heart, but believe that what you say will come to pass, it will be done for you. [24]So I tell you, whatever you ask for in prayer, believe that you have received it, and it will be yours. [25]Whenever you stand praying, forgive, if you have anything against anyone; so that your Father in heaven may also forgive you your trespasses."[26]

[27]Again they came to Jerusalem. As he was walking in the temple, the chief priests,

---

V22. *Have faith*: Jesus uses this small event beyond its symbolic value regarding official Jewish religion as a call to a faith that can work unlikely results.

V23. *Truly I tell you:* Again, a signal that what follows is important; ***if you say to this mountain***: Literalists who ignore the hyperbolic tone may herniate their souls to no avail; ***if you do not doubt in your heart***: This promise of the power of prayer demands an inner innocence few can muster.

V24. *believe that you have received*: When those of such crystalline faith pray, the request is as good as done. In this regard, to avoid the disappointment that comes from unanswered prayers, which might threaten what faith one has, it is at the very least prudent not to presume one's faith is of such purity. Moreover, remember that "No" is, in fact, an answer. And also, that Jesus himself prayed with bloody intensity in the garden, but the answer was "No."

V25. *Whenever you stand praying, forgive*: Here Jesus himself suggests an obstacle to fulfillment of prayer that one could carelessly ignore. Is anyone of us so innocent of grudges that we could expect instant gratification from prayer? One need not feel warm affection for those who disrespect us, but one must set them free from the wish for vengeance. An Alcoholics Anonymous adage says, "Resentment is like taking poison and hoping the other guy dies." Though Mark does not quote it in full, this segment suggests his community was familiar with the Our Father: "as we forgive those." St. Paul echoes both elements of Jesus' promise: "If I have all faith, so as to remove mountains, but do not have love, I am nothing" (1 Cor 13:2).

The Authority of Jesus: VV27-33

V27. *Again they came:* Difficult to determine if Mark intends this to be a fourth day; ***walking in the temple:*** Shows a degree of gall, since he so recently trashed it; ***the chief priests . . . elders***: These are the men most responsible for keeping order in Jerusalem and in the temple. After such a ruckus, the remarkable aspect of this incident is the officials' failure to arrest Jesus on the spot. Caiaphas

the scribes, and the elders came to him [28]and said, "By what authority are you doing these things? Who gave you this authority to do them?" [29]Jesus said to them, "I will ask you one question; answer me, and I will tell you by what authority I do these things. [30]Did the baptism of John come from heaven, or was it of human origin? Answer me." [31]They argued with one another, "If we say, 'From heaven,' he will say, 'Why then did you not believe him?' [32]But shall we say, 'Of human origin'?"—they were afraid of the crowd, for all regarded John as truly a prophet. [33]So they answered Jesus, "We do not know." And Jesus said to them, "Neither will I tell you by what authority I am doing these things."

---

was the high priest at the time; Annas was a former high priest. These are an aristocracy who constitute the leadership of the Jewish religion that Jesus has so summarily rejected.

V28. *By what authority*: It is clear that Jesus has gotten their attention by his noisy entry into Jerusalem and cleansing of the temple, but he has no accreditation from the official temple aristocracy. In this segment, he shows that he does not need it, that his power exceeds that of the temple and even of the emperor.

V29. *I will ask you*: Question for question.

V30. *the baptism of John*: Jesus cleverly turns the tables on the authorities: he will justify himself if they answer his question—then he puts them into the dilemma of either condemning themselves for rejecting something from God (John) or condemning John and losing favor with the many who received John enthusiastically as a prophet.

V31. *If we say . . .*: Mark pictures them like a clutch of high-school debaters huddling to find some clever way of avoiding the horns of this dilemma—by no matter what slippery means. They are interested not in the truth but in winning—or at least in not appearing to lose. Thus, they end up deflated and impotent.

V33. *We do not know*: What they are arguing for pits the visible structures and strictures of organized religion against the kingdom of God that John proclaimed to such favorable reception. Mark has been careful throughout to distinguish between the Jewish leaders who fear Jesus and the Jewish people who appreciate him.

Jesus consistently gives evidence that he was charismatic and persuasive enough that, had he wanted to provoke a civil uprising, he probably could have. But he didn't.

Review Questions for Chapter 11

1. How does Jesus' entry into Jerusalem differ from the entry of a victorious general into Rome or the visit of a modern dignitary to a big city?
2. Carefully list and explain each of the elements of the chapter that show Jesus' rejection of Israel—not as a legitimate conduit to God, but rather as God's *privileged* channel of human intervention—and his opening of God's favor to anyone who wishes it.
3. When the powerful people in his religion challenge Jesus' justification for interfering in "their" religion, how does he respond? What does this episode say to the "ordinary Christian"? In the strictest sense, remember, Jesus was a layperson.
4. In what ways was Jesus' "disobedience" like the challenges of Gandhi and Martin Luther King rather than the revolutions of Fidel Castro and Mao Zedong? Is there a point after which provoking civil unrest repels even those who agree with one's criticisms but not one's methods, e.g., Vietnam?

For Reflection

(1) *Verses 6-10.* When Roman generals were brought in triumph into the city of Rome, a slave boy holding the crown of victory over the general's head kept whispering in his ear, *Memento mori!*—"Remember, you are going to die." Death puts our heady triumphs into perspective.

This very crowd that shouts its hosannas at Jesus this Sunday will be crying for his crucifixion on the coming Friday morning. But Jesus doesn't need a boy whispering in his ear; he has an internal voice that keeps his perspective. That shows in the most telling aspect of the scene: he comes riding on an ass, the steed of a poor man—or a fool. There is no pomposity in this man, simply because he keeps his eyes firmly fastened not on surfaces but on substance.

Do you ever find yourself chuckling at the pomposity of the actors and athletes and rock stars who appear on TV talk shows, giving their ill-considered answers to the deepest questions of human life? Except for the notoriety, they're just like the rest of us; they put their socks on one at a time. But do you ever feel a tug of envy that they're "where it's *really* at"?

(2) *Verse 14.* Cursing the fig tree is, as the notes said, meaningless unless it is a symbolic act. Along with the episode that follows, cleansing the temple, it is a definite rejection of Israel as a unique channel of grace into the world. What is sobering about this act—as with the Last Judgment in Matthew 25—is that people *can* be rejected from the fulfillment of the kingdom.

In recent years, there has been a salutary rejection of the judgmental image of an angry God, which held sway for too long in the church. But perhaps the pendulum has swung too far toward a nonjudgmental God who is equivalently a pushover. True, God does love us as helplessly as a mother loves her child nine months before she has even seen it. But God, like the mother, is helpless when the child refuses that love, mocks it, turns away to "do it on his or her own." God does not reject us, but he will bow to our choice if we reject him.

(3) *Verses 15-17.* Pious artists and preachers who emasculate our Savior into "Jesus, the Warm Fuzzy" get their comeuppance here, and in many other places in the gospel. Such people turn the real flesh-and-blood Jesus into a kind of dewy-eyed extraterrestrial who did nothing but smile and look sad. For them, the Good Shepherd has swallowed up the Lion of Judah who said he had come to bring not peace but a sword. Jesus was gentle with the broken, the weak, the sick, but never with the self-righteous. He called the officials of his religion such uncomplimentary (and dangerous) things as "hypocrites," "whitewashed tombs," "nest of vipers." He showed no "proper" deference to wealth and pedigree. He called his own right-hand man, "you Satan." And here in the temple he shows that his divinity did not prevent him from losing his temper!

How much has your image of what Jesus—and therefore the good Christian—"ought" to be been influenced by those pious simplifications? Does rightful wrath in others make you nervous and rightful wrath in yourself seem unthinkable?

(4) *Verse 25.* Perhaps here is a clue to at least some of our unanswered prayers. Jesus says that, when we pray, we should forgive anything we may have against anyone in order for our prayers to be effective. Not that God is the slave of the economic metaphor we have burdened him with: making a list and checking it twice. But asking favors from a God to whom we owe everything—and yet ourselves keeping tight tabs on everybody who owes us—savors a bit too much of double-dealing. We who are in debt up to our ears with God come for yet another handout, resolutely refusing to forgive debts far smaller.

Grudges seem almost self-justifying. How can I be blamed for refusing to forgive someone who hurt me so badly, who perhaps doesn't even want my paltry forgiveness? The point is not what forgiving the perpetrator will do to him or her. The point is what it will do to you.

(5) *Verse 28.* People who have been liberated from an exaggerated concern about their own shortcomings, who realize that their acceptance and missioning from God is justification enough, often tend to rile the feathers of those who depend on their own law-abiding works for justification. "Who are they to stand

up and challenge so much of what we have held sacred all these years? Where is their authorization?"

Power is precious to small minds. Those in charge of the seating arrangements, the bylaws, the blackballing mechanisms have the weapons to keep on top of things, to run things the way they really "should" be run, "God's" way—which has long since become synonymous with "the way *we* want things run." Do you ever feel the temptation to challenge such petty-minded people? Jesus felt it, and yielded to the temptation.

12 ¹Then he began to speak to them in parables. "A man planted a vineyard, put a fence around it, dug a pit for the wine press, and built a watchtower; then he leased it to tenants and went to another country. ²When the season came, he sent a slave to the tenants to collect from them his share of the produce of the vineyard. ³But they seized him, and beat him, and sent him away empty-handed. ⁴And again he sent another slave to them; this one they beat over the head and insulted. ⁵Then he sent another, and that one they killed. And so it was with many others; some they beat, and others they killed. ⁶He had still one other, a beloved son. Finally he sent him to them, saying, 'They will respect my son.' ⁷But those tenants said to one another, 'This is the heir; come, let us kill him, and the inheritance will be ours.' ⁸So they seized him, killed him, and threw him out of the vineyard. ⁹What then will the owner of the vineyard do? He will come and destroy the tenants

---

Parable of the Wicked Tenants: VV1-12

V1. *planted a vineyard*: Isaiah 5:1-5 uses the same allegory of Yahweh as an owner whose vineyard (Israel) refused to bear fruit despite all his efforts, and he thus takes down the hedges and turns the land into pasture. This parable echoes cursing the fig tree and cleansing the temple; *leased it to tenants*: Before AD 65, tracts of land in Palestine were owned by absentee landlords and leased to small farmers for a hefty percentage of the yield.

V2. *a slave*: The many prophets whom the Jews repeatedly maltreated over the centuries.

V3. *seized . . . beat . . . sent him away*: The mission of a prophet is a thankless task (6:4), and the patience of the owner is beyond extraordinary.

V6. *a beloved son*: Jesus. This is the same term Mark has used at Jesus' baptism and transfiguration.

V7. *come, let us kill him*: Exactly the same words used by Joseph's brothers in their jealous rage against their father's favorite (Gen 37:20); *the inheritance will be ours*: If the father has no other heir, the land does not legally revert to the tenants at the owner's death. Having descended this low, they could probably lay claim to it by force.

V8. *killed . . . vineyard*: Jesus will not escape the same treatment Israel gave other prophets. They threw the son out, as the jealous leaders will hurl Jesus out of Jerusalem to his death.

V9. *What . . . will the owner . . . do*: The word "owner" is the Greek *kurios*, which shows that the referent is Yahweh. As usual, the parable is a curveball riddle, a provocation for the audience to figure it out for themselves; *come and destroy*: Had this been an addition of the early church, it might have mentioned the son's return; thus, it is probably Jesus' own answer to his question. The parable's point is that in rejecting Jesus Israel is rejecting her own

and give the vineyard to others. [10]Have you not read this scripture:
'The stone that the builders rejected
has become the cornerstone;
[11]this was the Lord's doing,
and it is amazing in our eyes'?"

[12]When they realized that he had told this parable against them, they wanted to arrest him, but they feared the crowd. So they left him and went away.
[13]Then they sent to him some Pharisees and some Herodians to trap him in what he said. [14]And they came and said to him, "Teacher, we know that you are sincere,

---

birthright; *others*: No justification for restricting this to Gentiles, since most leaders in the early churches were ethnic Jews.

V10. *"The stone . . . rejected"*: Psalm 118:22-23. The metaphor changes from vineyard workers to stone workers; *the stone* (Jesus), misshapen according to their limited viewpoint, is the very keystone of the new Israel: the Christian community.

V11. *amazing*: Even though it seems characteristic of God to bring triumph from failure.

V12. *wanted to arrest him*: It is clear that the temple authorities understand perfectly well what Jesus' message has been since his arrival in Jerusalem.

This parable is the whole scripture in miniature. It places Jesus at the *kairos*, the critical moment in the history of God's dealing with humankind.

Paying Taxes to Caesar: VV13-17

V13. *they sent:* The subject is, presumably, the chief priests, scribes, and elders who probably realize they were the wicked tenants in the previous parable. This also connects to the disposal of the money changers; ***Pharisees and some Herodians***: Again Mark emphasizes that opposition to Jesus spanned the spectrum from the anti-Romans to the Roman collaborators. After this, Pharisees and Herodians make no further appearance in Mark's gospel.

V14. *we know that you are sincere*: Multiple ironies here: they themselves are totally *insincere*; they are trying to prove Jesus is *not* sincere; unbeknownst to them he is completely sincere—like the Roman soldiers who mock Jesus as a "king" (15:18); ***show deference to no one***: A blunted barb, since Jesus shows no deference to the people who sent these hecklers; ***not regard people with partiality***: Thus far in his public life, Jesus has treated rich people and outcasts in exactly the same way; ***taxes to the emperor***: Since AD 6, citizens of Palestine had to pay a census tax. It not only was a yearly reminder of their conquered state but also provoked religious scruples about paying in coins with the image of an emperor the pagan Romans hailed as a god. Deuteronomy 5:8-10 forbade

and show deference to no one; for you do not regard people with partiality, but teach the way of God in accordance with truth. Is it lawful to pay taxes to the emperor, or not? [15]Should we pay them, or should we not?" But knowing their hypocrisy, he said to them, "Why are you putting me to the test? Bring me a denarius and let me see it." [16]And they brought one. Then he said to them, "Whose head is this, and whose title?" They answered, "The emperor's." [17]Jesus said to them, "Give to the emperor the things that are the emperor's, and to God the things that are God's." And they were utterly amazed at him.

[18]Some Sadducees, who say there is no resurrection, came to him and asked him a question, saying, [19]"Teacher, Moses

---

Jews to make an image of anything at all. Worse, the particular coins of the time read: "Tiberius Caesar, son of the *divine* Augustus, great high priest." Thus, it was an unsettling breach of their religion to have to carry such images around with them. But when religious belief threatens one's ability to do business, utilitarian motives often prevail.

V15. *Should we pay them*: They think they have Jesus trapped: If he says "pay," he upsets those who hate the Romans; if he says "refuse," he risks arrest as a rebel; *Bring me a denarius*: A workman's daily wage. Implies that Jesus himself carries none. All coins were considered property of the emperor; thus, if Jesus' antagonists were carrying these images, they themselves were implicitly admitting the power of the emperor and carrying images that called the emperor's father "divine" and called him "great high priest."

V17. *Give to the emperor*: The state has legitimate expectations even of Christians, unless they genuinely conflict with God. This, of course, was edited during the persecution of Nero.

Resurrection Debate: VV18-27

V18. *Some Sadducees*: An aristocratic, priestly sect more conservative than Pharisees, fiercely protective of priestly privileges. They denied any transcendent, other-worldly dimension to human life, including an afterlife. Caiaphas, the high priest who will condemn Jesus, was probably a Sadducee; *no resurrection*: The first Hebrew affirmation of this belief occurs in Isaiah 14:11 (ca. 747–736 BC). It did not become common until later; see Daniel 12:2 (ca. 165 BC) and Wisdom 5:1-16 (first century BC). Resurrection is *the* validation of Jesus (1 Cor 15:14).

V19. *Moses wrote*: Deuteronomy 25:5-6 orders that a childless widow must marry her brother-in-law and their first child must bear her first husband's name so that his heir might give him a kind of immortality; no doubt there were also some considerations about not letting land and goods escape the family control. If the man adamantly refused this duty, the widow could pull off the man's sandal

wrote for us that 'if a man's brother dies, leaving a wife but no child, the man shall marry the widow and raise up children for his brother.' ²⁰There were seven brothers; the first married and, when he died, left no children; ²¹and the second married the widow and died, leaving no children; and the third likewise; ²²none of the seven left children. Last of all the woman herself died. ²³In the resurrection whose wife will she be? For the seven had married her."

²⁴Jesus said to them, "Is not this the reason you are wrong, that you know nei-

ther the scriptures nor the power of God? ²⁵For when they rise from the dead, they neither marry nor are given in marriage, but are like angels in heaven. ²⁶And as for the dead being raised, have you not read in the book of Moses, in the story about the bush, how God said to him, 'I am the God of Abraham, the God of Isaac, and the God of Jacob'? ²⁷He is God not of the dead, but of the living; you are quite wrong."

²⁸One of the scribes came near and heard them disputing with one another, and seeing that he answered them well, he

in the presence of the elders, spit in his face, and shed him—to his permanent disgrace. There was seemingly no scruple if he was already married.

V20. *There were seven brothers*: The example is so far-fetched it sounds like the kind of tortuous example a brainy and bored sophomore boy might pose to trap a confident teacher. "If God is all-powerful, can God make a rock so heavy he can't lift it?"

V23. *In the resurrection*: Since the Sadducees disbelieved in resurrection, the question is cynical—and unanswerable. They are questioning both the scriptures (Isaiah) and the power of God (to raise the dead if he chooses). Once again, Jesus is warning about expecting God to follow humanly limited formulas. For Paul on resurrection, see 1 Corinthians 15:35-50.

V25. *they neither marry*: The Sadducees try to limit reality to the reality they themselves are capable of understanding and manipulating. Here, Jesus sides with the Pharisees.

V26. *I am the God of Abraham*: Jesus argues that, on the testimony of Yahweh himself, the dead do continue to live. The argument is a bit shaky, since the passage quoted could have been intended as meaning "I am the same God Abraham worshiped," in the past tense. But it is sufficient to dismiss the Sadducees. Nothing said about the afterlife of the wicked.

The Greatest Commandment: VV28-34

V28. *One of the scribes*: At last someone from the ruling religious groups who seems sincere; **Which commandment is the first**: Some combed the Torah and found 613 commandments, and rabbis for generations rightly argued over which were "light" or "heavy" and struggled to find which was the "root" commandment from which all others sprang.

asked him, "Which commandment is the first of all?" [29]Jesus answered, "The first is, 'Hear, O Israel: the Lord our God, the Lord is one; [30]you shall love the Lord your God with all your heart, and with all your soul, and with all your mind, and with all your strength.' [31]The second is this, 'You shall love your neighbor as yourself.' There is no other commandment greater than these." [32]Then the scribe said to him, "You are right, Teacher; you have truly said that 'he is one, and besides him there is no other'; [33]and 'to love him with all the heart, and with all the understanding, and with all the strength,' and 'to love one's neighbor as oneself,'—this is much more important than all whole burnt offerings and sacrifices." [34]When Jesus saw that he answered wisely, he said to him, "You are not far from the kingdom of God." After that no one dared to ask him any question.

V29. *Hear, O Israel*: Deuteronomy 6:4-5, the Shema, which devout Jews recite three times every day.

V30. *love the Lord . . . all your strength*: This is the "root" commandment, and since God is one, our love for him must be undivided. The piling-up of parts of the person emphasizes the totality of one's submission. Cf. Abraham and Isaac. Quite likely "mind" was added to the original to reflect the growing community's interaction with a more intellectual Greek audience.

V31. *love your neighbor*: Leviticus 19:18 commanded that Jews love other Jews. Even before Jesus, students of the Torah believed that command extended at least to *resident* aliens, like Palestinians in Israel today. Jesus' parable of the Good Samaritan (Luke 10:29-37) shows that the content of "neighbor" is unlimited. This double-rooted command is found in innumerable places throughout the OT, but Jesus seems the first to streamline it so clearly into a single moral principle; ***as yourself***: Some readers seem to misread the commandment to say that one must love the neighbor *more* than oneself. Pagan Pythagoras put it: "What is a friend? Another I."

V33. *heart . . . sacrifices*: The scribe acknowledges that fulfilling ritual without personal involvement and commitment doesn't "fool God" (cf. Matt 22:11-14). He seems to resonate with Jesus' conflicts so far with the spirit of the law and the rigidity of formal Judaism. Perhaps too fine a point: Mark has the Jewish scribe substitute the word *synesis* ("understanding") for the more rational *dianoia* ("mind"). The analytical, academic, Greek "knowing" is more heady than the Hebrew, experiential, "gut" sense, as in "He knew his wife." The only thing the scribe has added while repeating what Jesus has said, however, is the superiority of loving over ritual sacrifices. Only that would seem to justify Jesus' praise of the scribe's "wise" answer.

V34. *You are not far*: But there is still one last step: accepting Jesus as Lord.

35While Jesus was teaching in the temple, he said, "How can the scribes say that the Messiah is the son of David? 36David himself, by the Holy Spirit, declared,

'The Lord said to my Lord,

"Sit at my right hand,
    until I put your enemies under
        your feet." '

37David himself calls him Lord; so how can he be his son?" And the large crowd was listening to him with delight.

The Messiah and David: VV35-37

V35. *Jesus was teaching in the temple*: Again, since at his last appearance there Jesus raised havoc in the temple, this shows more than a measure of *chutzpah*; *the Messiah is the son of David*: This is a literalist statement, meaning a political Messiah who has a direct bloodline back to David, and hence a legitimate pretender to the literal throne of Israel. The same literalism has been applied to legitimate successors to St. Peter.

V36. *David himself . . . declared*: At the time of Jesus, all believed that King David was the original author of all the psalms; Psalm 110:1: "The LORD said to my lord." The Jews of Jesus' day did not pronounce the divine name, "Yahweh," but substituted the circumlocution, "Adonai," which is literally "my lords," a plural form used only for God; *by the Holy Spirit*: At the time of Jesus, the common belief was not only that David composed all the psalms (just as they believed Moses composed the first five OT books: the Torah), but also that he (and Moses) did so under the direct influence of God, thus unchallengeably; *Sit at my right hand*: The image is Yahweh inviting David the king to sit in the most privileged place in heaven after God

V37. *David . . . calls him Lord*: Jesus insinuates the Messiah is something far more than merely a human descendant of David, if David the supposed author of the psalm explicitly declares his inferiority to the final Messiah. Therefore, Jesus would have an even more exalted place than the greatest Hebrew king. Mark is suggesting that neither "Messiah" nor "Son of David" is a completely adequate way of describing the real identity of Jesus. In fact, he shares with Yahweh the title of *kurios*, "Lord," in a more intense way than any other human being. It is also quite clear that, contrary to any fears the Romans might have, Jesus is "beyond" any desire for mere political power. The kind of "lordship" Jesus claims will survive even degradation.

Even today, the British accept the title "my lord" (even for some who are quite short of being personally noble), yet they use the word in a quite different way when they say, "Bless us, O Lord, and these thy gifts." Early Christians faced a similar problem when the emperor was routinely called "Lord."

[38]As he taught, he said, "Beware of the scribes, who like to walk around in long robes, and to be greeted with respect in the marketplaces, [39]and to have the best seats in the synagogues and places of honor at banquets! [40]They devour widows' houses and for the sake of appearance say long prayers. They will receive the greater condemnation."

[41]He sat down opposite the treasury, and watched the crowd putting money into the treasury. Many rich people put in large sums. [42]A poor widow came and put in two small copper coins, which are worth a

---

The Scribes and the Poor Widow: VV38-44

V38. *scribes*: Again, these men not only read and wrote for the illiterate but also drew up legal contracts. What's more, since their only book was the scripture (which also was the repository of all laws), they were also theologians; *walk around in long robes*: They wore the *tallith* or prayer shawl outside religious occasions, making show of their piety, as if a bishop or priest walked the streets in liturgical dress.

V39. *best seats*: The reason for libraries is that human nature hasn't changed much over the centuries.

V40. *devour widows' houses*: Lawyers who "advertised" themselves publicly were more likely to be appointed trustees for women who (by rigid custom) were kept ignorant of "the ways of the world." Even their prayers are a form of preying. Jesus accuses the scribes not only of hypocrisy but also of money gouging. He made such accusations, to be sure, but the intensity of *tone* could well come from Mark and reflect a reaction against persecution of Christians by official Jewry in the empire. Still, Mark's anger is mild compared with Matthew's, which takes an entire chapter (23) in his version. This diatribe is clearly a setup to contrast with the next story. These two episodes are a stark contrast between two very different kinds of "religious" persons.

V41. *the treasury*: The Jerusalem temple was, in fact, also a bank—as were Roman temples. But also around the two huge porticoes on either side of the temple itself were thirteen trumpet-shaped collection boxes. Larger coins would of course make more noise going in.

V42. *poor widow*: Most widows had to depend on children or charity; thus the OT consistently urges care for them; *two small copper coins . . . worth a penny*: The tiniest coins in circulation in Palestine, each 1/64 of a laborer's daily wage. The explanation is evidence of its composition for a Roman audience.

V43. *Truly I tell you*: That solemn formula we have seen before indicates that this pronouncement of Jesus carries much more weight than this commonplace event suggests; *put in more*: This requires no superhuman knowledge.

penny. ⁴³Then he called his disciples and said to them, "Truly I tell you, this poor widow has put in more than all those who are contributing to the treasury. ⁴⁴For all of them have contributed out of their abundance; but she out of her poverty has put in everything she had, all she had to live on."

The woman was dressed in obviously poor clothing and her tiny coins make only a little tinkle in the receptacle.

V44. *everything she had*: The story is a pitiful one if taken literally: the woman has impoverished herself—to give to the money-gouging scribes just mentioned—and will surely die, or end up having to depend on the charity of others. Figuratively, however, the story is used here to say that, although Israel seems resolutely hardened against the message of God in the person of Jesus, there is some hope. Also, it is a small foreshadowing of Jesus' own total self-giving.

It would be unfair—not to mention un-Christian—to infer that all scribes were unprincipled hypocrites. Mark has already shown us an honest one (12:28-34). Judging from the formal construction of his book, it is quite possible that the author of Matthew had been a scribe. It would be even more unprincipled to accuse the entire Jewish nation of the death of Jesus because of one verse in Matthew's gospel (27:25). An unchallengeable stance of Jesus was refusing to condemn entire classes of individuals.

Similarly, it would be an unjustifiable wrenching of Mark's intention here to read the story of the widow as an example of organized religion's cynical manipulation of a gullible woman rather than as the obvious contrast between charity "with a hidden agenda" and openhearted generosity.

Review Questions for Chapter 12

1. List all the elements of this chapter that again repeat the themes of Jesus' rejection of official Judaism and the Jews' narrow vision compared to that of God.
2. Jesus refuses to specify which things are "the emperor's" and which things are "God's." Many people consistently ask a similar question about all kinds of moral issues: "How far can I go?" What does that imply about their relationship with God? Does anyone ask that question about dealings with a friend—much less with a Father? What comment does the generous widow make on that mind-set?
3. Have you ever known people who ask of their teachers the same kind of question that the Sadducees ask Jesus? Was their motive in asking their questions to find the truth or to achieve something else?

4. Jesus is remarkably empathic with sinners who fall because of weakness, but there is one sin he seems to have no empathy for: hypocrisy. Why?

For Reflection

(1) *Verse 9.* Like the episodes in the previous chapter, this parable is yet another statement of the opening of the kingdom to non-Jews as well. Though that might have some historical interest and theological significance, it has little to do with our ordinary lives. But like many of the parables about masters and stewards, it is an occasion for us to reflect on our own stewardship of our own little plots in the garden—and God's expectations of us.

Reading such parables, good people can feel inadequate to their Christian mission, wasting a great deal of valuable time and energy moaning over how disappointed God must be in their measly harvests, giving themselves no legitimate credit for what they have in fact been able to do for the kingdom, with what they had, at the time. We forget that God is not like us: grudge-bearing, perfectionist, nitpicking, thin-skinned, impatient for tangible results. Look at the vastness of the universe; against that background, don't our petty nastinesses assume a more realistic size?

(2) *Verse 17.* The history of the church is kernelled in this one verse: a cavalcade of persecution by Caesar, or unworthy collaboration from the church—and even attempts to dominate the civil government, crusades, the Inquisition. The conflict still exists in our day in the petty bickerings of whether Christmas cribs can be erected on courthouse lawns. (But what would happen if Christmas were no longer an official holiday?)

It is not so easy to separate what is the emperor's and what is God's. Should a Catholic elected official be forced to follow the will of his church rather than the will of those who elected him or her? Should a Christian protest that his or her taxes go to support repressive governments or build more armaments than it would take to blow up twenty planets the size of ours? The issues grow so complex that we merely throw up our hands and let "them" see to it. Can a Christian legitimately do that?

(3) *Verse 31.* Jesus says that the only other commandment beyond loving God is loving the neighbor "as you love yourself." First, if many of us gave to others the grudging love we give ourselves, there'd be precious little love of the neighbor around! Second, what does "love" even mean? Not palpitations of the heart, surely; that's just romance, being in love. Love is an act of the will; it takes over when the feelings fail, when the beloved is no longer even likable. Love is the wish that the other person grow, even at some cost to myself. That is what Jesus

means. Third, Jesus does not say we should love others *more* than we love ourselves. He does not expect us to impoverish ourselves for the poor or to kowtow to bullies or to turn the other cheek when a real injustice occurs.

Do you honestly respect yourself to the same degree and with the same justification as you respect your relatives and friends? Do you forgive yourself as readily as you forgive them? Someone wise once wrote that we ought to be very subjective about others and very objective about ourselves. Are you?

(4) **Verse 38.** Jesus warns us to watch out for teachers of the law. By that he wasn't condemning all attorneys! What he was condemning was people whose *only* norm was laws and rules, and especially those whose single-minded adherence to the law had given them the false conviction that they had achieved holiness: wholeness. Such people operate sheerly through their analytical left brains; they have no hearts. They make a ritual of their piety and yet hold everyone else for downs, which proves that their piety is merely surface, not heartfelt.

Something inside us resents that, longs for a speedy comeuppance for hypocrites, which is why we take such delight in hissing the villain when he is trapped and guffawing when the pompous folk step on the banana peels. But a subtler soul can see that such pious hypocrites have already been punished. Their punishment is to be soulless, heartless, loveless.

(5) **Verse 44.** Jesus obviously admired the wholehearted generosity of this widow—in stark contrast to the doctors of the law he spoke of immediately before. But something hard-nosed, perhaps "American," surely insufficiently redeemed, makes us wonder what's going to happen to this woman who has so totally impoverished herself. Will she become just one more welfare widow? Poach on her son and daughter-in-law?

The gospel statement that comes closer to the sanctity most of us can aspire to is: "If you have two coats and your brother or sister has none, give them one of your coats." If you give *both*, there will just be one more person out begging for still another coat!

13 ¹As he came out of the temple, one of his disciples said to him, "Look, Teacher, what large stones and what large buildings!" ²Then Jesus asked him, "Do you see these great buildings? Not one stone will be left here upon another; all will be thrown down."

³When he was sitting on the Mount of Olives opposite the temple, Peter, James, John, and Andrew asked him privately, ⁴"Tell us, when will this be, and what will be the sign that all these things are about to be accomplished?" ⁵Then Jesus began to say to them, "Beware that no one leads you

---

The Day of Fulfillment: VV1-37

V1. *one of his disciples*: This is a private lesson, not one for the crowds; *what large stones and what large buildings*: Herod the Great undertook the reconstruction of the temple about 20 BC. It was fully completed in only AD 63, six years before the Romans reduced it to rubble. The Wailing Wall in Jerusalem is one of the only large parts remaining today. The Roman historian Josephus (AD 37–100) described it: "covered all over with plates of gold of great weight, and, at the first rising of the sun, reflected back a very fiery splendor, and made those who forced themselves to look upon it to turn their eyes away." Despite Jesus' warnings about the seductions of riches, the country boys from Galilee can't help but be in awe at the splendor of the temple's wealth.

V2. *Not one stone*: Hyperbole; there is nothing to indicate that Mark was aware of the literal destruction of the temple in 70, but he could have been. Jesus' statement is symbolic of the fact that Judaism and Jerusalem and their temple will cease to be the privileged place of worship.

V3. *Mount of Olives*: Again, the association with oil and the Anointed One, and again the Temple Mount and the Messiah's Mount stand in opposition to one another like two opposing fortresses. The prophet Zechariah (14:4): "On that day his [Yahweh's] feet shall stand on the Mount of Olives"; *Peter . . . Andrew*: The first four apostles called.

V4. *when will this be*: The two questions are addressed to the specific case of the temple's destruction, but Jesus' answer broadens the perspective to the destruction of the world.

V5. *Beware*: This passage is apocalyptic in style, like nonobjective or surrealistic painting. It is always overabundant with hyperbole, an almost exclusively "underground" literature written with symbols meaningful only to those in on the "code." Therefore, it is frequently filled with exhortations to caution. This is Jesus' longest speech in Mark's gospel.

astray. ⁶Many will come in my name and say, 'I am he!' and they will lead many astray. ⁷When you hear of wars and rumors of wars, do not be alarmed; this must take place, but the end is still to come. ⁸For nation will rise against nation, and kingdom against kingdom; there will be earthquakes in various places; there will be famines. This is but the beginning of the birthpangs.

⁹"As for yourselves, beware; for they will hand you over to councils; and you will be beaten in synagogues; and you will stand before governors and kings because of me, as a testimony to them. ¹⁰And the

---

V6. *I am he*: Charlatans claiming to be Jesus come back to begin the end. Jesus is recommending calm discernment instead of panic in the face of the unheard of. Those words are also the translation of "Yahweh."

V7. *rumors of wars*: Of course, many of the signs of the end given here have been constant occurrences throughout human history; ***this must take place***: As in most apocalyptic literature, the view of history here is deterministic: that is, there is no need for the good to fear, since a good and just God is working out his will in history.

V8. *birth pangs*: Many of the prophets used this same metaphor for the preparations for the Day of Yahweh. Note that, although childbirth pains are agonizing, they are the price of something new and far better than before. Moreover, if the listeners face the pain calmly, like a woman prepared to accept them, it will not be as bad—since useless worry doubles the pain.

V9. *synagogues . . . governors*: Symbolizing both the Jews ("synagogues"), who considered converted Jews worse than dead, and the Gentiles ("governors"), who considered Christians disloyal to the empire, since they would not serve in the army, which required an oath on the divinity of the emperor and sacrifice to him as a god. These two predictions were being lived out as Mark wrote, but they are also foreshadowing Jesus' own fate, betrayed by one of his own, denied by another, then appearing before the Jewish Sanhedrin and before the Roman Pilate. St. Paul testifies to the power of synagogues even over converted Christian Jews: "Five times I have received from the Jews the forty lashes minus one" (2 Cor 11:24).

V10. *good news must first be proclaimed*: Although in Mark's time, belief in a literal end very soon was beginning to wane, there was still a strong belief in many that it would happen any day; ***all nations***: That is, the Gentiles. Any modern doomsayer using Mark to show that all these signs are *now* being fulfilled has to cope with the fact that there are still many, many Gentiles who have not yet heard the gospel. This qualification could likely be a later insertion by Mark—to cope with the failure of the end-time to occur. Also, if Jesus had been this dramatically explicit about the dependence of the end on universal

good news must first be proclaimed to all nations. [11]When they bring you to trial and hand you over, do not worry beforehand about what you are to say; but say whatever is given you at that time, for it is not you who speak, but the Holy Spirit. [12]Brother will betray brother to death, and a father his child, and children will rise against parents and have them put to death; [13]and you will be hated by all because of my name. But the one who endures to the end will be saved.

[14]"But when you see the desolating sacrilege set up where it ought not to be (let the reader understand), then those in Judea must flee to the mountains; [15]the one on the

---

conversion, it would be difficult to explain early churches' controversies about admitting Gentile converts (Acts and Paul's letters, *passim*).

V11. *do not worry beforehand*: Continuing the exhortation to calm confidence. Like most Christians today, defending one's faith in public would be intimidating, as any believer trapped into a college debate on religion can attest. Or consider the unschooled Joan of Arc forced to defend her beliefs against learned, ordained clerics of her own religion; ***Holy Spirit***: They will not endure persecution alone. If they maintain their faith, they will know that the Spirit of the risen Jesus will be with them. Like any disaster, this event shows what is *really* important.

V12. *Brother will betray brother*: Jesus' family treated him in the same way (3:31; 6:1-6). Within the week, his own disciples will run from him. In Mark's time, nonconvert Jews were turning in members of their own families whom they believed to be blasphemers and traitors. In his *Annales*, Tacitus calls them "Christians, hated for shameful deeds," among them the report that the Mass was a form of cannibalism, since it meant eating the Body of Christ.

V13. *you will be hated*: The "you" refers not just to Jesus' listeners but to Mark's as well; ***will be saved***: The apocalyptic contrast shows this means "ultimate salvation" rather than momentary rescue from a temporary threat.

V14. *the desolating sacrilege*: The object in question was both detestable and devastating; an allusion back to the OT book of Daniel, in which, under apocalyptic symbols, the author describes the erection of a pagan statue by the Seleucid emperor in 167 BC in the innermost room of the Jewish temple, the holy of holies, to show the Jews that they had no choice but to submit to pagan religion; ***where it ought not to be***: The "sacrilege" is neuter in Greek, but the subject of this "ought" is masculine: "where *he* ought not to be." Therefore, Mark likely refers to plans of the Emperor Caligula in AD 40 to have such a statue of himself erected in the same place, for the same purpose; ***(let the reader understand)***: Typical apocalyptic style, suggesting that only those in on the code—i.e., know the book of Daniel—will comprehend.

V15. *enter the house*: Presumably because it would collapse on top of him. Many of the signs and many of the concrete warnings here are taken from Jew-

housetop must not go down or enter the house to take anything away; [16]the one in the field must not turn back to get a coat. [17]Woe to those who are pregnant and to those who are nursing infants in those days! [18]Pray that it may not be in winter. [19]For in those days there will be suffering, such as has not been from the beginning of the creation that God created until now, no, and never will be. [20]And if the Lord had not cut short those days, no one would be saved; but for the sake of the elect, whom he chose, he has cut short those days. [21]And if anyone says to you at that time, 'Look! Here is the Messiah!' or 'Look! There he is!'—do not believe it. [22]False messiahs and false prophets will appear and produce signs and omens, to lead astray, if possible, the elect. [23]But be alert; I have already told you everything.

[24]"But in those days, after that
   suffering,
   the sun will be darkened, and
   the moon will not give its light,
[25]and the stars will be falling from
   heaven,

---

ish apocalyptic literature describing "the great tribulation." So too is the hope that the provident Yahweh will shorten the length of the suffering for the sake of his beloved ones. But *where* can they flee *to?*

V18. *winter*: The Palestine rainy season lasts from October to April.

V19. *creation . . . created*: One constant in Mark's unsophisticated style is such needless repetition.

V20. *if the Lord . . . cut short*: Awkward, since the only plan God could cut short is one God had himself already laid out. God changing his mind? And the next clause repeats it, just as in "*the elect . . . he chose.*" Some Protestant reformers made much of this unexplainable favoritism to a preordained few. The thorny, knotted, frustrating—and eventually insoluble—conflict between predestination and free will is too complex for these pages (and quite likely for our lifetime).

VV21-23. *Here is the Messiah*: The form and content of verses 21-23 are very similar to verses 5-8. The consistent message of this long passage is "Stay confidently calm!" That message is still meaningful today, when countless fake messiahs *produce signs and omens* and promise all kinds of temporary "fulfillment." One acid test is: What's in it for the messiah? We may have (justifiably) shed ourselves of the simplicities surrounding the symbol of "Satan" (horns, tail, sulfur), but that hardly justifies the delusion that an Antagonist-force no longer exists.

VV24-25. *sun . . . moon . . . stars*: (Cf. Isa 13:10.) In "those days" before the final days (verses 17-20), the signs were all earthly: wars, earthquakes, famines. Now they are cosmic, using hyperbole lifted from apocalyptic OT books like Daniel and Zechariah.

V25. *powers in the heavens will be shaken*: Whatever astrological powers the planets reputedly had would be neutered by the power of the almighty God.

157

and the powers in the heavens
will be shaken.
²⁶Then they will see 'the Son of Man coming in clouds' with great power and glory.
²⁷Then he will send out the angels, and
gather his elect from the four winds, from
the ends of the earth to the ends of heaven.

²⁸"From the fig tree learn its lesson: as
soon as its branch becomes tender and puts
forth its leaves, you know that summer is
near. ²⁹So also, when you see these things
taking place, you know that he is near, at the
very gates. ³⁰Truly I tell you, this generation
will not pass away until all these things have

V26. *Son of Man coming in clouds*: A direct allusion to Daniel 7:13 in which the Son of Man is summoned to the Ancient of Days (Yahweh) to inherit his kingdom, a new heaven and a new earth. In all apocalyptic gospel sections about the end of the world, many readers fail to see that the tribulations they describe are temporary, like the waters of the Great Flood at the time of Noah or the Jews' forty tormented years in the desert, and that God would then begin the whole grand experiment over again. The image will recur in Jesus' Jewish trial (14:62).

V27. *ends of the earth . . . heaven*: A new beginning not only for the living but also for the dead.

V28. *fig tree*: The reader knows how to read the signs of the seasons; he or she should learn to read the signs of the times. Fig leaves are a sign winter is over and summer is near.

V29. *when you see*: Easy to forget that "you" means only the four disciples mentioned in 13:3 (Peter, James, John, Andrew), not the full twelve or a crowd; *these things*: That is the prelude, events signaling the coming of the Son of Man and the vindication of the "elect"; *you know*: With the same sureness you know fig leaves portend summer; *at the very gates*: With the same decisive presence as an invading army.

V30. *Truly I tell you*: The signal for another solemn declaration; *this generation will not pass away*: The only reasonable explanation for the term "generation" is the people of Jesus' approximate age. Therefore, "all these things" should occur by about the time Mark is writing. The great problem is that the generation to whom Jesus was speaking did *not* see the literal end of the world. Therefore, unless Jesus was a charlatan, the meaning of "the coming of the Son of Man and the vindication of the 'elect'" must have meant something less dramatic than a literal enactment of these apocalyptic scenes. Beneath the apocalyptic veil, then, he must have been talking about some other "earth-shattering" experience: the birth of the new kingdom of God. Like the angels in the Bethlehem skies, these "special effects" are symbolic—since "no one knows the hour" and since "the good news must be proclaimed to all nations."

taken place. ³¹Heaven and earth will pass away, but my words will not pass away.

³²"But about that day or hour no one knows, neither the angels in heaven, nor the Son, but only the Father. ³³Beware, keep alert; for you do not know when the time will come. ³⁴It is like a man going on a journey, when he leaves home and puts his slaves in charge, each with his work, and commands the doorkeeper to be on the watch. ³⁵Therefore, keep awake—for you do not know when the master of the house will come, in the evening, or at midnight, or at cockcrow, or at dawn, ³⁶or else he may find you asleep when he comes suddenly. ³⁷And what I say to you I say to all: Keep awake."

V31. *Heaven and earth will pass away*: Obviously, "heaven" means the visible stars and planets, not the abode of God, who can't pass away.

V32. *that day or hour*: Thus, the need for vigilance; *nor the Son*: Jesus has already told the Zebedee brothers (10:40) that he doesn't know who will sit beside him in the new kingdom. (Recall chap. 4, "Jesus' Consciousness of His Divinity.") Mark was writing only thirty years after the events he was describing. He did not have the benefit of two thousand years of theologizing to understand the nature of the Son or of the relationship between the Son and the Father. It would take hundreds of years—and more than a few general councils of the church—to formulate (still inadequate) answers to those questions.

V33. *Beware, keep alert*: Ironic that three of these men specially chosen to hear this prophecy would also be specially chosen to witness Jesus' agony. And they fell asleep.

V34. *like a man . . . journey*: The parable concludes the teaching on the end and embodies the frequent exhortations to vigilance, not only in the face of the end but also in the face of death; *doorkeeper*: The theme of watchfulness joins this small parable with the preceding.

V35. *you do not know when*: Although fear of being caught out is not the most laudable motive, it is quite often the only effective one; *evening . . . dawn*: Palestinians divided the night into three watches; here Mark uses the fourfold division used by his readers in Rome.

V36. *he may find you asleep*: All analogies limp, even parables. Within the limits of the story, no master could expect a servant to stay wide awake 24/7, and yet some overly zealous Christians believe that the loving God expects them never to relax. Every instant must be stiff with apprehension of entrapment. That is hardly the God manifested by Jesus in his life.

V37. *I say to all*: The perspective goes far beyond a warning to just those four in Jesus' immediate audience or even just to the Jews of Palestine, but to Christians of all ages.

Mark's "Little Apocalypse" (contrasted to the book of Revelation, the Great Apocalypse) is copied in Matthew 24–25 and Luke 21. Jesus delivers it on the

Mount of Olives where the OT predicted Yahweh will begin his final assault. The next two chapters will be his passion and death.

Apocalyptic is the name given to a densely symbolic kind of prophecy that depends very heavily on the audience's knowledge not only of its patterns of seemingly bizarre symbols—numbers, animals, cosmic phenomena, visions—but also of its allusions to the Old Testament. It derives from the Greek *apokaluptein*, "to unveil." It is like a surreal painting by Salvador Dali: "horns" mean power, "eyes" mean knowledge, "wings" mean mobility, "trumpets" mean a divine voice, a "sword" means judgment. Apocalyptic is difficult for a beginner to decipher without the aid of a commentary. In fact, it often reads like the ravings of a maniac.

Apocalyptic is the underground literature of oppressed peoples. The element of prediction is actually a fiction: the author is interpreting his *own* time "as if" he were writing a prediction dating from a prior time. For instance, the prophet Daniel wrote to Jews living about 165 BC under the tyrannical Syrian invader Antiochus Epiphanes, but—for fear of reprisal—he never mentions his name. Rather, he speaks of King Nebuchadnezzar, a Babylonian conqueror of the Jews four hundred years before. To a curious Syrian, the book of Daniel is nothing but a historical "novel," but to the oppressed Jews every nasty thing the author says about Nebuchadnezzar reads as a nasty thing about Antiochus. The same kind of underground ruse was used in recent times by such writers as Albert Camus during the Nazi occupation of France. Camus wrote a play about the mad Roman emperor Caligula. Any German seeing it watched only a diverting historical drama, but the French audience saw its tyrant—and his ultimate destruction—not as Caligula but as Adolf Hitler. Apocalyptic views the present through the distorting mirror of history.

Rather than being predictions of dire punishments for those in the underground, it was a message of hope: it will all be over, hang on, stand firm.

From the beginning, Mark said: "The time is fulfilled, and the kingdom of God has come near" (1:15). He has used images of a hundredfold harvest and a fully grown mustard bush, and Jesus' healings and exorcisms have been inroads on the Antagonist. The title "Son of Man" has been prominent in this gospel, especially in the three passion predictions and the stark contrast of the transfiguration, which triumphs here in this fulfillment of what the passion was really for.

Whatever Christian sources went into Mark's final conflation, Mark's editorial input seems firmly committed to persuading his readers not to be carried away by either terror or enthusiasm, as witnessed by the many forms of warnings to be watchful, beware, be alert. He seems intensely committed to defusing the apprehension that the temple's destruction in AD 70 signaled the end.

Mark's apocalyptic chapter 13 is, like its predecessors, persecution literature, urging his audience to stand firm against the current persecution by Nero.
"Be calm; God's will is working its way out." Yes, all the signs are beginning
to become literally fulfilled; but that is a signal for *hope*, not despair! We are
about to be delivered!

Review Questions for Chapter 13

1. What is the difference between prophecies of the impending end of the world
   one hears occasionally from present-day doomsayers and Jesus' prophecy
   about the events that would precede a new heaven and a new earth?
2. Pick out the sections in the chapter that were in fact literally coming true in
   Mark's own day. What effect would that have on the expectations of the
   people to whom he was writing? What obvious facts proved that Jesus had
   never meant the prediction literally?
3. Reread the prediction. If the reader peels away the hyperbole of apocalyptic
   about a literal end of the world and changes the focus to the literal end of
   each individual at the time of death, what realistic lessons does it offer? Just
   as a new world was to follow the end of the world, what is promised to the
   individual after going through the torment and uncertainty of death?

For Reflection

(1) *Verse 2.* There is a pattern in Judeo-Christian history of God wiping out
what has proved to be one more failure in human evolution—and beginning
all over again: Adam and Eve, Noah and the Flood, Moses and the people leaving Egypt for the Promised Land, the Babylonian captivity and the return of
the people to rebuild Jerusalem. Here again Jesus is announcing yet another
and final destruction and rebirth: from Israel as God's privileged channel to the
kingdom, with Jesus as the model of the fully evolved human being God had
envisioned all along.

This whole chapter is so grandiose and apocalyptic that it is easy to hold
it at arms' length, as if it were merely a bit of historical interest of importance
only to scholars. But we can condense it to apply it to our own less dramatic
lives. As C. S. Lewis says, when we invite God into our lives, we invite him
almost as if we were hiring a carpenter or going to the dentist. We expect him
to spruce up a few things here and there and then go about his business elsewhere,
with less important customers. But God doesn't work that way. When we invite
God into our lives, God comes as the New Owner, firing directions this way

and that. He doesn't mean to have only a small part of our lives; he is after the whole thing! Are you ready for that?

(2) *Verse 7.* In the two thousand years since Jesus painted this dark picture, the scenario has been almost literally fulfilled, over and over: wars and rumors of wars, earthquakes, siblings against siblings in civil wars, large and small. Even if they aren't the signs of an immediate and literal end of the world, they surely ought to be warnings that our collective life is out of kilter.

The trouble is—especially now, when the world has grown smaller and our troubles have become more complicated—there doesn't seem to be any messiah powerful enough to whip things back into a less catastrophic order. Heads of state have their own self-interested agendas, and their promises and plans change sometimes from moment to moment. Where do we begin to "get a handle" on our worldwide chaos?

Since there is little likelihood that we will have a world state anytime soon, there is only one option left, only one agent for change over whom each of us has control: our individual selves. We will never, individually or collectively, conquer all the evil in the world. Our only hope is to lessen it, if only in tiny increments. And if each of us recruited just two or three more who would refuse to knuckle under to "what everybody else does," we can make a difference, however small. "Let there be peace on earth, and let it begin with me."

(3) *Verse 21.* Human history has never lacked for messiahs convinced they had the answer to all our woes, as long as they got enough power: Charlemagne, Napoleon, Hitler, Marx, Lenin, Mao. But "by their fruits you will know them." They proved their momentary messiahship by disappearing, while the world reverted once again to weeds.

Probably the present false messiah is science and technology—and their advance agents: the very convincing media. Just give science enough money and time at the computers and microscopes, and we will have paradise. The one thing this limited specialist view of our common plight refuses to take into consideration is sheer human persnicketiness: original sin. Adam and Eve were in a paradise even better than ours today, and their self-absorbed willfulness ruined everything. America in the fifties was about as close to paradise as we can ever hope to get, but we let it run away with us. It was great, but we wanted even more. Just as the faults in the foundations of communism finally toppled its hope of paradise, so too the cracks in the deification of materialism will one day topple it more thoroughly than the temple of Jerusalem.

Can you find any flaws in that argument?

(4) *Verse 28.* The only thing we learn from history is that we learn nothing from history. We keep making the same mistakes, over and over. When parents

say, "You're going to get in trouble if you keep on this way," they don't have some kind of crystal ball that lets them foresee the future. They've been there, probably more than once, and have seen that every single time such-and-such begins to happen, such-and-such is going to follow. It's as predictable as saying that every time I put out a pot of water and the thermometer goes below 32 degrees, the water is going to go stiff.

Do you have any resistance to advice from others who are more experienced? (If experience is the best teacher, they are automatically better taught than you are. Humbling, perhaps, but true.) Do you have an irrepressible urge to "go it on my own, without anybody else"? Adam and Eve had the same idea, with disastrous results. That's why it's called the *original* sin, because it's the pattern for every single sin that followed it.

(5) *Verse 35.* Again, applying the verse not merely apocalyptically—but to the relative smallness of our own lives, we don't know when the master is coming, and therefore we must be watchful. Further, we cannot limit our watchfulness to the arrival of death. God is coming to us every day, under the most unlikely disguises: the surly sales clerk, the sullen child, the overly critical relative, the short-tempered spouse. He's all over the place! The question is how we react to God's messages through each of these challenging people. One response is simply to limit our intake of "messages" so that we're unaware of—and therefore untroubled by—them. Another response is just patient endurance until the irritating stimulus recedes from our awareness. What tactful ways can you deal with people like surly sales clerks and so forth—not ways that will embarrass them and harden their already obvious anger, but ways that they might be unarmed against?

14

¹It was two days before the Passover and the festival of Unleavened Bread. The chief priests and the scribes were looking for a way to arrest Jesus by stealth and kill him; ²for they said, "Not during the festival, or there may be a riot among the people."

³While he was at Bethany in the house of Simon the leper, as he sat at the table, a woman came with an alabaster jar of

---

The Final Reckoning Begins: VV1-11

V1. *two days before***:** Therefore, between our Tuesday sunset and Wednesday sunset. To be honest, some problems with the niceties of making Mark's chronology perfectly fit the historical possibilities (so "essential" to a modern audience used to clinical preciseness in reportage) arise probably from the need to make Jesus' death come as close as possible to congruence with the Jewish Passover—of which it is the fulfillment. Theology sometimes domineers over the possible; *Passover*: The feast celebrating the time when, on the way to slaughtering the Egyptian firstborn sons, the Angel of Death saw the lambs' blood on the Hebrew doorposts and "passed over" them. It is a feast of sacrifice for deliverance. The feast began at sundown, after the slaughter of the lambs in the temple, followed by seven days of the feast of Unleavened Bread; *chief priests*: Since the Jewish priesthood was hereditary there were countless grades and orders, some very prosperous near the temple, others dirt poor in the hinterlands. The priests here were an aristocracy with great power over the temple—and its treasury. Their function was analogous to the Councils of Jewish Elders established by the Nazis in localities all over occupied Europe: to keep order in the subject people and to pass on orders from the despised invaders; *looking for a way*: This is the fourth time Mark mentions this theme (3:6; 11:18; 12:12; here), which has knitted together his story; *arrest*: "Capture" is a better translation, since there was nothing legal about the action—by "a crowd."

V2. *they said:* An editorial intrusion, unless someone present later revealed the substance of their secret agreement; *Not during the festival*: One Passover prayer is: "Next year, in Jerusalem!" Crowds of foreign Jews returned every year, tripling the population, and causing Pilate the Roman prefect to move his headquarters temporarily into Jerusalem. Jesus had proved himself very popular the previous Sunday. In Mark's time line, however, they *do* apprehend Jesus *after* the Passover meal and therefore during the feast, which begins at sunset. The Donahue-Harrington commentary puts it perfectly: from this moment, Jesus is a "dead man walking."

V3. *Bethany*: As noted before, about two miles from the city, on the far side of the Mount of Olives, with its association with anointing and the coming of Yahweh; *Simon the leper*: Nothing is known of him, although, since the man

very costly ointment of nard, and she broke open the jar and poured the ointment on his head. ⁴But some were there who said to one another in anger, "Why was the ointment wasted in this way? ⁵For this ointment could have been sold for more than three hundred denarii, and the money given to the poor." And they scolded her. ⁶But Jesus said, "Let her alone; why do you trouble her? She has performed a good service for me. ⁷For you always have the poor with you, and you can show kindness to them whenever you wish; but you will not always have me.

---

is back in society, one could assume he was a leper Jesus had cured. Matthew follows Mark closely. Luke locates the story earlier in the house of Simon "the Pharisee" and the woman is identified there as "a sinner." John puts the story in the house of Lazarus and the woman as his sister, Mary—not "Magdalene"; *costly ointment of nard*: expensive perfume, a scented oil native to India; *broke open the jar*: This could mean merely breaking the seal or, symbolizing a finality, shattering the neck; *on his head*: This has two symbolisms, especially considering its occurrence near the Mount of Olives. In the OT, kings' heads were anointed on their accession to the throne, but also the dying were anointed as a symbol of their choice by God. Kings were anointed always by other males. This is a significant departure. It is even more startling that the woman, against all custom, has burst in to an all-male gathering.

V4. *some . . . in anger*: In Matthew, it becomes "the disciples," and in John, it is only "Judas." Mark uses the same verb to describe their grousing about the Zebedee brothers.

V5. *three hundred denarii*: A year's wages; *given to the poor*: John (12:6) not only attributes the remark to Judas but also specifies the motive as greed; *scolded*: The verb is one used for the snorting of a horse.

V6. *performed a good service*: This translation is stiff and stilted. The sense is more that she has done something "beautiful" or "graceful"—an unexpected kindness.

V7. *always have the poor*: Deuteronomy 15:1-23 is a hymn to kindness and fair play to all human beings, even slaves. The passion story is salted with quotations from the OT, putting the events into a theological—rather than a strictly reportorial—context, not merely events but meaningful for all humankind. The existence of the poor will be a lifelong invitation and incentive to kindness.

V8. *done what she could*: The verb *poie* adds to "done" a more creative connotation as in the word "poet." Therefore, "she has brought out the symbolism of this moment." If no one else understands what's going on (i.e., the male disciples), she does. Moreover, her generosity echoes the self-forgetfulness of the widow who gave all she had. It also foreshadows the women at Jesus' tomb. Jesus seems to value unthinking generosity more highly than caution and reserve.

8She has done what she could; she has anointed my body beforehand for its burial. 9Truly I tell you, wherever the good news is proclaimed in the whole world, what she has done will be told in remembrance of her."

10Then Judas Iscariot, who was one of the twelve, went to the chief priests in order to betray him to them. 11When they heard it, they were greatly pleased, and promised to give him money. So he began to look for an opportunity to betray him.

V9. *wherever . . . told in remembrance of her*: Mark here assumes that the gospel will, in fact, be preached all over the earth. The irony is that, although we know the names of all the out-of-it male apostles, Mark does not identify this woman he says will be eternally recalled. There is no basis for equating this woman or Lazarus's sister, Mary, with the "Magdalene" of Luke 8:2 from whom "seven demons had gone out," who witnessed both Jesus' death and his resurrection and brought the news to the still-incredulous apostles. Nor is there any reliable evidence that *any* of these women was a prostitute or the consort of Jesus, as in the intriguing but silly *Da Vinci Code*.

V10. *Judas Iscariot*: "Iscariot" designates "a man from Kerioth," a town in southern Judea, which would make Judas the only non-Galilean apostle. Others relate it to the Latin *sicarius*, meaning "dagger," and imply that Judas was a "dagger man," a Zealot who advocated the overthrow of the invaders by force. Dorothy Sayers suggests Jesus had thoroughly converted Judas from Zealotry and belief in a political Messiah, but when Judas saw Jesus' acceptance of the homage on Palm Sunday, he believed Jesus himself had gone back on his own belief, willing to become a political Messiah himself, and Judas turned Jesus in to "save him from himself." Jesus has already warned them (13:12) that brother will betray brother.

V11. *give him money*: Another irony: Mark says Judas betrayed his friend for an unspecified sum of "money," whereas this unnamed woman sacrifices a year's wages worth of perfume to anoint Jesus for his burial. Matthew 26:15 specifies that the blood price was thirty pieces of silver, the price of a slave, about three months' wages for an ordinary worker.

The Farewell Meal: VV12-25

V12. *Passover lamb is sacrificed*: The chronology here gives further evidence that Mark was written in Rome (or somewhere distant from Palestine) by someone unfamiliar with the niceties of Jewish customs and feasts. Was the Last Supper on the Day of Preparation or the day before? The arguments and details are too bewildering to untangle here, and such precision is most likely unappetizing (and unnecessary) for this book's audience. Deuteronomy 16:7

¹²On the first day of Unleavened Bread, when the Passover lamb is sacrificed, his disciples said to him, "Where do you want us to go and make the preparations for you to eat the Passover?" ¹³So he sent two of his disciples, saying to them, "Go into the city, and a man carrying a jar of water will meet you; follow him, ¹⁴and wherever he enters, say to the owner of the house, 'The Teacher asks, Where is my guest room where I may eat the Passover with my disciples?' ¹⁵He will show you a large room upstairs, furnished and ready. Make preparations for us there." ¹⁶So the disciples set out and went to the city, and found everything as he had told them; and they prepared the Passover meal.

¹⁷When it was evening, he came with the twelve. ¹⁸And when they had taken their places and were eating, Jesus said, "Truly

---

orders Jews to cook and eat a one-year-old unblemished male lamb in memory of the lambs slain to provide blood for the first Passover doorposts. Since the Last Supper occurs in conjunction with Passover, it is one more way in which the new Israel replaces the old, and Jesus himself becomes both the new Moses and the new Paschal Lamb sacrificed for the new people of God.

V13. *he sent two of his disciples*: Almost the same words as when he sent for the colt (11:2); *a man carrying a jar of* **water**: In Palestine, men carried water in skins; women carried it in jars or jugs. This might indicate Mark's unawareness of such a custom, or it could be that this was a way of singling out this man from other men carrying water.

V14. *wherever he enters*: Perhaps the owner was a disciple and saying "the Teacher" would immediately identify the messengers; *with my disciples*: There had to be enough people at each Passover table to consume the lamb with no leftovers.

V15. *a large room*: Suggests there were more disciples at the Last Supper than the select twelve; *furnished*: At the first Passover, the Hebrews, on their way out of Egypt, had to eat the meal standing and in haste, but by the time of Jesus it had become a festive occasion where even the poorest reclined in comfort as a sign that Israel had been freed from bondage and fear.

V16. *prepared the Passover meal*: In the description of the actual meal, none of the Synoptics mentions any other food than the bread and wine. Nothing about lamb. Perhaps the reason is to symbolize that Jesus has now become the *new* lamb.

V17. *When it was evening*: The meal was to be eaten after sundown and before midnight.

V18. *Truly I tell you*: Again, the prelude to a solemn declaration; *one of you will betray me*: All the evangelists except Luke put the betrayal before the Supper, possibly to eliminate the idea that Judas had shared in the Eucharist; *who is eating with me*: Psalm 41:9: "Even my bosom friend in whom I trusted, who ate of my bread, has lifted the heel against me."

I tell you, one of you will betray me, one who is eating with me." [19]They began to be distressed and to say to him one after another, "Surely, not I?" [20]He said to them, "It is one of the twelve, one who is dipping bread into the bowl with me. [21]For the Son of Man goes as it is written of him, but woe to that one by whom the Son of Man is betrayed! It would have been better for that one not to have been born."

[22]While they were eating, he took a loaf of bread, and after blessing it he broke it, gave it to them, and said, "Take; this is my body." [23]Then he took a cup, and after giving thanks he gave it to them, and all of them drank from it. [24]He said to them,

---

V19. *distressed*: For all but one, this is a sudden, shocking revelation; ***Surely, not I***: The form of the response expects a negative reaction. Nevertheless, the mere fact that they ask betrays some inner fear in each of them that, given the right circumstances, it was at least conceivable.

V21. *the Son of Man*: Here once again, Jesus refers to himself not merely as the carpenter from Nazareth but as a cosmic figure; ***as it is written of him***: That is, the Suffering Servant (Isa 53). Throughout this passage, the Passover background gives scriptural overtones to many of the words and actions; ***woe to that one***: Although the traitor has been named as Judas in 14:10-11, the name is not specified here, nor does Mark picture Judas leaving; ***not to have been born***: A fearsome statement, especially coming from a Jesus who has said the only unforgivable sin is against the Holy Spirit (3:28-29). As noted above: "seeing goodness as wicked and therefore shunning it, effectively blocking God's Spirit." Recall that Jesus upbraided Peter as "Satan" (8:33) when, out of human kindness, Peter tried to thwart God's plan to bring Jesus to Jerusalem. This could give some credence to Sayers' insight that Judas betrayed Jesus "for his own good," to keep him from yielding to become a literal king.

V22. *While they were eating*: Mark telescopes here; ***he took a loaf of bread***: As the father figure, Jesus would pronounce grace over the unleavened bread; ***this is my body***: In all Synoptic accounts, the Greek words are precisely the same. At the Passover meal, the father explains the meaning of "the bread of affliction," unleavened because of the haste with which the forefathers had fled Egypt. Here Jesus also explains the bread: it is his body, his complete self-giving.

V23. *took a cup*: The third cup of the Passover meal, "the cup of benediction," and although the *Seder* meal has four different cup offerings, and there were surely several cups on the table, "*all of them*" drank from this single cup Jesus had specially blessed and offered.

V24. *my blood of the covenant*: An allusion to the blood sacrifice that sealed the covenant at Sinai between Yahweh and the first people. In Exodus 24:8, Moses sprinkled the blood of the sacrifice on the people and said, "See the blood of the covenant that the LORD has made with you." The covenant was one of the most

"This is my blood of the covenant, which is poured out for many. ²⁵Truly I tell you, I will never again drink of the fruit of the vine until that day when I drink it new in the kingdom of God."

---

fundamental institutions in Jewish history and identity. The frequent analogy to it in the OT is a marriage bond between Yahweh and Israel—not a legal contract but a love-bond; *for many*: Semitic languages use "many" to mean an unlimited number, thus, the whole world. The Eucharist is the food of the Christ-life in us. Even though he often stresses the necessity of Jesus' death, Mark does not expand on *why* Jesus "had" to die. (See chap. 5, "The Son of Man *Must* Suffer.")

V25. *when I drink it new in the kingdom of God*: At the Messianic banquet, both in the earthly eucharistic meal and in the future banquet where we will sit down with Abraham, Isaac, and Jacob in the fulfillment of the kingdom. They ate and drank; no mention Jesus did either.

Mark's version, the first of the lives of Jesus, was written thirty to forty years after the events it describes. There are, however, confirmations of the Lord's Supper as a habitual practice and focus of the Christian community as early as 1 Corinthians (11–23), written by Paul in about AD 55.

The NT formulas for the words of consecration are basically the same and yet verbally varied—which should put to rest the wrongful belief that the eucharistic words are some kind of magic incantation that need scrupulously perfect re-creation to have an effect. The words for consecrating the bread and wine, for instance:

1 Cor 11: —"This is my body that is for you."
 —"This cup is the new covenant in my blood."
Mark 14: —"Take; this is my body."
 —"This is my blood of the covenant, which is poured out for many."
Matt 26: —"Take, eat; this is my body."
 —"Drink from it, all of you; for this is my blood of the covenant, which is poured out for many for the forgiveness of sin."
Luke 22: —"This is my body, which is given for you."
 —"This cup that is poured out for you is the new covenant in my blood."

And John has no explicit words of consecration at all!

But it would be as ludicrous to quibble over the varying wordings of the same intentions as it would be to wonder if John the Evangelist disbelieved in the Eucharist!

²⁶When they had sung the hymn, they went out to the Mount of Olives. ²⁷And Jesus said to them, "You will all become deserters; for it is written,

'I will strike the shepherd, and the sheep will be scattered.'

²⁸But after I am raised up, I will go before you to Galilee." ²⁹Peter said to him, "Even though all become deserters, I will not."

Even more complex than disentangling the historical chronology of these events, the subject of what actually transpired—what "happened to" the bread and wine between the fingers of Jesus and happens in present-day liturgies—is too fine-tuned and complex to settle in such an introductory text. Nevertheless, a great many Christians and all Catholics believe that at the moment of consecration in the Eucharist, the bread and wine actually transform—*become*—bearers of the presence of the Risen Christ. Perhaps two suggestions might be sufficient for the moment: (1) if all Christians could just agree that Christ is *somehow* more intensely present in the Eucharist than anywhere else on earth, and (2) if we accept that God can draw a universe out of nothing without too much fuss, we should be able to accommodate some meaningful "Real Presence."

Finally, this "kingdom" Mark has been unveiling from the first, has both a "now" and a "later" component. With the Last Supper, crucifixion, and resurrection, the New Kingdom has, in fact, *begun*. But only like a mustard seed, which is real but bursting with further potential.

Prediction of Peter's Denial: VV26-31

V26. *they had sung the hymn*: The last hymn of the Passover meal is Hallel, a conflation of Psalms 114–18, all hymns of praise and thanksgiving to the one true God; *out to the Mount of Olives*: Again, the prophesied place where Yahweh would begin his final conquest. The garden of Gethsemane was probably at the foot of the hill but down a steep incline from the city.

V27. *"sheep will be scattered"*: A quotation from the prophet Zechariah (13:7). Jesus predicts what is about to happen, not only that he will be struck down, but also that they will flee him.

V28. *after I am raised up*: A restorative note of hope in contrast to the doleful prediction; *to Galilee*: Only Mark has the risen Jesus appear to the apostles *only* in Galilee and not in Jerusalem. Thus, the risen Jesus will gather with his disciples in the place where he had first called them. Neither his death nor their betrayal will be the last word.

V29. *Peter said to him*: Since Mark was likely his interpreter, Peter is most likely the source of this story. Here is another indication that if the early church "made up" the gospels they did not spare even their highest officials profound

³⁰Jesus said to him, "Truly I tell you, this day, this very night, before the cock crows twice, you will deny me three times." ³¹But he said vehemently, "Even though I must die with you, I will not deny you." And all of them said the same.

³²They went to a place called Gethsemane; and he said to his disciples, "Sit here while I pray." ³³He took with him Peter and James and John, and began to be distressed and agitated. ³⁴And said to them, "I am deeply grieved, even to death; remain

humiliation at their own braggart stupidity; *I will not*: As certain as when he blocked Jesus' intent to come to Jerusalem and death.

V30. *Truly I tell you*: A solemn proclamation; *this day, this very night*: The immediacy of the repetition underscores the fragility of Peter's resolve; *before the cock crows twice*: Peter's denial will come so fast that the cock will not have a chance to crow a second time before the denial comes forth. This is in direct contrast to Peter's stubborn—and ultimately pitiful—second assertion that he will "die with you," even after Jesus has declared, in the strongest terms, that he would deny him; *you will deny me*: Peter has sworn he would not desert Jesus, but he counters with the prediction that Peter will do not only that but actively renounce their friendship; *three times*: This could reflect later Roman practice, in Mark's time, of asking Christians three times, "Are you a Christian?" If they falter, they know their first pope had already preceded them. Moreover, their more steadfast brethren should accept them back as Jesus did Peter.

V31. *And all of them said the same*: This makes the scene all the more pitiful.

The Agony in the Garden: VV32-42

V32. *Gethsemane*: The word means "oil press."

V33. *Peter and James and John*: This privileged threesome had been taken off alone with Jesus before. They had witnessed a girl raised from the dead and Jesus' own glorification at the transfiguration. Then, with Andrew, they alone heard the frightening prediction of the end time. Peter bragged he would never desert Jesus, and the brothers had finagled for the top places in the kingdom. Here they are being invited to be the privileged witnesses of Jesus' weakness. What is remarkable is that, despite Jesus' clear prediction of Peter's fragility, Peter is still specially chosen for this moment. Their past experiences do not predispose them to be alert. They fall asleep. Again, the early church did not whitewash its heroes. This event is a "negative" of the transfiguration. Then, we saw the divine Jesus; here we see the polar opposite human Jesus—in the same man.

V34. *grieved, even to death*: (See chap. 4: "Jesus' Consciousness of His Divinity.") Here the Son of God is so terrified he wishes he could die at once

here, and keep awake." ³⁵And going a little farther, he threw himself on the ground and prayed that, if it were possible, the hour might pass from him. ³⁶He said, "Abba, Father, for you all things are possible; remove this cup from me; yet, not what I want, but what you want." ³⁷He came and found them sleeping; and he said to Peter, "Simon, are you asleep? Could you not keep awake one hour? ³⁸Keep awake and pray that you may not come into the time of trial; the spirit indeed is willing, but the flesh is weak." ³⁹And again he went away and prayed, saying the same words. ⁴⁰And once more he came and found them sleeping, for their eyes were very heavy; and they did not

---

rather than face what is to come, and it is clear that he did not hesitate to tell his apostles that. Psalm 42:3 captures the moment: "People say to me continually, 'Where is your God?' " Or consider the entire book of Job.

V35. *if it were possible*: When we find the plan of God insupportable, it is consoling to realize that the Best of Us faced the same test of his faith. He *will* be saved from death—but not until Sunday; *the hour*: *Kairos*, the appointed time of his final confrontation with the Antagonist.

V36. *Abba, Father*: The word "abba" is far less formal than "father," closer to "papa," and Jesus kept saying it over and over. This apparent "coziness" of Jesus with the utterly transcendent Yahweh is at least part of the objections of the sophisticated lawyers. There are echoes of the Our Father here: trusting in God the Father, submitting to his will rather than one's own; *this cup*: The cup is a symbol like "the hour," the burden of fulfilling God's will. He asked James and John if they could drink from it (10:39), but at the moment James and John are asleep; *not what I want, but what you want*: The same incautious submission as in the Our Father.

V37. *Simon, are you asleep?*: Peter is Jesus' clear favorite throughout the gospel, and here he is the one Jesus singles out as a disappointment. Also, since Jesus called him, he has never had any other name than "Peter." But "Peter" means "the rock," hardly fitting here. There is also a suggestion that, for all Jesus' hopes for him and for all his bragging, he has not been changed at the core by these three years. He is still "Simon"; *Could you not keep awake*: Recalls the warning in the parable (13:34) about remaining alert, even when the master goes away.

V38. *into the time of trial*: In a moment, they will in fact be tested, and they will run away in abject terror. If the gospels were a hoax, why would they picture themselves so detestably?

V40. *for their eyes were very heavy*: It is too easy to be judgmental: they have had a heavy meal, with several rounds of wine, and they have nothing really to occupy them; *did not know what to say*: Like Peter at the transfiguration (9:6). What could they possibly have said?

know what to say to him. ⁴¹He came a third time and said to them, "Are you still sleeping and taking your rest? Enough! The hour has come; the Son of Man is betrayed into the hands of sinners. ⁴²Get up, let us be going. See, my betrayer is at hand."

⁴³Immediately, while he was still speaking, Judas, one of the twelve, arrived; and with him there was a crowd with swords and clubs, from the chief priests, the scribes, and the elders. ⁴⁴Now the betrayer had given them a sign, saying,

---

V41. *a third time*: By the third time anyone with compassion could see Jesus' anguish and have the loyalty to find some way to stay awake, to offer Jesus at least that, even if they felt helpless to help in any other way. It will get worse. Before the night is over, Peter will not only prove himself unwary but will first swiftly desert Jesus but then recover—only to come back and disown him, with curses; *still sleeping and taking your rest?*: The repetition and the tone of "resting" while Jesus agonized makes the two statements close to bitter; *Enough*: It will have to do. Jesus has done all he can with them. The verb *apechai* was written on bills "paid in full"; *The hour*: *Kairos*. Again, his appointment with his destiny; *sinners*: Among them, one of his own.

V42. *let us be going*: As if he could count on these men to go anywhere but away; *is at hand*: The same Greek verb as in 1:15 when Mark said, "the kingdom of God has come near." The irony is that Jesus' doom is also his deliverance.

Oddly, the hopelessness of this unpromising moment is a source of hope. The hindsight of two thousand years shows that the enterprise Jesus began with these completely undependable deputies had to have something going for it beyond the talent and worthiness of its ministers.

The Arrest: VV43-52

V43. *one of the twelve*: Anyone who has read this far would not need that clarification, which suggests that the rest of Mark's version of Jesus' passion may have come to him from a preexisting source; *a crowd*: The overtones of the word suggest a rabble, like an unruly posse in a Western, but the next phrase shows they were sent; *from the chief priests, the scribes, and the elders*: The three groups representing the official religion did not come themselves.

V44. *I will kiss*: Judas himself clarifies the reason for the kiss: to pick Jesus out from the rest. But after Palm Sunday, it would not have been difficult to find people who would recognize Jesus. The Greek verb is *kataphilesen*, "to kiss lovingly." If Dorothy Sayers is correct about Judas's motivation, it could be that Judas kissed Jesus because he genuinely loved him and was, reluctantly, trying to save Jesus from a sudden worldly ambition.

"The one I will kiss is the man; arrest him and lead him away under guard." ⁴⁵So when he came, he went up to him at once and said, "Rabbi!" and kissed him. ⁴⁶Then they laid hands on him and arrested him. ⁴⁷But one of those who stood near drew his sword and struck the slave of the high priest, cutting off his ear. ⁴⁸Then Jesus said to them, "Have you come out with swords and clubs to arrest me as though I were a bandit? ⁴⁹Day after day I was with you in the temple teaching, and you did not arrest me. But let the scriptures be fulfilled." ⁵⁰All of them deserted him and fled.

⁵¹A certain young man was following him, wearing nothing but a linen cloth.

V45. *when he came, he went up to him*: Another example of Mark's unnecessary doubling, as is the next verse: *laid hands on him and arrested him*.

V47. *one of those who stood near*: Mark, again carelessly, does not even clarify that it was someone with Jesus. Only John specifies that the servant's name was Malchus and the swordsman was Peter. Nowhere has any disciple appeared to have a weapon; *slave of the high priest*: Shows this was not just a makeshift rabble but organized and purposeful; *ear*: The diminutive form of the word suggests it was merely an earlobe—hardly a major onslaught.

V48. *as though I were a bandit*: Bandits were armed and dangerous. One misused sword and an earlobe are hardly professional work. In 11:17, Jesus has described the temple that sent them as "a den of robbers." Even at this perilous moment, Jesus still has an ironic humor; he has never done anything to merit such treatment. In fact, from now on, he will be treated like a highwayman and will be hanged between two of them.

V49. *Day after day:* At least in Mark's account, Jesus has been in Jerusalem only three days in his life. Therefore, a more likely translation would be "in the daytime"; *in the temple teaching*: Which is where these people come from. Jesus is equivalently saying, "You could have arrested me right there, and saved yourselves such a long trip, so late at night." But he knows the reason for such caution: an arrest in a crowd might have provoked a riot; *let the scriptures be fulfilled*: The sentence is unfinished, nor does Mark suggest what parts of scripture Jesus meant, unless it is the one he quoted before (14:27) about striking the shepherd and scattering the sheep.

V50. *All . . . deserted . . . fled*: Carelessly, Mark does not say that this is the eleven, not the crowd as well. But the point is made: those who blustered that they would die rather than deny Jesus just hiked up their skirts and ran to save themselves. From this moment on, Jesus will fight this by himself. The next verse suggests that his sense of abandonment might have been deeper.

V51. *young man . . . following him*: This is not mere carelessness; Mark has already said that "*all*" those with Jesus had fled. Who could this puzzling "young man" be? For many years, scholars believed it was Mark's "signature,"

They caught hold of him, ⁵²but he left the linen cloth and ran off naked.

⁵³They took Jesus to the high priest; and all the chief priests, the elders, and the scribes were assembled. ⁵⁴Peter had followed him at a distance, right into the courtyard of the high priest; and he was sitting with the guards, warming himself

---

that the man was Mark himself. But Mark was quite likely not a Palestinian. What's more, the Greek word translated here as "following" is more like "shadowing," dogging Jesus' footsteps. The key is that the precise same words: "young man . . . wrapped . . . linen cloth" appear again in Mark's gospel: at the resurrection. While the other Synoptics have the women at the tomb greeted by an angel (Matt) or two men in brilliant clothes (Luke)—both of which are consistent OT symbols for the presence of God—Mark has the women met by "a young man wrapped in a linen cloth": exactly the same words as this passage. A case could be made, then, that Mark is using this puzzling young man to symbolize that Jesus' clear conviction of his relationship with the Father and his mission—which have not faltered since his baptism—now deserts him. His disciples fled; now he loses his surety. He goes the rest of the way alone, on sheer faith in a silent God.

The Sanhedrin Trial: VV53-65

V53. *to the high priest*: Matthew identifies him as Caiaphas, and John as Annas, who was high priest emeritus and retained the title, as some American political officials do. To expect modern historical accuracy from writers with no access to libraries—much less the internet—is as foolish as asking printed and stapled books from them. If Mark seems slipshod about such trivial details, his inaccuracy testifies that he was working from oral research and not from having been an eyewitness himself. Since in the next verse, Peter follows them ***right into the courtyard of the high priest***, Mark seems to place the trial at the high priest's residence, which was not usual. Moreover, the penalty for blasphemy was stoning, not crucifixion—which was a Roman practice—and under the occupation only Romans could execute (although that seemed not to inhibit Herod in killing the Baptist); ***all . . . assembled***: The temple aristocracy, called the Sanhedrin ("council"), seventy-one members with the high priest, who judged religious questions as well as legal and civic matters that did not concern the Roman governor. Since such a night trial was illegal, either Mark did not know that or he purposely put it at night to underline it as a travesty of justice no matter when it occurred. Whatever the time of the trial, it is most likely that Peter's denials did occur in the early morning (the cock crow).

V54. *Peter . . . at a distance*: Mark typically "bookends" Jesus' trial with the Peter episode. There is something touching about this blustering fellow,

at the fire. ⁵⁵Now the chief priests and the whole council were looking for testimony against Jesus to put him to death; but they found none. ⁵⁶For many gave false testimony against him, and their testimony did not agree. ⁵⁷Some stood up and gave false testimony against him, saying, ⁵⁸"We heard him say, 'I will destroy this temple that is made with hands, and in three days I will build another, not made with hands.'"

---

who turned tail and ran like the rest, yet here is drawn loyally to be near his friend—even though he has to move stealthily to do it. Nor is it often in the gospels one finds such homely, concrete details as the guards killing time and Peter *warming himself at the fire*. One can imagine him, hooded, cutting furtive glances at the others, wondering why in heaven's name he's taken this risk.

V55. *looking for testimony against*: In Jewish courts, defense witnesses appeared first, to give the accused the benefit of their support before he or she was attacked. There was no official prosecutor; rather, witnesses were the prosecutors, and at least two had to agree in order to be acceptable testimony. Here, the official court is actively trying to find attackers, but, since witnesses were interrogated separately, they could not find two who could tell the same lie. It is also interesting to note that the Sanhedrin arrested Jesus before they had a clear case against him. No defense witnesses are mentioned. The trial is rigged from the start, a pretense at legality. The rush is caused by the imminent Passover.

V56. *testimony did not agree*: Deuteronomy 19:15: "A single witness shall not suffice to convict a person of any crime or wrongdoing." The officials haven't had time to prep their witnesses.

V58. *I will destroy this temple*: Not just a prediction that it will happen, but that *he* will *make* it happen. (If this gospel were put into final form after AD 70, the audience would have known the prophecy had literally come true.) Jesus' opposition to the idea of religion held by the vested interests of Judaism was well known, but he would not be arrested for that, since there were many sects in Judaism that felt the same way. Mark says, however, that more than one witness ("some") agreed that Jesus had *said he* would destroy the temple. Perhaps Jesus spoke of its destruction more than one time, but Mark has recorded it only once (13:2) and that spoken to his disciples—though he might have been overheard. Perhaps the reason the testimony was not acceptable was that building a temple "*not made with hands*" seemed ludicrous to the judges—although there are many OT chapters (Isa 40–66; Ezek 40–48) that speak of a perfect sanctuary replacing an earthly one. It is intriguing to speculate why Judas, who had been "paid for" by these very men, did not—or would not—appear as a witness. (Only Matthew says that Judas regretted his act and killed himself.)

V60. *Have you no answer?*: Because of lack of agreement among the witnesses, the high priest has to intervene and ask Jesus to incriminate himself.

⁵⁹But even on this point their testimony did not agree. ⁶⁰Then the high priest stood up before them and asked Jesus, "Have you no answer? What is it that they testify against you?" ⁶¹But he was silent and did not answer. Again the high priest asked him, "Are you the Messiah, the Son of the Blessed One?" ⁶²Jesus said, "I am; and

'you will see the Son of Man
    seated at the right hand of the
        Power,'
and 'coming with the clouds of
    heaven.'"
⁶³Then the high priest tore his clothes and said, "Why do we still need witnesses? ⁶⁴You have heard his blasphemy! What is

---

V61. *But he was silent and did not answer*: Mark's typical unneeded repetition gives emphasis to his silence. But the outcome is foregone. "He did not open his mouth, like a lamb that is led to the slaughter" (Isa 53:7); *Are you the Messiah, the Son of the Blessed One?*: Note that the high priest scrupulously uses a circumlocution for "God." Here is the climax of Mark's gospel, the crucial question of the Messianic Secret he has been unfolding all along, coming from the least likely source: an enemy trying to get Jesus to condemn himself with his own testimony.

V62. *I am*: The unpronounceable name of Yahweh, the answer to the question: Who is Jesus? In two words, Jesus unabashedly affirms what Mark has said from the first sentence, what was testified by demons twice (3:11; 5:7), by Peter (8:29), and by the voice from heaven twice (1:11; 9:7); *seated at the right hand*: Psalm 110:1 says, "The LORD says to my lord, 'Sit at my right hand until I make your enemies your footstool'"; *clouds of heaven*: A clear allusion to the Messiah in the OT book of Daniel, at the right side of the Almighty. This claims that this man Jesus—standing before them at this moment—will one day act as judge of all humankind. Anyone who offers the ill-founded claim that Jesus was merely one of a line of wise moral gurus in history has to contend against this undeniable claim that he believed himself someone far greater.

V63. *tore his clothes*: It was not "blasphemy" to claim to be an "agent" of God, so that is not how the high priests understand Jesus' reply. If no one else can see Jesus' unequivocal claim, this man does. Ripping clothes is a ritual Jewish symbol to show utter rejection, as when a Jewish child marries a Christian and "dies" to the faith. To give his executioners credit, they did not rid themselves of a moral teacher but a man they were convinced was a blasphemer and a madman.

V64. *All*: A blanket accusation, although Mark himself says later (15:43) that "Joseph of Arimathea, a respected member of the council" persuaded Pilate to release Jesus' corpse to him. Presumably he withheld his approval; *deserving death*: According to Leviticus 24, the sentence should have been stoning. However, John 18:31 suggests that under the Roman occupation the Jews were not allowed to execute criminals.

your decision?" All of them condemned him as deserving death. ⁶⁵Some began to spit on him, to blindfold him, and to strike him, saying to him, "Prophesy!" The guards also took him over and beat him.

⁶⁶While Peter was below in the courtyard, one of the servant-girls of the high priest came by. ⁶⁷When she saw Peter warming himself, she stared at him and said, "You also were with Jesus, the man from Nazareth." ⁶⁸But he denied it, saying, "I do not know or understand what you are talking about." And he went out into the forecourt. Then the cock crowed. ⁶⁹And

---

V65. *spit . . . strike him*: Since no other noun intervenes, one is left with the conviction that, despite the fact Luke and John transfer this brutality to guards, Mark and Matthew believed that it was the infuriated priests and elders themselves who abused Jesus. Only after the priests and elders have played this sadistic children's game, *the guards also took him over*. That change of actors implies that Jesus has been dragged down to the courtyard where the guards—and Peter—were warming themselves. That certainly adds a painful intensity to what follows.

Peter's Denials: VV66-72

V66. *one of the servant-girls*: It is wise to recollect often that the first of the apostles knuckled under, not to a soldier with a knife at his throat, but to a powerless waitress—more than once.

V67. *You also were*: Mark does not say how the woman knew. One might guess from Peter's general character that he might behave out of place and countrified. Matthew says that it was Peter's Galilean accent that gave him away, since many guerrillas operated out of remote Galilee. Even a maid felt citified enough to mock a hillbilly.

V68. *I do not know*: Peter's denials build: first, feigning ignorance; second, a flat denial; finally, the denial augmented by cursing and swearing. At least for some time, the very first pope was an apostate, a defector. He is the model (versus the ideal) Christian: zealous and protective, but also obtuse, impatient, obstinate, and confused. No different from any of us; *into the forecourt*: Perhaps trying to get to the gate and escape; *the cock crowed*: Dramatically, this comes too soon, since the crucial moment of the scene should be the crowing that makes Peter realize what he has done. This is omitted from some manuscripts as a clumsy attempt to cover Mark for having the cock crow a second time (14:72) without having mentioned the first.

V69. *the servant-girl . . . again*: Presumably, the same maid has followed him, getting pleasure out of tormenting him, like a schoolyard bully.

the servant-girl, on seeing him, began again to say to the bystanders, "This man is one of them." [70]But again he denied it. Then after a little while the bystanders again said to Peter, "Certainly you are one of them; for you are a Galilean." [71]But he began to curse, and he swore an oath, "I do not know this man you are talking about." [72]At that moment the cock crowed for the second time. Then Peter remembered that Jesus had said to him, "Before the cock crows twice, you will deny me three times." And he broke down and wept.

V70. *again he denied it*: The imperfect tense of the verb signifies that he kept on denying.

V71. *he began to curse*: One can only imagine the specifics; **he swore an oath**: To grasp an equivalent, consider a witness, hand on a Bible, swearing: "I do not know this man you are talking about." Not only the man he left all to follow, whom he called "Messiah," but also his friend.

V72. *broke down and wept*: The verb is iterative, that is, he wept and wept, implying heaving sobs of shame. To all the evangelists, Peter is the model disciple; not the ideal disciple, only the typical one. Aristotle defined the turning point (*peripeteia*) of a well-made play as the moment at which the protagonist suddenly grasps the truth (*anagnoresis*) in a moment that changes his or her life utterly.

Review Questions for Chapter 14

1. What does the episode of the woman's anointing of Jesus "say" about expending money that could feed people's bodies for "purely religious" purposes? Have you ever heard people complain about so much money being spent to beautify church buildings? Do such complaints at least seem to reflect a belief that the physical is more important than the spiritual?
2. What are the parallels in Jesus' enactment of the Last Supper and the Jewish celebration of Passover? What is the great difference? What does this meal "say" about Judaism, its dominance, its rituals?
3. Give evidence from the chapter to show that, although the first Eucharist was indeed a ritual, it was not a very ornate or magnificent one.
4. Give evidence from the chapter to show that Jesus could not have had full use of the divine knowledge.
5. Why is it a cop-out to claim that Jesus was a very great moral teacher but not the Son of God? If he was not what he claimed to be, he must have been a madman or a charlatan trying to work the crowd, either for money or for power. What evidence in Mark's gospel shows that Jesus was neither insane nor a crook?

For Reflection

(1) *Verse 23.* In the present formula of consecration in the liturgy, the celebrant says, "[T]his is the cup of my blood, the blood of the new and everlasting covenant. It will be shed for you and for all so that sins may be forgiven. Do this in memory of me." Jesus, of course, meant re-create the last supper in his memory. But one wonders if he might also have meant "forgive sins in memory of me." It is at least plausible, since he wants his new people not merely to "act out" a ritual by which Jesus externalized his self-sacrifice but also to be ourselves imitators of his self-sacrifice.

We tend, however, to restrict self-sacrifice to acts or gifts that take up our time and money: checks to the missions, giving up candy for Lent, sitting with a sick friend. But an even greater—and therefore more profound—gift of self is giving up the bruised ego: forgiving.

(2) *Verse 38.* The spirit is quite often willing, yet it struggles against an unwilling flesh: fatigue and too much wine, as in this case, or frustration rooted in all the other times one has tried in vain, or resentment that only a couple of us pitch in to help wash the dishes while the others dawdle away the time with their dessert.

The first time Jesus returns to them, probably to get some solace from his best friends, the tone of his words sounds disappointed and a touch abrupt. But the second time he shows a remarkable understanding. Heedless of his own wearying prayers, he—whose flesh has every right to feel weaker than their own—has compassion for them.

"Well, I'm only human." Not so often do we offer that same forgiveness to others: "Well, *they're* only human, too"—especially if they have offended us.

(3) *Verse 50.* This is the instant when Jesus' passion—for which the garden was only a rehearsal—begins. First, all the men he had spent every minute of the last three years with desert him. Then the puzzling man wrapped in a linen cloth deserts him. Some see this as a symbol of Jesus' being deserted by his conviction of the protective presence of God.

Some of us have known those rock-bottom moments: when we stand all alone, naked to our enemies, deserted by our friends, bereft even of our former conviction that what we have been doing is truly the will of God. Is it arrogance, that we could be right when all the others tell us we are wrong? Thomas More knew that bleak prospect when all his friends had signed the oath making Henry VIII head of the church in England. Religious have known the feeling when their superiors are manifestly wrong and yet they must still obey.

But yielding to the will of God—however mystifying—is what we were made for. As John Donne wrote, "And I, except you enthrall me, never shall be free, nor ever chaste, except you ravish me." No one wants to face ravishment. But it is the only way Christ can be born in us. Are you willing that God ravish you?

(4) *Verse 62.* This is the short sentence that seals Jesus' fate: "I am." He had used the two words that named Yahweh, which no good Jew could speak—unless, of course, they were true. In claiming equality with God, Jesus had condemned himself out of his own mouth. This is the climax of Mark's gospel: Jesus' admission to the full Messianic Secret. And he could have gone free if he had just remained silent. But he answered, forthrightly, no matter the penalty.

All that's needed for the triumph of evil is that good men and women be silent. We are never going to overcome evil, but if those of us who are trying to do our best refuse to speak up, evil will overcome us all. Our silence betokens agreement with the Antagonist.

Few of us will ever be spotlighted so dramatically as Jesus was, but we are called upon nearly every week to speak up against some petty injustice: an unfair teacher, a colleague fired without any justifying reason, a government more devoted to its financial backers than to those they were elected to serve. The instances are nearly numberless. But if we are silent in small issues, there is little evidence to think we can be counted on for more personally costly issues.

(5) *Verse 71.* When we sin, it is heartening to remember this scene. Here is Peter, who an hour or two before had sworn, "I will never leave you, even though all the rest do! . . . I will never do that, even if I have to die with you!" It is easy to boast in the ready room before the battle.

But give Peter one thing: even though he fled with all the others, he is the only one who overcame his fear, at least momentarily, to come and at least be near where Jesus was. Not even John, "the beloved disciple," did that. There is a lesson there: even though we buckle, we tried.

What's more, as Peter dared more greatly than the others, he also failed more greatly. But that was not enough for Jesus to stop loving him. Nor is there any evidence that Peter tried to apologize; he just came back. One wonders what went on in his mind that Sunday evening when Jesus miraculously returned. Only later, according to John (21:15-19), the actions of Jesus seem to hint that Peter has never really apologized. Jesus doesn't say to Peter, "Well, are you sorry?" No. Instead, gently, he simply asks Peter, "Do you love me?"

For those of us who find it most difficult to forgive those who have betrayed us, it is a stunningly simple forgiveness.

15 ¹As soon as it was morning, the chief priests held a consultation with the elders and scribes and the whole council. They bound Jesus, led him away, and handed him over to Pilate. ²Pilate asked him, "Are you the King of the Jews?" He answered him, "You say so." ³Then the chief priests accused him of many things.

Jesus before Pilate: VV1-20

V1. *morning*: Either an attempt to legalize the night trial by an official morning decision or to reach a decision to take Jesus to the Roman authorities and charge him not for blasphemy—about which the Romans cared nothing—but for treason; ***Pilate***: Pontius Pilate, Roman governor (prefect, procurator) from AD 26–36, which testifies to his competence in the eyes of Rome. He was a tough-minded, stern ruler who cared nothing about his appeal to the people he governed. King Herod described him as "inflexible, cruel, and stubborn," and Josephus accused him of "graft, insults, robberies, assault, wanton abuse, and constant executions without trial." He is in the city at the moment from his usual headquarters at Caesarea, on the Palestine coast, for just such potentially dangerous cases at the feast. Ordinarily, on an internal matter, he would defer (scornfully) to the high priest's judgment. If Pilate is more cautious in condemning Jesus, it could be that Jesus impressed him with his dignity, but it also could be that he simply wanted to taunt these prominent Jews contemptuously with his own power.

V2. *Are you the King of the Jews?*: Again, telescoping: Mark has not even shown the Jewish officials making *any* charge whatever, and surely claiming kingship of the Jews was not what they had condemned him for in their own trial. But "Messiah" was one of the titles of the rightful king of the Jews, and the only accusation that might prick Pilate's interest. To that end, the leaders had to pervert the title from a religious sense to a purely political one—so that they can interest Pilate in a charge of political mutiny. Also the question is, once again, the focus of the Messianic Secret: Who is Jesus?; ***You say so***: It is not a wholehearted response. Jesus means something far different from what Pilate—and the Sanhedrin—mean by "King of the Jews," but it would be useless to try to explain it to the pagan Pilate if Jesus' own coreligionists do not understand. His own *disciples* don't really understand! Notice, too, that Jesus resorts here to the usual Jewish circumlocution to avoid saying, "I am," God's name, which he had not done at his Jewish trial. There, the precise issue was Jesus' right to use those words.

V3. *many things*: The statement is vague. At least as the evangelists recount it, Pilate is somehow intrigued by Jesus, not least by Jesus' dignity and refusal to "play the game," even when he is on trial for his life. At first, for Pilate this

⁴Pilate asked him again, "Have you no answer? See how many charges they bring against you." ⁵But Jesus made no further reply, so that Pilate was amazed.

⁶Now at the festival he used to release a prisoner for them, anyone for whom they asked. ⁷Now a man called Barabbas was in prison with the rebels who had committed murder during the insurrection. ⁸So the crowd came and began to ask Pilate to do for them according to his custom. ⁹Then he answered them, "Do you want me to release for you the King of the Jews?" ¹⁰For he realized that it was out of jealousy

---

Jesus is merely one more barbarian fanatic (Google Rev. Jim Jones of Jonestown or David Koresh) whose eruption into public attention comes at a particularly inopportune time. Unlike other cranks, however, he is remarkably calm.

V5. *Jesus . . . no further reply*: Isaiah 53:7 says of the Suffering Servant, "He was oppressed, and he was afflicted, yet he did not open his mouth"; ***Pilate was amazed***: Most likely on previous occasions when Pilate had been given someone accused of a Roman crime he had been buffeted with all kinds of defense arguments, accusations against his accusers, and so forth. Here he finds Jesus refusing to say a word in his own defense. Just as Herod with the Baptist (6:14-29), Pilate is reluctant to pass judgment on an innocent man but slowly yields to expediency.

V6. *he used to release*: The custom is not evidenced in other writings.

V7. *Barabbas*: The name is truly ironic; it means "Son of Abba," son of the father—which is precisely what Jesus is. The irony is compounded by the fact that a true rebel is set free in the place of a man accused of rebellion but innocent. Since the priests have to egg on the crowd to ask for him instead of Jesus, it is not likely Barabbas was a popular rebel like Fidel Castro or Pancho Villa but more of a local bandit; ***the insurrection***: Mark seems to presume his readers would know what "the" insurrection was. No modern scholar does.

V8. *the crowd*: Unlike the Sanhedrin trial, this one must have been public. It is difficult not to assume that at least some, if not many, of those in the crowd were the same people who cheered Jesus through the streets on Palm Sunday. The reason for their change of heart is obvious: on Sunday, like the apostles, they believed Jesus to be a political Messiah. Since then, however, Jesus has been reported to have claimed the unthinkable: that he is equal to Yahweh. There is no more bitter foe than a disillusioned fan. Like Judas; ***began to ask***: Obviously, a "crowd" had to have had only one or two spokesmen, not hundreds speaking in unison.

V9. *Do you want . . . King of the Jews?*: Pilate is baiting them, trying to get them to admit they want to execute their own "king."

V10. *realized . . . out of jealousy*: This is obviously Mark editorializing. No one had any way to read Pilate's awareness or motivation, or knew that

that the chief priests had handed him over. [11]But the chief priests stirred up the crowd to have him release Barabbas for them instead. [12]Pilate spoke to them again, "Then what do you wish me to do with the man you call the King of the Jews?" [13]They shouted back, "Crucify him!" [14]Pilate asked them, "Why, what evil has he done?" But they shouted all the more, "Crucify him!" [15]So Pilate, wishing to satisfy the crowd, released Barabbas for them; and after flogging Jesus, he handed him over to be crucified.

[16]Then the soldiers led him into the courtyard of the palace (that is, the governor's headquarters); and they called to-

---

Pilate had anything better than an educated guess about the motives of the people who turned Jesus over to him.

V11. *the chief priests*: Mark makes sure the reader sees who the ventriloquists are.

V12. *wish me to do:* As if these riffraff had such power; *the man you call*: Pilate too is not without his ironic humor; on the previous Sunday, "the crowd" had, indeed, called out "Hosanna in the highest" at Jesus.

V13. *shouted back:* The same verb was used for the crowd that hailed Jesus' entrance into Jerusalem; *Crucify him*: This was common Roman practice for rebels and runaway slaves. It is clear from 15:11 that the temple aristocracy was inciting the crowd and that, unlike Matthew's version, the guilt for Jesus' death cannot be laid on the entire Jewish population.

V14. *asked them:* The imperfect tense implies "kept asking." It is highly unlikely that a man of Pilate's reputation would spend this much time with an unruly crowd unless it were to avoid a serious problem for his soldiers; *what evil has he done?*: Also untypically, Pilate seems genuinely to be trying to protect an innocent person.

V15. *to satisfy the crowd*: Pilate was, if anything, a practical man; in his eyes, a riot was a more pressing problem than seeing justice done. The world has not changed much; *after flogging Jesus*: The translation belittles the action. Mel Gibson's *The Passion of the Christ* gives a better understanding, if erring in the opposite direction. Scourging is not merely whipping; it was done with whips that were studded with slivers of metal and bone and then dipped in molten lead and allowed to harden. Like the foreplay in a bullfight, this preliminary torment was meant to make the victim less trouble. A Roman citizen could be scourged only thirty-nine times; Jesus was not a Roman citizen.

V16. *the soldiers*: It is not completely unfair to compare Roman soldiers in Palestine with any soldiers warped by consistent brutality in any war and occupation. Whether from Rome itself or conscripted from conquered peoples, they did not want to be there and considered people they mastered as less than animals; *the whole cohort*: Somewhere between two hundred and six hundred

gether the whole cohort. [17]And they clothed him in a purple cloak; and after twisting some thorns into a crown, they put it on him. [18]And they began saluting him, "Hail, King of the Jews!" [19]They struck his head with a reed, spat upon him, and knelt down in homage to him. [20]After mocking him, they stripped him of the purple cloak and put his own clothes on him. Then they led him out to crucify him.

---

men; this is quite likely hyperbole that so many would concentrate their sadism on a single prisoner. At least some of them were off duty. There is no indication that the crowd is not still witnessing this.

V17. *purple cloak*: The soldiers are mocking Jesus as a pseudo-king, but Matthew's reading, "scarlet," is probably closer to the truth, since Roman soldiers wore scarlet cloaks and one was ready to hand; ***thorns into a crown***: Branches of thorn bush were used commonly for fires and were also probably ready to hand in the courtyard.

V18. *"Hail, King of the Jews!"*: A double irony—at least. The soldiers mean it with mocking irony: this battered man a king? But with an irony that doubles back on them—and on all expectations of political kings—it just happens to be the truth. This whole episode is a stark reminder of the differences between outward appearances and genuine value.

V19. *struck his head with a reed:* Since a "reed" is slender and supple, this cannot be intended to intensify his physical pain. Quite likely, they had taken a reed from the kindling and poked it into Jesus' fist in mockery of a royal scepter. Then they slap it against his thorn crown in childish ridicule; *spat . . . knelt*: Which associates the pagan Romans with the religious leaders who did the same to Jesus (14:65). Moreover, Mark used the same verb before when the Gerasene demoniac knelt before Jesus (5:6-7) and called him "Jesus, Son of the Most High God." Recall that at the time Mark was writing, the Body of Christ—the Christian community—was also being tormented by both Jewish and Roman officials.

There is no question that Mark has shaped this material editorially, both in his treatment of Pilate's less than characteristic sensitivity to innocence and his insistence on echoes from the Suffering Servant songs of Isaiah 40–55. "He did not open his mouth" (Isa 53:7); "He had done no violence" (53:9); "I did not hide my face from insult and spitting" (50:6). Although some Christian denominations do not accept it, the Wisdom of Solomon (2:12-20), composed in the first century before Christ, resonates in perfect harmony with this Christian episode. Mark was not writing merely an objective report. His major motive was illumination and persuasion.

²¹They compelled a passer-by, who was coming in from the country, to carry his cross; it was Simon of Cyrene, the father of Alexander and Rufus. ²²Then they brought Jesus to the place called Golgotha (which means the place of a skull). ²³And they offered him wine mixed with myrrh; but he did not take it. ²⁴And they crucified him, and

---

Jesus Is Crucified: VV21-32

V21. *compelled*: Roman soldiers could command any subject person to do any service, which gave rise to Jesus' saying, "If anyone presses you into going one mile, go two miles"; *coming in from the country*: An odd qualification, which seems this man is coming in from field work, which is strange at midday; and if he is a field worker, why the reference to his African home? But the clear reference to his sons seems to suggest he is someone known; *carry his cross*: The condemned were forced to carry at least the crossbar, while the uprights were permanently embedded at the place of execution. It appears Jesus was incapable of carrying it farther; **Simon of Cyrene**: A colony of dispersed Jews lived in Cyrene in North Africa, near the modern Benghazi, Libya. Perhaps Simon was visiting Jerusalem for Passover. The fact he is identified as the father of Alexander and Rufus suggests that at least his sons may have become Christians, known to Mark and his Roman audience, and therefore a connection to an eyewitness. One scholar makes the point that this is, indeed, one "Simon" who does, in fact, "take up the cross" of Christ.

V22. *Golgotha:* A Greek form of the Aramaic word for "skull," *gulgulta.* The English word "Calvary" comes from the Latin word for "skull," *calvaria.*

V23. *wine mixed with myrrh*: Although Mark does not mention it, myrrh is one of the gifts brought by the wise men in Luke's account. It was a painkiller. But Jesus refused it: "I will never again drink of the fruit of the vine until that day when I drink it new in the kingdom of God" (14:25).

V24. *they crucified him*: In three words, the deed is done. No gory Mel Gibson details, coolly blunt and objective. In none of the four accounts is there any dwelling on the grisly specifics: the relentless sun, the torn back against the rough wood, spurting blood. The only hint of nails is in the postresurrectional story of doubting Thomas and the nail holes. For such an early narrative—considering even such far later stories as *Beowulf*—there is no "playing to the audience." Cicero called crucifixion "the most cruel and repulsive punishment," hardly the kind of degrading penalty the writers would have invented for a hoax messiah. St. Paul says that Christ, crucified, is "a stumbling block to Jews and foolishness to Gentiles" (1 Cor 1:23). (Google: Joseph Zias, "Crucifixion in Antiquity.") The omission of nails here makes some believe Jesus must have been tied, which was more usual. Nevertheless, in 1968, a skeleton

divided his clothes among them, casting lots to decide what each should take.

²⁵It was nine o'clock in the morning when they crucified him. ²⁶The inscription of the charge against him read, "The King of the Jews." ²⁷And with him they crucified two bandits, one on his right and one on his left. [28] ²⁹Those who passed by derided him, shaking their heads and saying, "Aha! You who would destroy the temple

---

was unearthed in Jerusalem of a young male with a four-and-a-half-inch spike through his ankle bone; *divided his clothes*: Roman custom allowed the executioners to divide the prisoner's valuables when he died, but there are resonances here, alluding back to Psalm 22:18: "They divide my clothes among themselves, and for my clothing they cast lots." Much of Mark's passion stresses fulfillment of the ancient prophecies. (The scene is replete with allusions to Ps 22.)

V25. *nine o'clock*: If Mark is correct, Jesus was on the cross not three hours but six. In our chronology and Mark's (unlike John's), Jesus appeared before Pilate at about six o'clock in the morning and was crucified at nine. There was darkness at noon; Jesus died at about three and was buried at six.

V26. *King of the Jews*: This was the custom, to label the criminal with his crime, but Pilate is also making a cynical comment about the Jews and the type of king they have. Such a charge was often hung in a sign around the condemned man's neck to discourage any other would-be offenders. Still, with heavy irony, the moment says, "A *real* king looks like this. The others are gilded fakes."

V27. *two bandits*: Rebel guerrillas, *sicarii* or "dagger men" of whom Judas may have once been a member; their placement on Jesus' right and left could well be a bizarre parody of the transfiguration, where Moses and Elijah were on his right and left, like supportive counselors, and this is where James and John asked to be (10:35).

V28. Note: There is no verse 28 here. Some ancient authorities add a verse: "And the scripture was fulfilled that says, 'And he was counted among the lawless'" (Isa 53:12). The most reliable manuscripts omit it, suspecting a later copyist inserted it from Luke 23:27.

V29. *passed by*: Executions were often just off a roadside where the victims could be public warnings against misbehavior. These sneering passersby did not come out specifically to see the "show." They merely happen to be on their way somewhere else but unable to resist taunting a helpless victim; *shaking their heads*: To their minds, Jesus is the worst of religious criminals: a blasphemer. Psalm 22:7-8: "They shake their heads; 'Commit your cause to the LORD; let him deliver—let him rescue the one in whom he delights!'" Using so many allusions to the OT, Mark is not just a reporter but a commentator.

and build it in three days, [30]save yourself, and come down from the cross!" [31]In the same way the chief priests, along with the scribes, were also mocking him among themselves and saying, "He saved others; he cannot save himself. [32]Let the Messiah, the King of Israel, come down from the cross now, so that we may see and believe." Those who were crucified with him also taunted him.

[33]When it was noon, darkness came over the whole land until three in the af-

---

V31. *the chief priests . . . scribes*: The cynicism is vicious, even if Jesus were a criminal. If anything, it shows the stark contrast between a religion of justice and a religion of love. These are also the same men who, in the name of religion, have been pictured by Mark and Matthew as beating a blindfolded man. These are not "the Jews." They are men who have surrendered their souls in the name of righteousness; ***He saved others***: They don't seem to sense the ugly irony in their own words; they have condemned and now mock a man whose "crime" was to save others.

V32. *so that we may . . . believe*: If Jesus had in fact saved himself, he would have—by that very fact—*denied* that he was the authentic Messiah: the Suffering Servant. But that is what the priests and scribes and passersby wanted, not what God wanted. Yet again another conflict in points of view; ***Those who were crucified with him***: Only Luke, the gentlest of the Synoptics, has one of Jesus' fellow victims sympathize with him (23:40) and be welcomed into the kingdom. If the earlier suggestion that the young man who fled at Jesus' arrest is a symbol for Jesus' felt awareness of God's support, then Mark's version of Jesus' end is even more intensely harrowing. Even those who were suffering the same agony had no compassion for him. His is an abysmal loneliness.

Jesus Dies: VV33-41

V33. *darkness*: This is probably a legendary detail added by Mark, symbolizing what Luke (22:53) described as "the power of darkness," meaning the moment when evil seems to triumph. The OT prophet Joel wrote that, on the day when Yahweh comes: "The earth quakes before them, the heavens tremble. The sun and moon are darkened" (2:10). The prophet Amos (8:9-10) writes: "On that day, says the Lord GOD, I will make the sun go down at noon . . . like the mourning for an only son." Matthew is the one who lays on the apocalyptic details. Anyone who tries to find meteorological data to validate the darkness on that date has lost all sense of the truth power of symbols.

V34. *cried out*: a better word might be "screamed," except for the evident exhaustion of someone so badly used; ***Eloi, Eloi***: The Greek translation of an Aramaic version of Psalm 22:1. It is the same question embodied in the OT

ternoon. ³⁴At three o'clock Jesus cried out with a loud voice, "Eloi, Eloi, lema sabachthani?" which means, "My God, my God, why have you forsaken me?" ³⁵When some of the bystanders heard it, they said, "Listen, he is calling for Elijah." ³⁶And someone ran, filled a sponge with sour wine, put it on a stick, and gave it to him to drink, saying, "Wait, let us see whether Elijah will come to take him down." ³⁷Then Jesus gave a loud cry and breathed his last. ³⁸And the curtain of the temple

---

book of Job: How can the upright man suffer such degradation? How could God himself be so devalued? Could the Son of God possibly teeter like this on the edge of despair? (See chap. 4, "Jesus' Consciousness of His Divinity.")

V35. *calling for Elijah*: Jesus' speech is, naturally, garbled by his torment. Like St. Jude in later times, Elijah was considered by ordinary Jewish believers to be the "patron saint" of hopeless cases. The OT prophet Sirach said that Elijah would come to the aid of the wrongly accused. Again ironically, Elijah has already come, in the person of John the Baptist. And they killed him too.

V36. *someone ran*: Soldier or Jewish onlooker? Mark does not say; *sour wine*: Used by the poor, which the soldiers probably had with them. Psalm 69:21: "When I was thirsty, they gave me vinegar to drink"; *Wait, let us see*: Again, the same shallow cynicism: using this moment of agony as a show.

V37. *a loud cry*: A violent final effort; Luke interprets by quoting Jesus as saying, "Father, into your hands I commend my spirit" (23:46), and the early church fathers believed it to be a cry of triumph. In fact, if the first line of Psalm 22 calls to mind the entire hymn, it continues to say, "in the midst of the congregation I will praise you" (22:22), and "before him shall bow all who go down to the dust" (22:29), and "future generations will . . . proclaim his deliverance to a people yet unborn" (22:30-31); *breathed his last*: All over the ancient world, one's breath was identified with one's spirit, the life force within. With the exception of a few hyperbolic details—the darkness, the rending of the curtain—this is a remarkably sober description of such a focal event to the early church, written at a time when such religious stories did not hesitate to overpaint the picture of the hero's death.

V38. *the curtain*: No one else records what would have been such a historic event, therefore it is surely a symbolic not a historical detail, *interpreting* the event. The Greek word for "torn" here is the same one Mark used at Jesus' baptism, when the sky was "torn" and the voice of God broke through. The curtain hung at the doorway of the holy of holies, where the presence of Yahweh lived and where only the high priest could enter and only once a year. Josephus describes it as being painted with the stars of heaven. Thus, God was held at arm's length from the ordinary folk. Here, Mark is saying that, at the death of

was torn in two, from top to bottom. ³⁹Now when the centurion, who stood facing him, saw that in this way he breathed his last, he said, "Truly this man was God's Son!"

⁴⁰There were also women looking on from a distance; among them were Mary Magdalene, and Mary the mother of James the younger and of Joses, and Salome.

Jesus, God is no longer inaccessible. Instead, at the moment of Jesus' fulfillment, God's Spirit rushed forth from the confines of the heavens and of the temple.

V39. *the centurion*: Commander of one hundred soldiers; ***God's son*:** Again, perhaps a symbolic addition, or an expansion on the centurion's declaration that Jesus was innocent, as in Luke 23:47. Coupled with the question of the high priest, this is the climax of Mark's gospel. It is heavily ironic, since the Jewish priest rejects Jesus' claim but the Gentile soldier accepts it (whatever the term means to him). It symbolizes again Israel's denying itself the Messiah while non-Jews accept him. Some argue that a pagan could not have meant what Christians mean by the term, i.e., the unique Son of God. That missed the whole point. It was unarguably the meaning the *author* intended.

V40. *Mary Magdalene*: The woman "from whom seven demons had gone out" (Luke 8:2); ***mother of James the younger*:** There is little justification for speculating who these are, although Mark does have two apostles named James (3:17-18), the second of whom is designated after his father, Alphaeus, to distinguish him from James the brother of John and son of Zebedee. Levi has also been called "son of Alphaeus" (2:14). No explicit mention is made in Mark of Mary, the mother of Jesus, at the crucifixion. In fact, Jesus' mother is mentioned in Mark (3:31) but never by name. Some scholars are tempted, however, to believe that the "Mary" mentioned here as "the mother of James the younger and of Joses" is the mother of Jesus, whom Mark clearly identifies (6:3): "Is not this [Jesus] the carpenter, the son of Mary and brother of James and Joses . . . ?"

V41. *used to follow . . . provided*: The verb "followed" qualifies these women as much as the males as "disciples." Their "ministry" was likely the "women's work" presumed in that society; ***many other women . . . to Jerusalem*:** Therefore, the witnesses were not only the three women singled out to be named. Moreover, one is left to wonder if they came accompanying their husbands or on their own, having left their own families. If they were *un*married, their presence here would be even more scandalous.

It is well to remember that Mark is not a modern reporter, or even a scrupulous modern historian. His purpose is openly apostolic, to answer two questions: (1) Who was Jesus, really? and (2) What does it mean to be his disciple?

The crucifixion answers both questions.

⁴¹These used to follow him and provided for him when he was in Galilee; and there were many other women who had come up with him to Jerusalem.

⁴²When evening had come, and since it was the day of Preparation, that is, the day before the sabbath, ⁴³Joseph of Arimathea, a respected member of the council, who was also himself waiting expectantly for the kingdom of God, went boldly to Pilate and asked for the body of Jesus. ⁴⁴Then Pilate wondered if he were already dead; and summoning the centurion, he asked him whether he had been dead for some time. ⁴⁵When he learned from the centurion that he was dead, he granted the body

---

Jesus Is Buried: VV42-47

V42. *evening had come*: This is puzzling since, if it was the evening of Preparation day, that is, the day before the Sabbath, then the Sabbath had already begun at dusk. Therefore, no pious Jew would think of doing what Joseph does, asking for the corpse. Equally unfitting even to bury the dead on such a day. Nonetheless, Deuteronomy 21:22-23 says: "When someone is convicted of a crime punishable by death and is executed, and you hang him on a tree, his corpse must not remain all night upon the tree; you shall bury him that same day, for anyone hung on a tree is under God's curse. You must not defile the land that the LORD your God is giving you for possession." Since, according to Mark's chronology so far, Jesus died at three o'clock in the afternoon by our reckoning, we are talking about sometime near four. The whole problem would also be resolved if Mark were merely mistaken about the hour—or if he were translated "as evening was approaching," so the burial occurred before sundown.

V43. *Joseph of Arimathea*: Arimathea is an unknown town. Matthew describes Joseph as a rich man and a disciple of Jesus, omitting designation as a member of the Sanhedrin, perhaps because Mark 14:64 says "*All* of them condemned him." Mark makes it fairly clear that this Joseph was not in any way a "Christian," since he was "*waiting expectantly for the kingdom of God*." He was, rather, just a worthy Jew who had the courage—and influential position—to ask the leader of the occupation forces for the body of a man who had been executed as "King of the Jews."

V44. *Pilate wondered*: Often the condemned hung on for days, and Roman officials left them there to rot even after death, as an object lesson to passersby. Unlike the two crucified highwaymen, however, Jesus has been mercilessly scourged and is far weaker. Pilate's easement here probably does not argue to any kindness on his part, but rather his efficient desire to have the incitement to unrest out of sight and out of mind—especially on a feast.

V45. *body*: The Greek is more precise: "corpse." The details here—the corpse, the shroud, the tomb, the heavy rock—all testify that Jesus was genuinely dead.

to Joseph. ⁴⁶Then Joseph bought a linen cloth, and taking down the body, wrapped it in the linen cloth, and laid it in a tomb that had been hewn out of the rock. He then rolled a stone against the door of the tomb. ⁴⁷Mary Magdalene and Mary the mother of Joses saw where the body was laid.

V46. *bought a linen cloth*: Despite the proximity of the holy *Shabbat*, there were enough merchants willing to make a quick sale. All the verbs indicate haste. There is no washing of the body, no anointing, merely bundling him into a shroud; ***hewn out of the rock***: The soft limestone hills around the city were honeycombed with tombs. The corpse was left to decompose for a year, then the bones were gathered into an ossuary ("bone box") with an inscription. Unlike Matthew, Mark does not indicate the tomb belonged to Joseph.

V47. *Mary Magdalene*: The women are official witnesses to Jesus' death and burial, not Jesus' male disciples. There were many burial caves in the area, and the women are witnesses who returned on Sunday—thus not to the wrong cave, which just happened to be still empty.

There is no explicit mention of "mourning," no formalities.

Review Questions for Chapter 15

1. In the last two chapters, list the details that point to the illegality of Jesus' execution. Never once in Mark's version, however, does Jesus complain on that point. Why?
2. Judging from the way nonscriptural sources paint Pilate, he was not a very sensitive man. What are the reasons that he might have been historically different dealing with Jesus, and what reasons could Mark—as not merely a reporter but someone bringing out theological dimensions—have in "making" him more sympathetic?
3. List the very few details with which Mark most likely embellished the events in the chapter to bring out their cosmic meaning. Without them, the story is remarkably unadorned, unlike many other epic tales.
4. What does the presence of only women from Jesus' followers "say"?

For Reflection

(1) ***Verse 15.*** Andy Warhol said that everybody gets fifteen minutes in the spotlight during their lives. This is Pontius Pilate's, though he never could have guessed it at the time. To his eyes, this was merely a wandering Jewish carpenter turned preacher, obviously being victimized by the Jewish elders for moving in too successfully on their turf. The fact that he tries several times to offer

these leaders a scapegoat shows that, at least in the eyes of the evangelists if not in fact, he was a man not totally without compassion and a sense of justice. But Pilate was also a man of the world, practical, with a job to do. Given the choice between justice to one peasant and a wholesale riot, Pilate made the only "sensible" choice, didn't he?

People in business face similar choices every week: between justice to people and profit/loss. Advertising is good for the economy, even if it paralyzes the listeners in infantile greed; plastic is cheap and efficient, even if it buries us in litter; sanitized porn on the daily soaps gets viewers, even if it also makes children believe sex is an impersonal game. They pacify their consciences by saying, "Church is church, and business is business." How could you prove them wrong?

(2) *Verse 20.* Like Pilate, these nameless soldiers don't know that this is their fifteen minutes in the spotlight; they don't even know the man they are degrading and mocking will be someone whose name and power will outlast them, much less that they are degrading and mocking their Creator.

Jesus said (Matt 25) that the only question to determine whether our lives were worth living would not be, on the one hand, how much money we made, how many times we had our names in the paper, how many awards we got. Nor, on the other hand, would it be how many times we missed Mass, practiced birth control, married. The only question will be: "I was hungry, I was thirsty . . . what did you do about that?" They didn't realize, but I was the one they beat, spat upon, mocked. I was the one they called nerd, slut, faggot. What did you do about that?

(3) *Verse 29.* As with verse 20, we'd like to think of ourselves as unwilling to degrade Jesus himself, though we sometimes find ourselves degrading him in others. We would not like to think of ourselves sadistically mocking Jesus—surely not when he was in agony, kicking him even after he had been totally defeated. But are there times when you find yourself hungry for vengeance, wanting someone to go on "paying" even after he or she has apologized? Have you ever found yourself saying, "I warned you" or "I told you so," when someone has not heeded your advice and now lies wallowing in anguished embarrassment? That isn't Jesus' way of dealing with weakness.

(4) *Verse 34.* At this moment, Jesus is not merely quoting a psalm for the edification of the crowd. He feels a genuine, agonizing sense of abandonment. Could I have been wrong? Does the Messiah die like this?

One of the greatest appeals of Christianity—as opposed to other forms of seeing God and worshiping God—is that we are the only religion whose God endured betrayal, desertion, and even the temptation to despair. Yet he clung on, in faith, to the will of his Father, which had brought him to this end.

At times we all feel betrayed, deserted, tempted to despair, when we are sure that what we are doing is the will of God and everyone else calls us fool, walks away, shuns us. Is your trust in God—and in your own ability to discern his will—strong enough that at those times you can say, "Father, into your hands I commend my spirit"?

(5) *Verse 42.* Joseph of Arimathea is obviously a man of some means; he has enough position in Jerusalem to gain admittance into the office of the governor, whom he boldly asks for Jesus' body. Thus, it is a rich man who secures the body of Jesus. Joseph has found his way through the needle's eye, without surrendering his worldly goods. The question the gospel poses to us is not wealth or poverty but how we use our wealth or poverty. Poverty, of itself, is no virtue; there are as many connivers, thieves, rapists, and terrorists spawned of poverty as there are from those with material excess. Does the poor woman use her poverty to achieve dignity or to become a whining, grasping shrew? Does the rich man, like Joseph, use his excess wealth to ease the pain of those in need, or does he hoard his wealth, like Aesop's dog in the manger, squatting on the straw he cannot eat while all around him the cattle starve?

16 ¹When the sabbath was over, Mary Magdalene, and Mary the mother of James, and Salome bought spices, so that they might go and anoint him. ²And very early on the first day of the week, when the sun had risen, they went to the tomb. ³They had been saying to one another, "Who will roll away the stone for us from the entrance to the tomb?" ⁴When they looked up, they saw that the stone, which was very large, had already been rolled back. ⁵As they entered the tomb, they saw a young man, dressed in a white robe, sitting on the right side; and they

---

The Empty Tomb: VV1-8

V1. *When the sabbath was over*: Thus, at dusk on our Saturday; *Mary . . .*: Note that it is the same three women who witnessed Jesus' death. Also, in every mention of these women, Magdalene, out of whom seven devils had been cast, is always named first, indicating a position of prominence among them—but no more; *bought spices*: They could not be purchased on the Sabbath; *anoint*: One reason some mistakenly assume that Mary Magdalene must be the woman who anointed Jesus earlier, but that woman had already performed this task.

V2. *very early on the first day*: Thus, the day after purchasing the spices, our Sunday. Even though Jesus had predicted his resurrection, these loyal women came to anoint a corpse, not to greet a resurrected man. According to Jewish tradition, it was customary to visit the burial place three days after death, not only to mourn but to be certain the person was indeed dead. This was the reason for Jesus' puzzling delay for three days after the death of his dear friend Lazarus—so there would be no doubt that he had indeed revived a dead man, not someone only wrongly believed to be deceased. Hosea 6:2 says, "on the third day he will raise us up, that we may live before him."

V3. *Who will roll away the stone?*: Huge circular stones were set into a track at the cave entrance. To ask why they hadn't thought of this before misses the whole point of the story.

V4. *the stone . . . rolled back*: None of the gospels picture the actual resurrection itself, which seems, at first, odd, and yet on the contrary it gives greater credence to the story. If ever a scene begged for hyperbolic and apocalyptic overdoing it is this one. Yet the gospel writers resist a temptation each has yielded to at least a few times in their other episodes. Their silence testifies they honestly did not know how Jesus rose, and yet they died rather than deny that he had.

V5. *they entered the tomb*: The caves were fitted with several shelves or large slots for corpses; *young man*: As in the episode in the garden, after the flight of the disciples, the same words: "a young man, dressed in a white robe"—symbolizing the presence of God and the realization within the women of what the empty tomb really means.

were alarmed. ⁶But he said to them, "Do not be alarmed; you are looking for Jesus of Nazareth, who was crucified. He has been raised; he is not here. Look, there is the place they laid him. ⁷But go, tell his disciples and Peter that he is going ahead of you to Galilee; there you will see him, just as he told you." ⁸So they went out and fled from the tomb, for terror and amazement had seized them; and they said nothing to anyone, for they were afraid.

[And all that had been commanded them they told briefly to those around Peter. And afterward Jesus himself sent out through them, from east to west, the sacred and imperishable proclamation of eternal salvation.]

[⁹Now after he rose early on the first day of the week, he appeared first to Mary Magdalene, from whom he had cast out seven demons. ¹⁰She went out and told those who had been with him, while they

---

V6. *He has been raised*: Death has yielded up life: the profoundest conversion of all, requiring a responding conversion within ourselves of what is possible.

V7. *tell his disciples and Peter*: Singling Peter out has several purposes: to show him set apart from them and to call up echoes of Peter's denials; *Galilee*: The story ends where it began.

V8. *terror and amazement*: And little wonder! It is also worth noting, however, that the first "apostles" to preach Jesus risen were women; *nothing to anyone*: Puzzling, since obviously they told the disciples.

As Mark stands at this point, there is no appearance of the risen Jesus himself, even to the women. And they have only the word of "the young man, dressed in a white robe." Like ourselves, they have to take the word of someone else. And the last word in this segment is the Greek *gar*, meaning "for" or "because," which is a puzzling way to end a book—a cliffhanger. One distinct possibility was that further verses were somehow lost.

Later Endings: VV9-20

The "Old" Ending: Verses 9-20 were declared part of the Catholic canon of scripture by the Council of Trent (1546). It is quite likely, however, that Mark ended his gospel at verse 8; the style, vocabulary, and subject matter of all three endings are very unlike Mark. Note, for instance, that the first words repeat the fact that Jesus rose on the first day of the week, which Mark has already told us. Note also that it says "Jesus rose" rather than "was raised," that is, by the Father. Also, the angel has said Jesus would meet them in Galilee, not in Jerusalem. Further, there is no indication that church authorities like Clement of Alexandria (d. AD 215) or Origen (d. 254) knew those later verses. The point of those original first eight verses of chapter 16, however, is enough: Jesus is risen.

There are four resurrection appearances in the appended segment: (1) appearance to Magdalene (16:9-11, perhaps added from Luke 24:10-11 and/or

were mourning and weeping. [11]But when they heard that he was alive and had been seen by her, they would not believe it.

[12]After this he appeared in another form to two of them, as they were walking into the country. [13]And they went back and told the rest, but they did not believe them.

[14]Later he appeared to the eleven themselves as they were sitting at the table; and he upbraided them for their lack of faith and stubbornness, because they had not believed those who saw him after he had risen. [15]And he said to them, "Go into all the world and proclaim the good news to the whole creation. [16]The one who believes and is baptized will be saved; but the one who does not believe will be condemned. [17]And these signs will accompany

---

John 20:14-18), (2) appearance to two men on the road to Emmaus (16:12-13, perhaps added from Luke 24:13-25), (3) mission of the Eleven (16:14-18, perhaps from Matt 28:16-20; Luke 24:50-51; or John 20:26-29), and (4) the ascension (16:19-20, perhaps added from Luke 24:50-51; or Acts 1:9-11).

There should be no uneasiness about such an "intrusive addition" not written by whoever wrote what we have already seen of Mark's gospel. Those four addenda *are* clearly attested to by other New Testament writers we have no hesitation in accepting as authentic. Nothing in the passage (*logion*) is untrue; it is just not genuine Mark.

V11. *they would not believe it*: One of the reasons could quite likely be that the first herald of this best of the good news was a woman, and one formerly (according to this ending) possessed. God "would not have done that." God's ways; our ways.

V12. *two of them*: This reminds the reader of the Emmaus episode in Luke 24:13-35. It is common in all the gospels that the witness does not recognize the risen Jesus at once. This is Jesus finally transfigured.

V13. *did not believe them*: It is easy to be condescending about their lack of faith, but encountering a man once dead was no more commonplace in their day than it is in our own.

V14. *he upbraided them*: Again, far too gentle; the Greek word, *oneidizo*, is the same verb used to describe the snarling of the thieves condemned with Jesus (15:32).

V15. *to the whole creation*: This addition is post-Mark, but it certainly testifies to the belief that the community saw itself as universal and not merely a new sect of Judaism.

V16. *condemned*: This is not the place to go into a long study of the fate of those who "refuse to believe." Suffice it to say here that the church has condemned as heretical the proposition that "outside the church there is no salvation."

V17. *these signs*: These marvelous works are signs that the kingdom of God is now established. Nor should one take them literally or read them with solely materialist eyes, as if the only demons were *Exorcist*-type demons, the

those who believe: by using my name they will cast out demons; they will speak in new tongues; [18]they will pick up snakes in their hands, and if they drink any deadly thing, it will not hurt them; they will lay their hands on the sick, and they will recover."

[19]So then the Lord Jesus, after he had spoken to them, was taken up into heaven and sat down at the right hand of God. [20]And they went out and proclaimed the good news everywhere, while the Lord worked with them and confirmed the message by the signs that accompanied it.]

---

only serpents were literally fanged, and the only poisons are poisons that kill the body.

V19. *spoken to them*: This would seem to have been just after this single appearance—and in Jerusalem, not Galilee; *was taken up*: A passive verb; raised up by the Father. We know now, of course, that heaven is not "up there," since the word "up" has meaning only in terms of where the speaker is standing; if Jesus went literally "up" to heaven, a person in China would go "up" in the opposite direction. Jesus returned to another way of existing, compared to which our own is a shadow of reality.

V20. *the Lord*: It is not the historical, flesh-and-blood Jesus who worked with them but the glorified risen Lord.

Review Questions for Chapter 16

1. What does the lack of a dramatic description of Jesus "exploding" out of the tomb do to the credibility of Mark's declaration of the resurrection?
2. The additions to Mark's original text (verses 9 on) are not authentic Mark, but that doesn't negate their credibility. Explain.
3. St. Paul says that, if Jesus did not rise from the dead, our faith is completely in vain. Why?

For Reflection

(1) *Verse 1.* The anointing the women intended to perform would do Jesus no good. He was three days dead. But it would do the women some good; at least they had tried to offer the memory of Jesus some shred of dignity and respect. Women often are better at this kind of thing than men. Traditionally, it has been the women who take care of corpses, prepare a meal for the funeral guests, clean up. In many cultures, it's the women who "take care of the religion end." Can you say why? Is it that women are more sensitive to others' needs? More empathic? What is there in the upbringing of males and females even today that fosters this sensitivity in most of one sex and fewer of the other? Males

generally establish a sense of self by setting up ego boundaries, while women generally establish a sense of self by reaching out and including others. Is there something "unmanly" in being sensitive, inclusive . . . Christian? How could we change that?

(2) *Verse 11.* It is easy to believe that the disciples scorned Magdalene's news because she was "only an easily suggestible woman." But remember that we have heard for most of our lives that Jesus rose from the dead. Despite Jesus' predictions, the disciples would have reacted to her news exactly as we would if someone ran in breathlessly and said she'd just had a long chat with Elvis Presley. That lifetime of repetition of the truth of the resurrection has also deadened our capacity for surprise over the resurrection, an indifference amplified by our distaste for considering the fact of our own inevitable and unpredictable deaths.

Each of us has a finite number of days we will wake up, and the fact that the number of our days is limited should make each of those days indescribably precious. Yet so many of us drag ourselves through the work week like sullen automatons, little realizing that this one could very well be the last.

Nor, if we shield ourselves from the reality of our own deaths, can we appreciate why "The Good News" is very good news, indeed. If we honestly contemplate the utter annihilation of death in a godless universe, the realization that—because of Jesus—it is not an annihilation at all, that is something worth celebrating every Sunday!

(3) *Verse 15.* It is easy to distance ourselves from this command to bring the good news out into the world. Somehow we hear it as given only to twelve men—or at the most to those who have become priests or religious: the professionals. But at our baptism, each of us was ordained to be not only a healer but also an apostle of the good news: to declare the Amnesty of God. We cannot say, "Oh, I'm only a layperson." We cannot merely sit in the pews and have our *own* individual souls revitalized by a homily and by ingesting the Body and Blood and Spirit of Jesus. We are missioned. We are not Christian sheep but Christian shepherds, sent out to find the strays.

(4) *Verse 17.* Some of the most spiritual Christians read the gospel with exclusively materialist eyes, as if the only poor were the literally, physically poor. Such reading would make this segment of Jesus' message impossible to all but the rarefied few saints among us.

But you—*you* who hold this book in your hands—have the power to work miracles, if you are able to scale down the drama of the statement to the relative smallness of your own life. At your own elbows there are people plagued with the demons of self-doubt, self-absorption, self-distaste. There are people to whom only someone like you can speak and get a hearing, people who would turn away from a priest or nun with scorn or fear. There are snakes and poisons abounding all around us—greed, lust, anger, envy, inertia—which immobilize their victims unless we challenge them. There are people sick with confusion, betrayal, anonymity. You cannot heal them all, but you could start with just one.

Who, if not you? When, if not now?

Addendum

Opening Up the Scriptures

Today, even intimidatingly well-educated people still naively believe the commonplace depiction of an atom—electrons whizzing around a central nucleus with the same comfortable predictability of planets circumnavigating our sun. Like their study of scripture, they have left any serious inquiry into science back in college because they've been detoured from such leisurely pursuits by understandably more pressing questions of career, family, and survival. Despite their considerable erudition, they never fully grasped what it meant when Werner Heisenberg won the Nobel Prize for Physics in 1923 (nearly one hundred years ago) for proving that pellet model as "false" as pictures of an Old Man on a throne trying to "capture" an ineffable God. Both the solar-system atom and the Ancient of Days are highly inadequate *symbols*—very remotely suggesting something of the truth but no more "accurate" than medieval maps of Europe.

For centuries, the same held true, on principle, about the Bible. Except for a relatively few scriptural experts, often more interested in preserving purity of permanently determined doctrine, Catholics were sidetracked from reading the scriptures for themselves. This was done with "the best of intentions," lest they become confused—or worse, inconveniently obstructionist. Everyone agrees, "A little knowledge is a dangerous thing." After all, many who believe in "the priesthood of all believers," who disparage intrusions into private conscience by despotic clerics, encourage ordinary believers to read scripture and make up their own minds what it rewards and forbids. As a result, they've splintered into uncountable sects, spurning not only Mother Church but also one another. Safer to restrict scripture to approved texts at Mass and recommend owning a Bible in each home, kept in a place of reverence, safely unread but reassuring as a talisman. "Reassuring" was pretty much the church's role in most Catholic lives, like a mother's warm bosom in thunderstorms.

Perhaps this protectivism, restricting scriptural access to the clergy (even at times when many of them were illiterate), began to stir first at the rise of the middle class in the late Middle Ages. Sons of the wealthy, who lacked the bloodlines that had guaranteed tutored literacy only to the nobility and clergy, went to the monasteries (or were boarded out to impoverished nobles) to broaden their horizons—which began to create a small group not so easily persuaded or controlled. And envious of the clergy's unmerited wealth and power. But certainly that unrest with class distinctions in access to learning—and therefore to freedom and independent thinking—burst out full force with the eighteenth-century Age of Enlightenment, which stressed the primacy of rational thinking over brute obedience, and also with the Age of Revolutions, which trumpeted the rights of individuals over dominant power structures. It is utterly impossible to have reassuring uniformity—of either doctrine or practice—if every man jack in the street is allowed to learn and think for himself. (See George Orwell's *1984*.)

Unlike "those Protestants," Catholics were discouraged from reading scripture on their own, and that protectiveness came from the highest authority: Pope Leo XIII (1878–1903). On 18 November 1893, he issued a papal encyclical, *Providentissimus Deus*, in order to counter the growing influence of "godless rationalism"—especially the natural sciences of evolution and geology that contradicted the traditional scriptural belief that the earth could be only six thousand years old and the utter difference between humans and the highest level apes. The basic assertion was that, if there were a conflict between the "New Learning" and the literal message of the scriptures, the obvious error must be with "mere" rational assertions, unenlightened by divine inspiration. That inspiration—and its reassuring inerrancy—put the scriptures beyond the capacity of unaided reason and asserted the Roman Church as their privileged interpreter. The encyclical says, clearly: "The sense of Holy Scripture can nowhere be found incorrupt outside of the Church, and cannot be expected to be found in writers who, being without the true faith, only gnaw the bark of the Sacred Scripture, and never attain its pith" (15). Leo XIII was nonetheless the same intelligent, humanistic teacher who had written the great labor encyclicals. He did not outright condemn modern ways of discerning. He was, though, acutely cautious of them.

Leo's successor, however, Pius X (1903–1914) solidified the battlements of the church all along the intellectual spectrum against what was now called "Modernism," the use of rational tools in the exploration of sociology, anthropology, psychology, and especially scripture and theological reflection. In September 1910, he mandated a formal Oath Against Modernism, sworn in a church, from every priest in the world on condition of ordination and continued license to perform the sacraments. Among its concessions:

I reject that method of judging and interpreting Sacred Scripture which, departing from the tradition of the Church, the analogy of faith, and the norms of the Apostolic See, embraces the misrepresentations of the rationalists and with no prudence or restraint adopts textual criticism as the one and supreme norm.

. . . I firmly hold, then, and shall hold to my dying breath the belief of the Fathers in the charism [divine power] of truth, which certainly is, was, and always will be in the succession of the episcopacy from the apostles. The purpose of this is, then, not that dogma may be tailored according to what seems better and more suited to the culture of each age; rather, that the absolute and immutable truth preached by the apostles from the beginning may never be believed to be different, may never be understood in any other way.

This was not (quite) a blind rejection of any newly discovered avenue to the Truth. It stopped short of that in such phrases as modern methods acting as the "one and supreme norm," excluding any hierarchical intrusions. But it left little "wiggle room." Catholic scholars who tried to discover some middle ground where "the new learning" and "tradition" could cross-feed one another were suspect and virtually silenced. The encyclical *Spiritus Paraclitus* by the next pope, Benedict XV (1914–1922), was even more constricting.

When I began in 1960 to study scripture and theology prior to ordination, I was twenty-nine years old, and yet still a "child" of that church—which, with Vatican II, had begun to churn into a quite new, less glumly certain but more exhilarating Body of Christ. As I began, however, I clung to "the old Church" like a shipwreck survivor. Despite what I knew from paleontology, I was unswervingly convinced that all the evil on earth came from a pair of rather dumb nudists who ate one piece of fruit at the behest of a talking snake. I really, *really* believed that, with the same unquestioned certainty that I knew my mother loved me.

I never allowed myself to be troubled by the occasions for which the all-loving God required death by stoning: touching Mount Sinai (Exod 19:13), saying "Oh, my God!" (Lev 24:16), adultery (Deut 22:23), gathering sticks on the Sabbath (Num 15:32), a betrothed woman who doesn't scream during rape (Deut 22:24), or—what is particularly dicey these days—a woman found not virginal on her wedding night (Deut 22:21). Is there a reason why we now see those punishments as obviously exaggerated and yet hold homosexual actions (Lev 20:13) to it literally? It never crossed my loyal mind that every one of those misdeeds, from the horrific to the trifling, got exactly the *same* punishment. If I ever was aware of them, I had chosen till then not to investigate further why there are two *different* accounts of creation in Genesis or why the four evangelists differ from one another quite clearly on who greeted the women at Jesus' tomb. I remained resolutely untroubled by the fact that in Genesis 1, God created light before he got around to creating anything that could produce light.

I find it hard to admit now that I did, in fact, kneel next to the seminary rector just before ordination and swore the Oath Against Modernism. (But with my fingers crossed! Really!)

But just as the explorations of modern physics had been outdistancing the awareness of even highly educated people, so too the work of Catholic scripture scholars found more and more grounds on which to place trust in the discoveries of the new biblical studies, trying to understand the Bible not merely as an unchanging monolith but as a whole library of documents speaking in highly specialized ways to an audience whose understandings were quite different from our own. Many of those rigid former interpretations had been psychically lethal.

Two tiny examples: the Greek word *hubris* for centuries was incautiously translated as "pride," as in "I will break your proud glory" (Lev 26:19). To a Greek, however, *hubris* meant not simple pride in a job well done, but arrogance—the narcissism of Adam and Eve, Oedipus, Hitler—of people who thought they could be independent of God. But because of that seemingly trivial slip, countless simple-minded preachers and their listeners have disparaged anyone who has simply tried their best! Similarly, "perfect," as in "Be perfect [*teleioi*] . . . as your heavenly Father is perfect" (Matt 5:48) could not possibly have meant flawless, in our sense of that word—simply because such a statement would be blasphemous, since only God can be flawless. Rather, *teleioi* means "complete, all together, mature—as opposed to childish." But again, the small semantic difference has savaged souls who attempted to be what their Creator never could have intended.

Without the awareness of all but the most sophisticated Catholics, in 1943, Pope Pius XII delivered the encyclical *Divino Afflante Spiritu* ("With the Inspiration of the Divine Spirit"), the Magna Carta of modern biblical studies. It summarily rejects those Catholic conservatives who "pretend that nothing remains to be added by the Catholic exegete [expert interpreter] of our time to what Christianity has brought to light" (32). Honest understanding arises from within the work, not from outside, "intended and expressed by the sacred writer" (26). The letter also approved methods that "endeavor to determine the peculiar character and circumstances of the sacred writer, the age in which he lived, the sources written or oral to which he had recourse and the forms of expression he employed" (33).

The gains made by *Divino Afflante Spiritu* were finally solidified with Vatican II's Dogmatic Constitution on Divine Revelation (*Dei Verbum*), but not without a final campaign by entrenched Vatican theologians. Just as Pius XII had to avoid "stepping on the toes" of the long-dead Leo XIII, the council had to be cautious against such fierce opposition from around the very Throne of Peter. The Roman cardinals tried to insert into a draft version of the document such warnings as "[the council] condemns those errors" which assert that the Evangelists or, "what is far worse," the primitive communities attributed statements to the historical Jesus that he did not utter. Moved by Inspiration of the Divine Spirit, the world's bishops rejected that.

The church can be unafraid of any conflicts with modern science since, as Pope John Paul II later declared, "The truth cannot contradict itself." *Dei Verbum* states that "the books of Scripture must be acknowledged as teaching firmly, faithfully and without error that truth which God wanted put into the sacred writings for the sake of our salvation" (11). Literal understandings of the Bible cannot be used to validate culturally conditioned attitudes from centuries ago toward sexual or social oppression, like slavery or marginalization. Learning, personal religious experience, and communal discernment by the *laity* are an integral part of the development of tradition. The hierarchy is *part* of a larger process of growth, not its *sole* agent.

Lincoln's Emancipation Proclamation only *began* the long, long process of acceptance of African Americans into full participation in our society. Similarly, Pius XII and Vatican II only *began* the process offering due respect to the intelligence of the Catholic laity. There is still constant effort even by highly placed people to "reform the reform." *The Catechism of the Catholic Church* (1997) is an encyclopedic effort to codify Catholic belief, but only the most devoted would deny that there is much there that is hardly essential. There is little suggestion of a spectrum of doctrines from the nonnegotiable (like the divinity of Christ) through the important (like his presence in the Eucharist) to the trivial (like the conduct of the liturgy). In reviewing the *Catechism*, Luke Timothy Johnson, a leading Catholic scripture scholar, observes "how completely this catechism ignores the results of biblical scholarship. The code for reading the Gospels is the same used by Augustine and Aquinas" (*Commonweal,* May 7, 1993). We remain a pilgrim church.

A Sort-Of Conclusion

Perhaps a handful of very (very) devoted Catholics would face a firing squad rather than deny the immaculate conception or the assumption (even of those who go out of their way to worship on those feasts). Most laypeople have perspectives and priorities more realistic than the theological and doctrinal experts. Not many are troubled by the question of whether Jesus is of the same "nature" as his father or of the same "substance." They testify (at some cost) to their belief that Christ is more intensely present in the Eucharist than anywhere else on earth, without having time to ponder arguments to defend the power of the Creator of the Universe to concentrate himself wherever he chooses. Nor do many fret about "where Jesus goes" when Mass is over or if he gets lonely in his small gold prison. Most have long since disposed of the birth control issue, definitively, and with little residual guilt, despite the futile insistence of many clergy and more dedicated lay folk. The well-being of their present children unquestionably outweighs any might-have-been children—and surely takes precedence over the natural claims of a brainless pair of invisible cells.

What they do cling to—again without much rational analysis but at some personal cost—is that, "somehow," Jesus of Nazareth is The Answer, that his words and actions model the ways in which they can improve their grateful service of The Mind Behind It All, to whom they owe absolutely everything. Many of them have far more impressive academic degrees than their pastors or even their bishops. Almost all of them hold the unquestionable right to vote for the executive and legislators who hold tenuous control over the continued existence of the planet. It would be a grave insult to deny them direct access to understanding their Savior's wishes with the same directness they have to him in prayer—with no ordained intermediaries.

Nonetheless, to believe that anyone with significant secular education ought to be able to discern the original intentions of someone writing twenty centuries ago, in a different language and culture, would be as foolhardy as the same person reading Shakespeare without footnotes. As Raymond Brown, SS, wrote:

> Since scripture is inspired and presumably this inspiration was for the good of all, there has arisen the fallacy that everyone should be able to pick up the Bible and read it profitably. If this implies that everyone should be able to find out what the sacred author is saying without preparation or study, it really demands of God in each instance a miraculous dispensation from the limitations imposed by differences of time and circumstance. (*Jerome Biblical Commentary*)

Hubristically, I have established O'Malley's Law: "The less you know, the more certain you can be." Arrogant bigots are untroubled by disconcerting counterarguments simply because they refuse to allow them to be true. Fanatics decline to be swayed by common sense. Totalitarian leaders—sometimes even at the highest levels and from the most protective motives—would rather see their adherents safe than sorry. (See Dostoevsky's "The Grand Inquisitor.") But God graced us with intelligence long before he found need to allow "authorities" to emerge. It seems unarguable that God—whose purposes seem manifest in the history of an evolution culminating (thus far) in human ability to understand—wants us to use that gift to go in quest of him.

Perhaps we can join the prayer of Empress Helena, mother of Constantine, who like ourselves was burdened with learning and material security. Evelyn Waugh's novel, *Helena*, pictures her praying to her patron saints, the wise men of Christ's Nativity:

> Dear cousins, pray for me, for his sake who did not reject your curious gifts. Pray always for the learned, the oblique, the delicate. Let them not be quite forgotten at the throne of God, when the simple come into their Kingdom.

Welcome, then, to the quest we share with the communion of all saints!